ADVENTURES IN NATURE

PANAMA

William Friar

William Friar

**AVALON
TRAVEL**
publishing

Adventures in Nature: Panama
FIRST EDITION

William Friar

Published by
Avalon Travel Publishing, Inc.
5855 Beaudry St.
Emeryville, CA 94608, USA

Text and photos copyright © 2001 by
William Friar. All rights reserved.

Please send all comments, corrections,
additions, amendments, and critiques to:

Adventures in Nature: Panama
AVALON TRAVEL PUBLISHING
5855 BEAUDRY ST.
EMERYVILLE, CA 94608, USA
email: info@travelmatters.com
www.travelmatters.com

Excerpt from Chapter 9, "The Spirit of the *Uaga*," by Cacique General Carlos López, recorded by Valerio Núñez, from *Plants and Animals in the Life of the Kuna* by Jorge Ventocilla, Heraclio Herrera, Valerio Núñez, translated by Elisabeth King, copyright 1995.

ISBN: 1-56691-240-7

ISSN: 1531-4189

Editors: Jeannie Trizzino, Marisa Solís
Copy Editor: Nancy Gillan
Index: Emily Lunceford
Graphics Coordinator: Erika Howsare
Production: Karen McKinley
Map Editor: Michael Balsbaugh
Cartography: Doug Beckner

Printing History
1st edition— February 2001

5 4 3 2 1

Front and back cover photos: San Blas Islands—Michael Brands—Photographers/Aspen

Distributed in the United States and Canada by Publishers Group West

Printed in the United States by Publishers Press

CONTENTS

CONTENTS

CONTENTS

ABOUT THIS BOOK

Adventures in Nature: Panama is a guide to the crossroad between the Atlantic and the Pacific Oceans, one of the most exciting destinations for active travelers who are interested in exploring the natural wonders of the isthmus. Along with the best places for hiking and birding and prime spots for surfing or exploring rainforest canopy, author William Friar recommends outfitters and local guides that can provide gear and lead you to the more remote parts of the country. He also points out places to eat and stay that will help you enjoy local cultures and cuisine.

Like all Adventures in Nature guides, this book emphasizes responsible, low-impact travel. Restaurants, accommodations, and outfitters that are particularly eco-friendly—those that strive to operate in ways that protect the natural environment or support local ecotourism efforts—are highlighted in most chapters.

AUTHOR'S NOTE

This book is dedicated to my mother, Willie K. Friar, whose love, enthusiasm, and hard work for the Panama Canal are exceeded only by that for her children. You're an inspiration.

The author's note is where you're supposed to say your book could never have been completed without the help of many people. It's not true in this case. One way or another, I would have gotten the thing done. But I can only imagine what a mess and a chore it would have been without the expertise, guidance, and friendship of more people than I can possibly thank here. The following are just a few of them.

First, I have to thank Mary Coffey, my dinner partner and tireless source of great information. The way she cheerfully puts up with the many demands of the Friar family goes way beyond the requirements of friendship. The same is true of Sandra Snyder and David Wilson, as well as Rodrigo Gómez and his lovely family. Many thanks to them for helping me readjust to my homeland. I also want to thank Scott Doggett, whose impressive work and collegial spirit set a standard that's hard to match. A special thanks goes to Egbert N. ("Beets") Grazette and Clotilde O. de Guerra, who took far better care of me during this project than anyone deserves, especially a scruffy travel writer. Leslie Zellers had to deal with all the logistical headaches of managing my life in the U.S. while I was bopping around Panama. I will always be grateful to her for that, and for much more besides. My colleagues and editors at Contra Costa Newspapers showed me great support and understanding throughout this project, something that's all too rare in our profession. I thank them all. With John Muir Publications and Avalon Travel Publishing, I have had the rare good luck to work with skilled, good-natured, and patient professionals, some of whom I've never met. I hope one day I'll be able to thank them personally. Finally, I want to thank Teresa Tulipano, who helped me out of more than one jam, and who never used too much force.

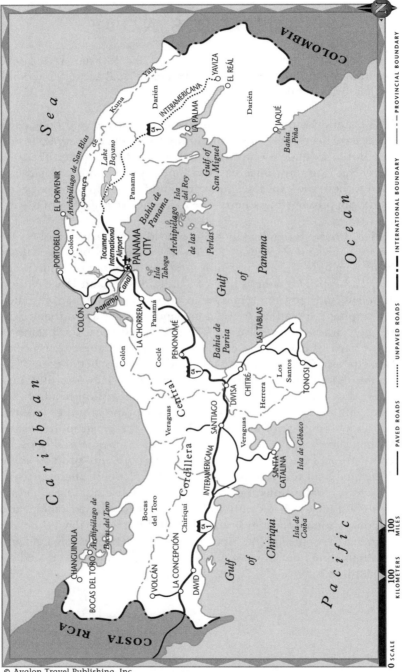

CHAPTER 1

Panama: An Overview

That you've picked up this book means you're at least toying with the idea of going to Panama. Do it.

There may never be a better time. It's hard to think of a single country on the planet that has the peculiar combination Panama offers: incredible natural beauty, a modern infrastructure, good roads, clean water, year-round warm weather, a peaceful atmosphere, a rich history—and almost no tourists.

In fact, Panama has more of almost everything that has made its more famous Latin American neighbors such a hit with ecologically minded and adventurous travelers.

There's a tropical forest within the limits of Panama City, the country's cosmopolitan capital. Another, particularly impressive one is just a half-hour drive away. In the highlands to the west and the Darién to the east lie virgin forests bigger than some countries. The Darién in particular is one of the most spectacular forests in the tropics, and no road has ever been cut all the way through it.

Panama's two oceans are so close together you can swim in both in a single morning. And in both you'll find endless islands, coral reefs, and mangrove forests. Visitors into water sports can enjoy world-class diving, snorkeling, surfing, and deep-sea fishing, as well as great sailing, kayaking, and white-water rafting. Onshore you can explore everything from cool cloud forests to sweltering rain forests.

Among the incredible diversity of Panama's flora and fauna are hundreds of species found nowhere else on earth. Though their numbers are dwindling, jaguars, pumas, and other big cats still prowl close to settled areas. And little Panama is a bird-watcher's dream with close to a thousand species, more than you'd find in all of North America.

Panama has long been known as a "crossroads of the world," which shows in the international sophistication and ethnically mixed population of its capital city. Panama also has seven indigenous peoples who have, to varying degrees, managed to preserve their cultures. The Kunas of the San Blas Islands, off the Caribbean coast, have survived by adapting to wave after wave of foreign visitors over hundreds of years without ever giving up their autonomy. Many of the Emberá and Wounaan, on the other hand, still live in the Darién forests in much the same way they have for thousands of years.

Visitors fascinated by history will soon learn that a surprising amount of it has been played out on the narrow isthmus of Panama. Balboa discovered the Pacific here. Sir Francis Drake was buried at sea off the Caribbean coast. The 49ers risked malaria and yellow fever as they struggled across the isthmus on their way to the gold fields of California. A late-1800s scandal that nearly destroyed France began in Panama. And on and on.

You can find reminders of Panama's remarkable history throughout the country. The ruins of old Spanish forts still guard the coastlines of both oceans. Even in Panama City, the cobblestone streets and colonial architecture of the Casco Viejo neighborhood will make you feel you've gone back in time.

And then there's the Panama Canal, still one of the wonders of the modern world. A transit through the canal, across the mountains and jungles of Panama, is unforgettable and easily arranged even for those who avoid cruise ships.

Perhaps the best thing about Panama for the adventurous traveler is that most tourists haven't yet caught on to what it has to offer. It's easy to find a white sandy beach without another human being on it for miles in either direction. Some lovely natural sights are so little advertised that even many Panamanians hardly know of them.

Virgin turf, however, does come at a price. Tourism of any kind, let alone ecotourism, is still so new to parts of Panama that visitors will face challenges they wouldn't find in more traveled parts of Latin America. At times you may feel like a pioneer, with all the excitement and frustration that implies.

But if the going gets rough, Panama City is never more than a day's journey away. It's a metropolis with the resources you'd find in any large U.S. city and with better restaurants than most.

The first ecotourism tours and resorts are just beginning to appear in Panama. You may be among the first to enjoy them, experiencing the natural riches of the land and oceans in a sustainable way. In doing so, you may help steer the course of Panama's future development, ensuring that the country's startling beauty is preserved for its people and the generations of visitors who come after you.

LAY OF THE LAND

The Republic of Panama covers 75,517 square kilometers (29,452 square miles), which makes it slightly bigger than Ireland and slightly smaller than South Carolina. Panama is a young country in geological terms. It emerged from the sea just 2.5 million years ago, dividing the Atlantic from the Pacific and forming a natural land bridge connecting the North and South American continents. The bridge has allowed North and South American species to intermingle. Known as the Great American Interchange, this mingling had a profound effect on the ecology of South America; the effect was much more modest in North America. The only originally South American animals that continue to thrive up north are armadillos and opossums.

Panama's peculiar, snake-like shape—which resembles the letter "S" turned on its side—is confusing to many visitors. It takes a while to get used to the notion that the Caribbean Sea is to the north and the Pacific Ocean to the south. Many also find it strange

The private island of Achutupu, San Blas Islands

to be able to watch the sun rising in the Pacific and setting in the Caribbean, or to realize that when you transit the Panama Canal from the Pacific to the Caribbean you actually end up slightly west of where you started. (Look at a map.)

Panama is at the eastern end of Central America, bordered to the west by Costa Rica and to the east by Colombia. It's far longer than it is wide. The oceans are just 80 kilometers (50 miles) apart at the Panama Canal, near the middle of the country, and that isn't even the narrowest spot on the isthmus. But the country stretches surprisingly far to the east and west; Panama has nearly 3,000 kilometers (over 1,800 miles) of coastline along its Caribbean and Pacific flanks.

People often wonder which body of water is the "higher" of the two. The reality is there's no difference in elevation—sea level is sea level. A locks canal was necessary in Panama not to keep the oceans from spilling into each other but to carry ships over the land mass of the isthmus. However, there is a dramatic difference between the tides on the Caribbean and Pacific sides. The Caribbean tide aver-

4

ages less than half a meter (1.5 feet); Pacific tides can be more than ten times that high.

Many visitors are surprised to discover how mountainous Panama is. The most impressive mountain range is the Cordillera Central, which bisects the western half of the country, extending from the Costa Rican border east toward the canal. It contains Panama's highest mountain, Volcán Barú, an extinct volcano that is 3,475 meters (11,400 feet) high. Another impressive range runs along Panama's eastern Caribbean coast, starting at the Comarca de Kuna Yala and ending at the Colombian border. It officially comprises the Serranía de San Blas to the west and the Serranía del Darién to the east, where it enters Darién Province.

Besides the humid tropical forests that people expect to find, which compose a third of Panama's remaining forests, Panama has a great variety of other ecosystems, ranging from cloud forests to deserts. Extensive mangroves, coral reefs, and hundreds of islands can be found on both the Pacific and Caribbean sides of the isthmus. Panama also has at least 500 rivers.

FLORA AND FAUNA

Panama's role as a narrow land bridge between North and South America makes it home to a particularly rich variety of animal and plant life. Sadly, the future of this abundant life is by no means secure: The World Conservation Monitoring Centre's Red List of threatened animals includes 112 species found in Panama.

Panama is especially well known for its incredible array of bird species, of which 960 have been identified so far. Panama is also home to well over 200 mammal and 200 reptile species, close to 200 amphibian species, and more than 10,000 species of plants. Some of these are found nowhere else in the world.

Panama has a wide array of animals that thrill nature tourists, though many are not easy to spot. There are five species of big cats on the isthmus, including the jaguar. Other mammals include giant anteaters, white-lipped and collared peccaries, howler monkeys, white-faced capuchins, spider monkeys, Geoffroy's tamarins, two- and three-toed sloths, and Baird's tapirs. Several species of sea turtles still come ashore in large numbers on both coasts. The seas are filled with brilliant tropical fish as well as impressive large specimens, including white-tip, hammerhead, tiger, and whale sharks; dolphins; orcas; humpback whales; marlins; manta rays; jewfish; moray eels; barracudas; big snappers; and much more.

Stunning birds include five species of macaws; toucans; the harpy eagle, the world's most powerful bird of prey; and the resplendent quetzal, which has been called the most beautiful bird on the planet.

HISTORY

It has been said of Panama that there are few other places where so much history has passed through a land and left so little trace behind. Much of what little the tropical forests and rains spared has been looted by grave-robbers and other treasure-seekers.

Humans have lived on the isthmus of Panama for at least 10,000 years, possibly far longer. They left behind no massive structures, such as the pyramids found elsewhere in the Americas, and information on a number of lost civilizations is sketchy. But archeologists found one of the most ancient sites in the Americas at Monagrillo, on Panama's Azuero Peninsula; it dates back to 3,000 B.C. The Barriles culture of western Panama lasted from 734 B.C. to A.D. 600, when the eruption of Volcán Barú put an end to this long-lived civilization. Intriguing, mysterious stone sculptures damaged by the eruption but still largely intact can be seen at the Reina Torres de Araúz Anthropological Museum in Panama City.

The arrival of the Spanish in 1501 spelled the end of the indigenous peoples' dominion over the isthmus and the beginning of the European conquest. The first arrival was an explorer named Rodrigo de Bastidas, whose crew included a seaman by the name of Vasco Núñez de Balboa; 12 years later Balboa would become the first European to hack his way through the Darién and lay eyes on the "Southern Sea," the Pacific Ocean. In 1502 Christopher Columbus also stumbled upon the isthmus, on his fourth and final voyage to find a westward passage to the Indies.

Panama City was founded on August 15, 1519, by Pedro Arias

de Ávila, the governor of the young Spanish colony. Better known as Pedrarias, he has gone down in history as a cruel man who treated the indigenous peoples horrifically. He also had Balboa, his rival, put to death on a trumped-up charge of treason in January 1519.

Panama's great importance to Spain was as a transshipment point for the silver, gold, pearls, and other treasures plundered from South America. These riches were brought to Panama City, on the Pacific coast, and then taken across the isthmus to the Caribbean coast, where Spanish ships transported them to Europe. The loot was taken by land on a narrow, muddy trail, or else by land for about a third of the way across the isthmus and then down the Río Chagres to the coast. Parts of this second route, the Camino de Cruces (Las Cruces Trail) still exist and can be walked to this day.

All this wealth made Panama a target of pirates and buccaneers for hundreds of years. The most famous of them all, Sir Francis Drake, died in Panama in 1596. His leaded coffin, which has never been found, is said to be lying somewhere in the waters off Portobelo, near where he performed some of his most famous exploits. In 1671, Panama City was sacked and burned by the Welsh pirate Henry Morgan. The city was rebuilt eight kilometers (about 5 miles) west of the original city, in what is now known as Casco Viejo.

Panama gained its independence from Spain in 1821 as part of a South American confederacy that soon dissolved, leaving just Colombia and its backwater province, Panama, in an uneasy union known as New Granada.

The California Gold Rush brought Panama back onto the world stage in another quest for treasure. For 49ers eager to reach California's gold fields, crossing the isthmus shaved thousands of miles off the arduous trip across the North American continent. It was a brutal journey that took many lives. But the flood of gold-seekers willing to pay any amount to cross the isthmus was the impetus for the building of the Panama Railroad. Though only 80 kilometers (50 miles) long, the railroad was an incredibly costly undertaking, both in dollars and lives. It was said that every railroad tie represented one worker dead from disease. That's an exaggeration, but untold thousands did die building the little railroad through the jungle; it was completed in 1855.

For hundreds of years, visionaries had dreamed of building a canal across the isthmus. The French finally undertook the challenge in 1882. They attempted to build a sea-level canal across Panama's forbidding terrain, and they failed disastrously. It has been estimated that 20,000 workers died, mostly of disease, during the seven years the French spent on the effort. The French canal company ran out of money in 1889, and the ensuing financial crisis nearly bankrupted France.

The United States then decided to try building a canal of its own. It bought out the French concession, but clashed with the government of New Granada (Colombia) over payments and the granting of rights over the proposed waterway. When negotiations stalled, the United States, under President Theodore Roosevelt, decided to support a small independence movement in Panama. In a display of literal "gunboat diplomacy," America sent a warship to Panama to intimidate the Colombian forces on the isthmus. It was a relatively peaceful civil war: the only casualty was a Chinese shopkeeper asleep in his bed, killed by an errant shell from a Colombian gunboat. On November 3, 1903, Panama declared its independence from New Granada.

The United States immediately signed a controversial treaty with the new Panamanian government that gave America the right to build a canal in Panama. The treaty granted the United States control over the canal and an 80-by-16-kilometer (50-by-10-mile) strip of land surrounding it "in perpetuity."

The American effort was quite different from the French one. Instead of a sea-level ditch, the U.S. plan called for a lock canal that would lift ships over the isthmian land mass. All work on the canal had to be halted, however, until disease could be controlled. The Americans eliminated yellow fever from Panama, brought malaria under control, and introduced clean water and modern sanitation methods.

The U.S. canal effort cost $352 million and took 5,600 lives, most of them West Indians who made up the bulk of the labor force. But the canal opened for business on August 15, 1914, under budget and ahead of schedule.

A growing sense of nationalism in Panama led to a new treaty being signed in 1977 that turned the canal over to Panama during a long transitional period. Panama assumed full control of the canal at noon on December 31, 1999.

Panama's political history through much of this century has been a repeated cycle of democratically elected governments overthrown by military dictatorships. The repressive military regime of General Manuel Antonio Noriega during the 1980s led to increasing unrest in Panama and a clash with the United States. On December 20, 1989, U.S. forces invaded Panama in a mission dubbed "Operation Just Cause." Noriega was eventually captured, brought to the U.S. for trial on drug charges, and sentenced to 40 years in a Florida prison.

Today Panama has a democratically elected government and its first female president, Mireya Moscoso.

Though Panama has a high income percapita for a Latin American country, there is a wide disparity between the haves and have-nots, as a tour around Panama City quickly makes clear. The unemployment rate among those 15 and older considered "economically active" is believed to be around 14 percent. Far too many Panamanians still live in poverty, especially given the country's relative affluence. More than a third of the population is below the poverty line, according to the World Bank. That figure rises to more than half the population in rural areas, with the indigenous peoples the poorest of all.

Still, Panama is a prosperous country by Latin American standards. It's an international banking capital with a growing economy that has largely recovered from the upheavals of the Noriega years. The Panama Canal, an oil pipeline across the isthmus, and the Colón Free Zone (a major free-trade zone on the Caribbean side of the isthmus) ensure Panama's status as an important center for international commerce. Panama's main export is bananas, followed by seafood, sugar, coffee, and leather.

CULTURE

Panama's official language is Spanish, and the predominant religion is Roman Catholicism.

9

Kuna women and girls

The population of Panama was estimated to be 2.8 million in 2000. The majority of the population is mestizo, of mixed Spanish and indigenous descent. There is also a substantial black population. Most are descendants of African slaves from the Spanish colonial era or English-speaking West Indians (also called Afro-Antilleans) brought over by the French and then the Americans to dig the Panama Canal, or, in Bocas del Toro Province, by the banana companies to work on plantations.

As befits "the crossroads of the world," many other ethnic groups from around the globe have been added to the mix over the years. There's an especially large Chinese population, whose presence dates back to the grueling days of the construction of the Panama Railroad in the 19th century.

Indigenous peoples make up about 8 percent of Panama's population. Seven different indigenous groups are recognized in Panama: the Ngöbe-Buglé (or Guaymi), Kuna, Emberá, Wounaan, Bokota, Teribe, and Bri-Bri.

The Ngöbe-Buglé are by far the most numerous, with a population of about 125,000. Most live in the highlands of western Panama, a large part of which was carved out recently for a semi-autonomous *comarca*, or reservation. The second-largest group is the Kuna, who number about 50,000. Most live in the islands and mainland of the Comarca de Kuna Yala, along Panama's eastern Caribbean coast. The Emberá and Wounaan, once known collectively as "Chocos," live primarily in the Darién and number about 18,000. All these numbers are rough, as reliable census figures do not exist. The populations of the other groups are very small.

As in other Latin American countries, machismo is a fact of life in Panama. Women may find they have to deal with unwanted male attention. Generally this doesn't get too obnoxious; if you ignore the guy making a comment or honking his horn, he usually won't persist.

Despite Panama's undeserved reputation as a dangerous place, you'll find that it's actually a remarkably mellow and low-key place to travel. It's extremely rare to encounter hostility or belligerence. Courtesy is considered quite important, however. Locals may take offense if they feel they're not being treated with dignity and respect.

You should be cautious of petty crime in the cities just as you would in a city back home. But except for Colón and a few poor parts of Panama City, you're unlikely to have any problems.

Foreigners sometimes complain that the Panamanians they encounter in stores and offices seem unfriendly or sullen. This complaint is most often made about Panama City; in the countryside, visitors are frequently overwhelmed by the warmth and friendliness they encounter. If you feel you're being treated rudely, do not raise your voice or snap at the offending party—this will get you absolutely nowhere. Be patient and polite, and if you have the option take your business elsewhere the next time. Similarly, the less you expect punctuality and speediness the happier you will be.

It'll be very tempting for you to wear skimpy, sloppy clothes in the Panamanian heat. Resist the temptation. Panama is still a rather formal place, and in some ways it's getting more formal: The widespread use of air-conditioners has made business suits much more common in recent years.

You will be treated much better if you dress neatly and conservatively. You'll notice that even the poorest Panamanians tend to be as

11

well-dressed and clean as they can afford to be. That a tourist with far more resources isn't willing to make a similar effort doesn't go over too well in Panama. You should be especially careful about what you wear in government office buildings and churches.

Shorts and revealing tops are to be worn only on the beach. Sneakers are not considered acceptable footwear in restaurants, bars, and nightclubs. And driving in Panama without a shirt is against the law.

CUISINE

Traditional Panamanian food leans heavily on starches and on red meat, chicken, and pork. Green vegetables do not grow well in the tropics, so outside of better restaurants in the cities don't be surprised if fried plantain is as close as you'll come to a veggie side dish. And even in cosmopolitan Panama City vegetarians will have a tough time finding a balanced meal.

Fish is excellent in Panama. The most common one you'll find on the menu is also one of the most delicious: corvina. It's a delicately flavored saltwater fish that even those not crazy about seafood will probably love. If you eat fish, you shouldn't leave Panama without trying it. Restaurants often prepare it a dozen different ways, but usually simplest is best. Prepared well, corvina *a la plancha* (grilled corvina) is hard to beat. Guabina is similar to corvina; you'll tend to find it at the fancier restaurants.

Other seafood you're likely to come across include shrimp *(camarones)*, prawns *(langostinos)*, squid *(calamares)*, octopus *(pulpo)*, crab *(cangrejo)*, and lobster *(langosta)*. You may want to think twice about eating lobster in Panama since it's terribly overfished; see Chapter 2, Conservation and Responsible Tourism, for more information. Ceviche in Panama is delicious. Traditionally it consists of raw corvina marinated in lime juice, peppers, and onions, which chemically "cook" the fish. It's increasingly common to find shrimp or octopus ceviche, or ceviche made from a combination of all three.

A staple of the Panamanian diet is yuca or manioc. It's a root vegetable prepared in a variety of ways. Most commonly you'll encounter deep-fried yuca, which when done right is crispy and golden-brown on the outside and chewy on the inside. *Carimañolas* are a kind of roll made from ground and boiled yuca that is generally stuffed with meat then deep fried.

Plantains *(plátanos)*, which are similar to bananas, are even more common. By the end of your trip you will probably have had more than your fill of *patacones*, which are green plantains cut crossways into discs, fried, pressed, and then fried again. These can be tasty when hot; they turn into concrete when cold. Ripe plantains are typically sliced lengthwise and then either fried or sprinkled with cinnamon and baked or broiled with butter. Fried plantains are called *tajadas*; the baked or broiled plantain dish is known as *plátanos maduros* or *plátanos en tentación*.

Other typical treats include empanadas, a kind of turnover made with flour or corn pastry that is stuffed with spiced ground meat and fried; tamales, which are made from boiled ground corn stuffed with chicken or pork and spices, then wrapped in banana leaves and boiled; and tortillas, which in Panama are thick, fried corncakes often served with breakfast in the countryside.

The Panamanian palate doesn't tend to favor lots of spices, and you may find some of your meals to be rather bland. But done well, even the simplest country fare can be delicious. Try *sancocho*, a thick and hearty soup usually made with chicken, yuca, and whatever vegetables are around. *Ropa vieja* ("old clothes") is also good; it consists of spiced shredded beef served over rice. *Arroz con pollo* (rice with chicken) is also a common dish.

Outside of Panama City, you'll tend to find the same dishes over and over again on menus. Main dishes will typically involve beef (usually referred to as "*carne*," though literally this just means "meat"), chicken *(pollo)*, and pork *(puerco)*. A good strategy to keep from getting bored with your options is to take advantage of the very good international restaurants in Panama City and save more traditional fare for trips into the countryside.

OUTDOOR ACTIVITIES

Panama is a great place for hiking, trekking, snorkeling, scuba diving, sailing, surfing, windsurfing, water-skiing, white-water rafting, sea and

13

river kayaking, bird-watching, fishing, biking, and horseback riding.

The catch is that it's not always easy to find an outfitter for everything you want to do. Hiking and diving are generally easy to arrange, but in most places you'll find it impossible to rent kayaks, surfboards, sailboards, and even bikes. This is slowly changing, however, and there may be several more options by the time you visit.

HOW MUCH WILL IT COST?

You can travel in Panama on almost any budget.

If you're an extremely bare-bones traveler who doesn't mind spending the night in rock-bottom places, you can find a room for $5 to $10 a night even in the cities. And if you eat where the local workers eat, you can stuff yourself silly for just a couple of dollars.

However, this book is written with the idea you'll want to stay and eat at places at least several notches up from the bottom, which can get kind of dodgy in Panama. Most hotel rooms listed start at upper-end economy or mid-range and may not be as cheap as you're used to in other parts of the developing world. Expect to pay $25 to $40 for a decent double room, with accommodations in Panama City toward the high end of that range. You can find quite nice hotels in Panama City for under $100 per couple, and if you want to indulge there are plenty of fancy places where you can get far more for about $200 per couple than you'd get in a comparable place in the States.

The good news for economy-minded travelers who like a bit of comfort is that, while prices don't start out super cheap in the countryside, they tend not to go sky-high either. Except for the luxury resorts, you'd be hard-pressed to find even good hotels that charge more than about $40 to $70 per couple outside the cities. This is partly because of a shortage of great accommodations in the hinterlands, but in many places you can stay at surprisingly nice places for little money. And even the luxurious places are not generally outrageous.

If you eat at an elegant restaurant in Panama City you will pay about what you would at a comparable restaurant in a U.S. city. Main dishes will cost you around $10 to $15 at the higher-end

AUTHOR'S TOP PICKS

These are my choices for the top spots in Panama for a variety of outdoor activities. The choices take into account both the quality of the experience and the ease of having that experience. For instance, the diving around Isla de Coiba is more spectacular than that around Bocas del Toro, but the latter is far more accessible and affordable.

Scuba Diving—Parque Nacional Isla de Coiba, San Blas Islands (when allowed), Perlas Archipelago, Bocas del Toro Archipelago

Snorkeling—Perlas Archipelago, San Blas Islands, Parque Nacional Isla de Coiba, Bocas del Toro Archipelago

Sea Kayaking—Bocas del Toro Archipelago

Windsurfing—Punta Chame

White-water Rafting/Kayaking—Río Chiriquí and Río Chiriquí Viejo

Bird-watching—Cana, Pipeline Road, around the Canopy Tower, around Cabañas Los Quetzales, around the Fortuna reservoir area, in and around the San Lorenzo Protected Area

Wildlife Viewing—Parque Nacional Darién, Parque Nacional Soberanía, Parque Internacional La Amistad, Fortuna reservoir area, Isla Boca Brava, Barro Colorado Island, Punta Patiño

Hiking—Parque Nacional Darién, Parque Internacional La Amistad, Parque Nacional Volcán Barú, around the Fortuna reservoir

Sea Turtle Nesting Spots—Bocas del Toro Archipelago, Isla de Cañas

Surfing—Playa Santa Catalina, Morro Negrito Surf Camp

Horseback Riding—El Valle de Anton, Boquete, Cerro Punta.

Sport fishing—Piñas Bay and around Isla de Coiba

places. Outside Panama City you'll rarely pay more than $7 for a full dinner, and there are plenty of quite decent places that offer food for far less.

Travel within Panama is generally cheap. The costliest round-trip airfare from Panama City to the most distant regions served by commercial small planes is about $100. You can travel by comfortable air-conditioned bus from Panama City to David, near the Costa Rican border, for less than $11, and most nearer destinations cost a fraction of that.

Traveling to the Darién, however, is not cheap. Package deals including all meals and transportation to the most remote parts of the Darién can add from $400 to more than $1,000 per person to your travel budget for a multiday trip. But if you can possibly afford it, you really should consider adding a Darién trip to your itinerary. It's the experience of a lifetime.

Advance purchase round-trip airfare between Miami, the most popular U.S. gateway city, and Panama City averages around $350, though deals are often available.

WHEN TO VISIT

Panama has two seasons, the rainy and the dry. The rainy season, which in Panama is also known as the winter *(invierno)*, generally lasts from about mid-April to mid-December. The rains tend to be heaviest at the end of the rainy season, as though the heavens are wringing out every last drop of moisture. October, November, and the beginning of December can be downright torrential.

Yearly rainfall averages around 3,000 millimeters (for those not metrically inclined, that's nearly 10 *feet* of rain). It's far rainier on the Caribbean side than the Pacific. Even in the rainy season, though, the rains in most parts of Panama tend to come in the afternoon or early evening, so it's often possible to enjoy clear mornings. When the rains do arrive, they typically dump an unbelievable amount of water in an hour or even less—sometimes storms last just a few minutes—and then move on. Storms tend to last longer, and come earlier, late in the rainy season.

Those who've never experienced a tropical downpour may want

to consider visiting Panama in the rainy season; the storms can be quite stupendous. The skies dump a veritable waterfall on the landscape, often accompanied by earth-shattering thunderclaps. However, it's not a great time to go on long hikes or drive on rough roads, as the mud can be overwhelming and rising rivers can make some routes impassable.

The dry season, also known as the summer *(verano)*, is Panama's high season. The weather is especially lovely just after the rains finally stop. Flowering trees all over the country burst into bloom, and everything seems fresh and luminously green. Later in the dry season the lowlands turn brown and slash-and-burn agriculture can fill the sky with smoke.

It's much easier to get around in rugged country during the dry season. Dirt roads that a good four-wheel-drive vehicle would have a tough time tackling in the rainy season are often tame enough for regular cars once the mud bakes dry. Note that the rain never stops completely in some parts of the country. You should be prepared for some precipitation year-round along the Caribbean coast, in the western highlands, and on the islands of Bocas del Toro.

You'll hear many different theories about the best time of year to go diving and snorkeling in Panama. The consensus is that the rainy season tends to be a better time to dive. In the dry season, strong winds stir up the ocean and bring sediment from the bottom, spoiling visibility. This is much less of a problem in the rainy season, and a light rain can actually help calm the waters. However, if you're diving in an area where many rivers empty into the sea, runoff following a rain can also wreck visibility.

Panama lies between seven and 10 degrees north of the equator. The climate is typically tropical, and days and nights are almost equally long throughout the year. Expect about 12 hours of night and 12 hours of daylight; sunrise and sunset vary by only about half an hour during the year.

Temperatures in Panama are fairly constant year-round. In the lowlands, these range from about 32°C (90°F) in the day down to 21°C (70°F) in the evening. It never gets cold in the lowlands, and the dry-season breezes in the evening are very pleasant. It gets considerably cooler in the highlands. Panama can be quite humid year-round, but especially so in the rainy season.

Panama is south of the hurricane zone so is spared those terrible storms.

Panama's biggest holiday is Carnaval, which is held each year in the four days leading up to Ash Wednesday. The country comes to a complete halt during Carnaval. If you're into massive parties this may be for you, but bear in mind that hotels in the Carnaval hot spots book up a year ahead of time, and plane reservations can be hard to come by as well. Besides the usual Christian holy days and New Year's day, other major holidays include Martyr's Day on January 9, Independence from Colombia Day on November 3, and Independence from Spain Day on November 28.

ORIENTATION AND TRANSPORTATION

Most international visitors arrive by air at Panama's Tocumen International Airport. Travelers often get a poor first impression of Panama based on this dreary, disorganized place. Don't worry: You'll probably be pleasantly surprised when you get to Panama City proper, which is congested and chaotic but also modern and glittery.

There is an IPAT (Instituto Panameño de Turismo, the Panamanian government tourist bureau) information booth inside the baggage claim area that may or may not be staffed when you arrive. It has a few hotel brochures but little else.

Once you clear customs and immigration and come out into the arrivals area, you'll see an IPAT-sponsored taxi booth straight ahead. This is the airport's best feature. If you want to take a taxi into the city, tell the person at the booth where you want to go. He or she will take your money (expect to pay about $25 to downtown Panama City, less if you're willing to share the ride), print out a receipt, and call over a neatly dressed driver who'll take you to your destination in a clean, late-model car. You may be able to work out a better deal with an independent cabbie—several of whom will probably approach you as you exit the airport—but beware of scams.

For information on Panama City's domestic airport and transportation within the city, see Chapter 3, Panama City. Long-distance bus information is included in Appendix A.

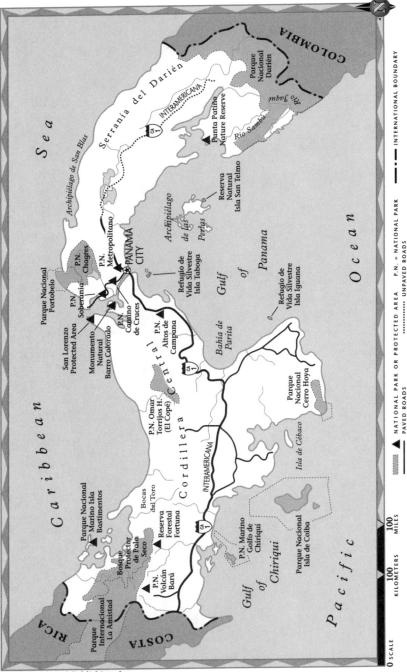

© Avalon Travel Publishing, Inc.

CHAPTER 2

Conservation and Responsible Tourism

Environmental destruction in the tropics is a terrible, disheartening thing to witness. There's plenty of it going on in Panama, as you'll see below.

But anyone who's had a long association with Panama can't help but feel at least some optimism these days. There's greater environmental awareness among the average Panamanian than ever before. While it's still a far-too-common sight to see citizens trashing their own country, there are also people out there cleaning up the mess—or at least refusing to add to it.

New environmental protection laws and organizations are being created, and new protected areas are being set aside. It's true that resources and the political will to back up the good intentions are often lacking. It's also true that greed and the march of "progress" often undo the modest achievements that are made. But there is a genuine environmental movement in Panama now, a claim that would have been hard to make 20 years ago.

The message that natural beauty is something to love and cherish is finally being heard, in everything from TV public-service ads to handwritten pleas posted by citizens determined to save a favorite bit of nature.

Panamanians are waking up to the realization that they live in

one of the most incredibly rich havens for life on the planet. One hopes that a pride in preserving that richness will outweigh the traditional belief in "taming" the wilderness.

WHAT IS ECOTOURISM?

"Ecotourism" is one of those amorphous words that seems to mean something different to everyone who uses it. For the purposes of the Adventure in Nature series, ecotourism means low-impact, environmentally responsible travel. This book is written for travelers who, given the choice, would rather stay in a small, locally owned hotel than a five-star resort, and who want their visit to Panama to cause as little stress on the environment as possible. The book also attempts, when appropriate, to point out ways in which those so motivated can become better educated about Panamanian environmental issues and perhaps even help out in some way.

ENVIRONMENTAL PROBLEMS IN PANAMA

Forty percent of the Republic of Panama, a little over three million hectares (nearly 7.5 million acres) of land, was still covered by forest in 1998, the most recent date for which figures were available at the time of writing. That's the good news.

The bad news is that 50 years ago, the figure was 70 percent. In other words, in the last half of the 20th century Panama lost nearly half its remaining forests—about 2.2 million hectares of wild, species-rich nature wiped out.

Even more disturbing, the trend continues even in an era of increased environmental awareness and new environmental protection laws. Between 1992 and 1998, Panama lost another 4 percent of its forests.

These forests have mostly been converted into farms and cattle ranches, or paved over to make way for cities and towns. Once the forest cover is gone, the soil erodes easily under Panama's incredible downpours. This is worsened by the fact that nearly 78 percent of Panama's land is mountainous, with a high potential for erosion.

The soil is generally of poor quality in any case and is quickly overexploited, leading to the need for more land and thus more deforestation. This process is accelerated by a traditional culture that honors "conquering the jungle" and by antiquated laws still on the books that actually encourage the destruction of the forest, including one that establishes the cutting down of trees as proof of ownership of land.

Len Kaufman

Cows grazing

Loss of Panama's forests is a critical problem not just for the country but also for the Americas in general. Panama is a natural land bridge linking the species of North and South America. While the Pacific side of the isthmus has been severely deforested, the forests on the Atlantic slopes, along with the Darién in eastern Panama, are under attack but still more or less intact, forming a vibrant biological corridor through the country. The loss or fragmentation of these forests, which some see as all but inevitable unless immediate steps are taken, could have profound, far-reaching effects. Consider birds alone: 122 migratory bird species regularly pass through Panama, and many more make the trip occasionally. What happens to them if the biological corridor disappears?

Water pollution and the shrinking of Panama's watersheds are also serious problems. Raw sewage and industrial waste are dumped directly into Panama Bay, for instance, turning what was once a tremendously vital body of water into a contaminated zone. It wasn't all that many years ago that kids used to go swimming in Panama Bay right across the street from bustling Panama City. Now no one in their right mind would so much as stick their toe into the water. Fishing in the bay has long been banned. At low tide, the smell wafting off the bay can be overpowering.

You can go to the most remote, untouched islands and beaches of Panama and find a ring of trash on the shores, carried there by currents that pass near cities and towns where garbage is dumped indiscriminately. Pollution is also damaging coral reefs, and over-fishing is doing even more damage to the biodiversity of the seas.

Mangroves are a vital and fragile component of marine ecosystems, and they help prevent coastal erosion. But in the last 30 years, Panama has lost nearly 6,000 hectares of mangroves, cut down to make way for construction projects, resorts, cattle ranches, shrimp farms, and the like. Mangroves have also been lost through pollution and direct exploitation.

The Panama Canal watershed is the most important in Panama. It supplies the water needed to run the Panama Canal, and provides drinking water to Panama City, Colón, and their environs, where most of the country's population live. A 1999 joint report by the Smithsonian Tropical Research Institute, the National Authority of the Environment (Autoridad Nacional del Ambiente, or ANAM), and USAID (United States Agency for International Development) found that the severe deforestation in the watershed that had been underway since the 1950s has been curtailed in recent years. But it also found that the watershed is hardly out of danger. It's in the middle of a densely populated area and is under great human pressure. Two divided highways completed in the late 1990s cut right through Parque Nacional Soberanía and Parque Natural Metropolitano, "protected" areas that are important parts of the watershed. And in years to come it's going to be important not only to preserve the watershed but also to expand it as the demands for fresh water increase. Panama's thirsty population is growing, and a proposed third set of locks at the canal would greatly increase the amount of water needed for transiting ships.

The purity of Panama's drinking water, a legacy of the Panama Canal Company's strict hygiene standards, has long been a source of pride. You can turn on a tap almost anywhere in the country and be sure what you're drinking is safe. But water quality has deteriorated dramatically in recent years. The watershed report concluded that if immediate steps aren't taken, city dwellers will soon find themselves forced to drink bottled water.

Those who've traveled extensively in the developing w⌐⌐ not be overwhelmed by air pollution even in Panama's most congested urban areas. But this problem is also growing, particularly as more and more cars clog Panama's roads. Parts of Panama City register well above acceptable limits for airborne toxins. This is noticeable even to the casual observer. In the past, strong winds have kept Panama City's air relatively fresh. In my trips to Panama in recent years, however, I've finally noticed a brown haze hanging over the city on bad days.

ECOTOURISM IN PANAMA

Panama is experimenting with an ambitious approach to ecotourism known as TCR, which stands for Tourism, Conservation, and Research. (It's known in Spanish as TCI: Turismo-Conservación-Investigación.) The idea is to treat ecotourism, or "sustainable heritage tourism," as its proponents prefer to think of it, as part of an integrated approach to tourism that also emphasizes conservation and scientific research and focuses not just on nature but also on the history and culture of a region.

TCR strategists are proceeding slowly and carefully with their plans, and at the time of this writing the only practical accomplishment was the identification of 22 "heritage routes" in Panama around which future TCR projects might be based.

These range from historical, human-made routes, such as the "Route of the Treasures of the Americas"—the paths used by the Spanish to transport silver, gold, and other treasures brought up from South America—to natural routes, such as "the Bridge of the Quetzals," which focuses on the habitats of the resplendent and golden-headed quetzals.

The TCR initiative has impressive partners, including the Panama-based Smithsonian Tropical Research Institute and internationally respected architect Frank Gehry, who has signed on as a consultant, and it enjoyed support from the previous Panamanian administration. But it is currently unclear how strongly the new Panamanian government will embrace this strategy. Even if the policy receives continued support, exactly what projects will actually grow out of the initiative, and just how eco-friendly they'll actually be, are impossible to predict.

But "ecotourism" in general has become fashionable in Panama. Increasingly you see the "eco" tag added to the sales pitch of all kinds of hotels, tours, and attractions, sometimes with little justification. Just how far this can go became apparent when I visited an aging highland resort hotel on my most recent trip to Panama. The resort boasted that it now had an "ecological miniature-golf course"—consisting of a grass ramp on a sloping lawn.

Because hotels and tour operators know that "eco" can spell money for them, they have an incentive to exaggerate just how ecologically conscious their operations are. This is not yet a big problem in Panama, but it's easy to see how it could become one if nature tourism really takes off in the country. To help readers make informed decisions about who to go with, this book attempts to highlight the features of a place or an operation likely to appeal to a low-impact tourist (e.g., small-scale, locally owned hotels that tread lightly on their surroundings) as well as those features that may be off-putting (e.g., a private zoo on the property).

Environmentally sensitive tourism is so new to Panama that it's hard for tourists to be entirely pure about where they stay and how they travel. Even Panama's finest ecotourist lodges tend to have their shortcomings. One place I visited in the highlands seemed great; it even composted and recycled its waste, which is all but unheard of in Panama. As I was leaving, though, a friend pointed out the necklace worn by the son of the Guaymi Indian caretaker: it appeared to be made of jaguar teeth.

Because there's no way to know for sure how old those teeth were or where they came from, and it would be unfair in any case to blame the owners of the lodge for the traditional ways of its caretaker, I still recommend this place. More disturbing was a hike I took with a native guide who worked for another lodge. He was a terrific guide, a gentle soul who loved the beauty that surrounded him and was eager to share his knowledge. One morning, though, we came across what we thought might be a rare owl. Hoping to give my companions and me a look at the owl in flight, he threw a stick at it.

It's tricky to know how to handle something like this. If we had told the owner of the lodge about this incident, there was a very real possibility the guide, a poor man with a wife and several small children, would have been fired on the spot. We chose to ask him gently not to throw sticks at animals in the future.

The answer is almost definitely not to boycott those places and tour outfits that don't fit all our criteria for a low-impact, environmentally aware operation. Probably the most useful thing to do is to seek out those that are on the right track, and through our own actions encourage those qualities we like and discourage those we don't. Most of the best operations are owned and run by intelligent businesspeople who take great pride in what they're trying to accomplish. Don't be afraid to give them feedback, including criticisms. They're all still trying to figure out just what it is low-impact tourists want, and they'll likely be eager to hear your comments.

Panama has historically favored high-end resort tourism, and many large, fancy resorts were still being built as this was written. There has at times been a downright prejudice against backpacker-types as an unkempt lot perceived as adding little to the Panamanian economy. Nature tourists to Panama in the next few years may well

Pension y Restaurante Bastimentos, Bocas del Toro

play a critical role in shaping the future of Panamanian tourism. If entrepreneurs see a demand for responsible, low-impact nature travel, and they are shown that it can pay, in a few years there may be more simple eco-lodges and fewer sprawling five-star resorts.

PARKS AND PROTECTED AREAS

Panama has set aside nearly four dozen protected areas covering nearly two million hectares (close to five million acres) of land, or about 25 percent of Panama's total area. Most of this land is part of an extensive national parks system that also includes marine parks and one international park, the giant Parque Internacional la Amistad, that extends over the border into Costa Rica.

These protected areas are a relatively new phenomenon. The first one, Parque Nacional Altos de Campana, was set aside in 1966, and all the others have been created just in the last 25 years.

The parks and other protected areas are managed by the Autoridad Nacional del Ambiente (ANAM), which was created in 1998 to replace the even more imposingly named Instituto Nacional de Recursos Naturales Renovables (INRENARE), aka National Institute of Renewable Natural Resources. You will sometimes still hear people refer to ANAM as INRENARE.

Panama contains 12 of the 30 Holdridge life zones found on the planet. As you might imagine, by far the most common in Panama is humid tropical forest, which accounts for 32 percent of Panama's remaining forest cover. All of these zones but one, humid premontane forest, are represented in the system of protected areas. That system, by the way, is known in acronym-happy Panama as SINAP: Sistema Nacional de Areas Silvestres Protegidas, or National System of Protected Wilderness Areas.

As anyone who travels extensively in Panama's national parks will soon discover, just being named a protected area does not necessarily confer much protection. Illegal hunting, fishing, logging, and even farming continue in many of the protected areas, including the national parks. Although Panama enacted a series of strong environmental laws in the 1990s, so far the money, people, and political will to enforce them have not materialized.

William Friar

Dolphins, San Blas Islands

ANAM has only a couple hundred workers spread throughout the entire system of protected areas; it's been estimated at an average of one employee for every 7,000 hectares (more than 17,000 acres) of "protected" area. Sometimes they're spread far more thinly than that: there are only a handful of rangers at three rustic ranger stations to guard the entire 579,000 hectares (1.4 million acres) of Darién National Park. And a third of the protected areas do not have so much as a single ranger assigned to them. The rangers ANAM does have are very poorly paid, have little education, and often lack the most rudimentary of resources to work with. And there are still many ecologically important parts of Panama that are not even nominally protected.

There are laws on the books to protect endangered or threatened animals. Eighty-two species of vertebrates, for instance, are protected by Panamanian law. But don't be surprised if you see hunting going on rather openly. On my last trip to Taboga Island, for instance, I saw a local skin diver heading home to his wife, a sea turtle tucked under his arm. I told a young policeman what I had seen and pointed out the house. The policeman got a pained look

on his face and shook his head, but I didn't see him heading toward the man's home.

CONSERVATION GROUPS

Panama's largest conservation group is the nonprofit Asociación Nacional para la Conservación de la Naturaleza (National Association for the Conservation of Nature), or ANCON. Since its founding in 1985 it has played a key role in Panama's attempts to protect its environment.

ANCON has helped make the national parks more than just good ideas on paper by taking on such basic but critical projects as demarcating park boundaries and training park rangers. It also played an important role in creating Parque Internacional La Amistad and Parque Nacional Marino Isla Bastimentos, among other protected areas.

ANCON owns the country's largest private nature reserve, the 65,000-hectare Punta Patiño Reserve on the Darién coast. Its other holdings include Isla San Telmo in the Perlas Islands, which protects endangered moist premontane forest and is a sanctuary for brown pelicans and other animals. ANCON also owns several nature lodges around the country that are managed by Ancon Expeditions, a private for-profit organization that spun off from ANCON as a separate entity.

Other ANCON projects include mobilizing large groups of volunteers for reforestation projects and annual beach cleanups, providing training for other conservation groups, and spearheading public education campaigns. It also has a Conservation Data Center that uses satellite photos and other data sources to identify parts of the country most in need of environmental protection.

ANCON welcomes foreign volunteers who'd like to work on its projects. If you're interested, the best approach is to send ANCON a letter or email detailing your skills and saying when you'd like to come down and how long you'd like to stay. Try to be as specific as possible about how you think you can help. Write to Oscar Vallarino B., Director Ejecutivo, ANCON, Apartado 1387, Panamá 1, República de Panamá; or email ancon@ancon.org. You can get more information from the ANCON website: www.ancon.org.

ANCON works with the U.S.-based Nature Conservancy on some projects in Panama. For more information contact the Nature Conservancy at 4245 N. Fairfax Dr., Arlington, VA 22203-1606. You can also call 800/628-6860.

The prestigious Smithsonian Tropical Research Institute (STRI) is based in Panama. STRI is one of the world's leading centers for the study of tropical animals, plants, marine life, evolution, conservation, and much more. It's world famous for its research into lowland moist tropical forests on Barro Colorado Island, which is in the middle of the canal. Access to the island is strictly controlled, but STRI does offer some tours. Visitors are also welcome to visit its Centro de Exhibiciones Marinas (Marine Exhibition Center) on the Panama Canal Causeway and its research library at its headquarters near downtown Panama City. For information on all three, see Chapter 4, Panama Canal and Environs. STRI has many other projects in Panama, most of which are not open to the public.

The Panama Audubon Society (Sociedad Audubon de Panamá) hosts regular bird-watching tours, and nonmembers are invited to join them. The society is also a good source of information on nature hikes and backcountry places to stay, and some of its members are freelance guides. For information write to Sociedad Audubon de Panamá, Apartado 2026, Balboa-Panamá, República de Panamá; or email audupan@pananet.com. The society's phone number is 507/224-9371, fax 507/224-4740; its website is www.orbi.net/audubon.

TIPS FOR RESPONSIBLE TRAVEL

An overseas trip is supposed to be fun, not an exercise in political consciousness. But you'll get a lot more out of Panama, and help keep it an enjoyable destination for those who come after you, if before you go you make at least some effort to get to know the place and how your actions may affect it.

Start by reading up on the fascinating history of Panama, which for hundreds of years has earned its reputation as the "crossroads of the world," and learning a bit about its flora and fauna. A list of suggested starting points is included in Appendix B.

It would be nice to think that it goes without saying that buying souvenirs made from the body parts of endangered animals—jaguar teeth, tortoiseshell jewelry—is a big no-no. If not, remember that possessing these products is a serious crime in Panama. The same thing goes for possession of pre-Columbian pottery and other historic artifacts. Obviously, it's also illegal to eat endangered animals; do not partake of tortoise eggs or the like if these are ever offered to you.

Think about what you eat while in Panama. Lobster, for instance, has been terribly overfished in the San Blas Islands (Kuna Yala). You'll be tempted to try one while you're on the islands, but bear in mind that what was once a subsistence food for the Kuna is now in danger of extinction, which would have serious consequences for the Kuna and their environment. And it's not just in the San Blas that you should consider this: poor lobster divers sell their catch to fancy restaurants in Panama City. If nothing else, avoid lobster during the mating season, which runs from March to July. Consider that a female lobster carries thousands of eggs, but divers scoop up the expectant moms right along with the other lobsters. It'd be a shame if your dinner meant the end of a whole generation of baby lobsters.

Personal recreational watercraft (Jet Skis and the like) panic marine life, shatter the tranquillity of other beachgoers, and pollute the environment. Resist the temptation to go for a spin.

Be skeptical of tour operators and hotels that advertise themselves as eco-conscious. Ask them exactly what they mean by that, and what kind of environmentally conscious services they offer.

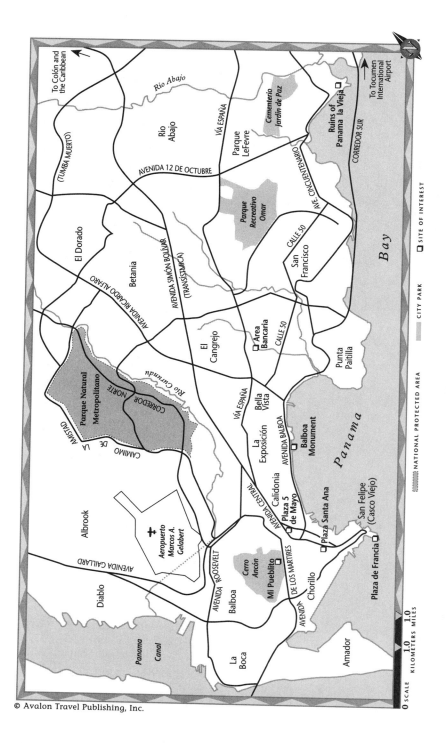

To Colón and the Caribbean

Río Abajo

Río Abajo

VÍA ESPAÑA

Cementerio Jardín de Paz

Parque LeFevre

Ruins of Panama la Vieja

To Tocumen International Airport

CORREDOR SUR

AVENIDA 12 DE OCTUBRE

(TUMBA MUERTO)

El Dorado

Parque Recreativo Omar

CALLE 50

San Francisco

Betania

AVENIDA SIMÓN BOLÍVAR (TRANSÍSTMICA)

AVE. CINCUENTENARIO

AVENIDA RICARDO ALFARO

Bay

Parque Natural Metropolitano

Río Curundú

CORREDOR NORTE

El Cangrejo

Area Bancaria

CALLE 50

Punta Paitilla

CAMINO DE LA AMISTAD

VÍA ESPAÑA

Bella Vista

La Exposición

AVENIDA BALBOA

Panamá

Albrook

Aeropuerto Marcos A. Gelabert

AVENIDA CENTRAL

Calidonia

Plaza 5 de Mayo

Plaza Santa Ana

Balboa Monument

Diablo

AVENIDA GAILLARD

AVENIDA ROOSEVELT

Cerro Ancón

Mi Pueblito

DE LOS MÁRTIRES

Chorillo

San Felipe (Casco Viejo)

Panama Canal

Balboa

La Boca

AVENIDA

Plaza de Francia

Amador

© Avalon Travel Publishing, Inc.

0 SCALE

1.0
KILOMETERS

1.0
MILES

NATIONAL PROTECTED AREA

CITY PARK

SITE OF INTEREST

CHAPTER 3

Panama City

Visitors who come to Panama for its natural treasures will be tempted to blast right through its capital on their way to the country's forests, mountains, islands, and beaches. But it'd be a shame not to spend at least a day or two in Panama City. Hundreds of years of history live on in its streets, and you'll find its more modern attractions appealing after roughing it in the wilderness for a while. Besides, it has its very own tropical forest within the city limits.

LAY OF THE LAND

The greater Panama City area is a growing metropolis of one million people, all of whom seem to be in cars 24 hours a day. Roads and public transportation have not kept pace with the city's growth, and the streets are choked during morning and evening rush hours. In recent years the city has grown east toward Tocumen International Airport, but with the U.S. turnover of the Panama Canal to Panama, urban sprawl has begun to creep west as well.

The part of Panama City that interests most visitors extends from the ruins of Panama la Vieja (Old Panama), west about eight kilometers (five miles) to Casco Viejo, where the city was moved after the Welsh pirate Henry Morgan sacked Panama la Vieja in 1671.

Most of the city's high-rises are in the ritzy Punta Paitilla district and the areas to its north and west. The heart of modern Panama City is in the area around Vía España, near which you'll find most of the upscale hotels. An older commercial center is found along Avenida Central in the Calidonia district. Part of this area, from Plaza Cinco de Mayo to Plaza Santa Ana, is now a walking street. Its shops deal mainly in electronics, jewelry, discount clothing, and the like, but it's worth a stroll for the people-watching even if you're not in a shopping mood. It's well patrolled by police, but be alert for pickpockets anyway.

Avenida Balboa sweeps along the edge of Panama Bay from Paitilla to Casco Viejo. A well-maintained promenade along the avenue, with an enormous statue of Balboa "discovering" the Pacific midway along, makes this a pleasant place for a morning or evening stroll. Try to time your stroll to coincide with high tide, when the view is nicer and the smell less potent (Panama City dumps its sewage into the bay).

Panama City skyline overlooking Panama Bay

William Friar

WHAT'S IN A NAME? QUITE A BIT.

The country of Panama gets its name from the city of Panama, but what does "Panama" mean? No one knows for sure.

The Spanish apparently got the name from a native fishing village not far from the modern capital. It's little wonder that the most common explanation is that Panama (or, to be proper, Panamá), is a forgotten Indian word for "abundance of fishes." Another theory is that the word means "abundance of butterflies." Yet another posits that the striking (and abundant) Panama tree gave the city, and later the country, its name. A personal favorite is that the word means "to rock in a hammock."

Take your pick: Any of the definitions still fits.

Transístmica (Avenida Simón Bolívar) cuts across the city then heads north across the isthmus. However, if you're planning to head north toward the Caribbean you'd do much better to take the new toll road, Corredor Norte, which extends about a third of the way across and supposedly will one day be completed clear across to the city of Colón. It'll save you a lot of time and hassle for just $2.50. Another toll road, Corredor Sur, leads from Tocumen International Airport to Panama City. Again, it's well worth the minimal expense.

You can see most of Panama's tourist attractions, from Casco Viejo to Panama la Vieja, in a single day if you're pressed for time.

NATURE AND ADVENTURE ACTIVITIES

Hiking in Parque Natural Metropolitano is about the extent of the natural as opposed to human-made excitement in Panama City. This city is a place to prep for your adventures elsewhere.

Statue of Balboa, Spanish explorer and conquistador

William Friar

FLORA AND FAUNA

Wildlife fights to maintain a foothold even within the limits of Panama City. Anywhere you can find a tree in crowded Panama City—and it's not always easy—you're likely to see bird life more interesting than you'd find in a quiet forest back home. And Parque Natural Metropolitano is a refuge for a surprising array of plants and animals. For details, see that entry under Nature and Adventure Sights, below.

VISITOR INFORMATION

Tour operators are your best source of information about Panama City; see Appendix B for some suggestions. Panama's government tourism department, IPAT, has its administrative headquarters at the Atlapa Convention Center in Panama City, but they're not really set up to deal with actual visitors. If you're eternally optimistic, you can try calling the office at 507/226-3544 or 507/226-7000.

You can find just about anything in Panama City you'd find in any other modern city, from ATM machines to pizza delivery in your hotel room. Internet cafés are a popular new fad. If you're in the centrally located El Cangrejo district try Bienvenido, S.A., 507/263-3188, on the corner of Calle D (Via Venetto) and Calle 55. It's close to the Las Vegas Hotel Suites and across from a branch of Cafeteria Manolo. An odd place, it's combined with a perfume shop, not a coffeehouse, and offers five PCs that are often occupied. Rates are $3 an hour, $1.50 for a half-hour. Hours are 8:30 a.m. to 10 p.m. Monday through Saturday, 3 to 6 p.m. Sunday.

GETTING THERE

For information on Panama City's international airport, Tocumen, see the Orientation and Transportation section in Chapter 1. For information on the city's domestic airport, Marcos A. Gelabert, see Appendix A.

Traffic in Panama City is bad and getting worse all the time. If possible, avoid car trips during morning and evening rush hours, especially from about 8 to 9 a.m. and 4:30 to 6:30 p.m. A couple of new toll roads that cut through the city are a quick escape from the congestion, since they're priced out of reach of the average Panama City driver. Unless you're on a severe budget (most tolls will run you about 35 to 75 cents) you'll save a lot of time and aggravation by taking them. If you're in a cab, offer to pay for the toll if the route gives you the option, e.g., to or from the international airport.

There are approximately two zillion taxis in Panama City, all eager for your business. Most are small Japanese cars that will take you just about anywhere in town for $2 or less. Agree on a price before getting in. (Taxis are not metered in Panama City or anywhere else in the country.) A few larger, air-conditioned cabs lurk around the more upscale hotels and charge several times what the smaller guys do. You can always just walk down the street to find a cheaper ride.

Taxis offer by far the easiest way to get around the city. Taking buses within Panama City is an exercise in frustration, especially when you can zip around in a cab for next to nothing. Don't be alarmed if your driver stops to pick up another fare heading the same way. It's a normal practice, but you can tell your driver not to do it if it makes you uncomfortable.

Attempting to drive in Panama City is a good way to spoil your entire trip. Drivers are extremely aggressive, streets are confusing and poorly marked, and there's a severe shortage of traffic signals (which most drivers treat merely as friendly suggestions in any case). Streets have been known to change from two-way to one-way literally overnight, without anyone bothering to change the signs. It's no fun to turn a corner of what you thought was a two-way street and see a battalion of SUVs barreling down on you. Again: take cabs.

Adding to the confusion of getting around Panama City is the fact that many streets have multiple names. The names used in this chapter are generally those most likely to be recognized by taxi drivers and other locals.

NATURE AND ADVENTURE SIGHTS

Parque Natural Metropolitano—Amazingly enough, you don't even have to leave the limits of Panama City to find a tropical forest. This 265-hectare park is just minutes from downtown, and it's a lovely little place with a surprising amount of wildlife given its location and size. Only brief day hikes are available here. You can skip this park if time is short and you plan to venture out at least as far as Parque Nacional Soberanía, which is only about a half-hour drive away from the city. (See Chapter 4, Panama Canal and Environs.) But if not, Parque Metropolitano will give you a quick sample of what Panama's forests have to offer.

Most of the park is dry lowland Pacific forest, now rare in Central America because of deforestation, and it's home to about 45 species of mammals, 36 species of reptiles, and 14 species of amphibians. These include such colorful creatures as two- and three-toed sloths, tití monkeys (Geoffroy's tamarin), and boa constrictors. As usual, however, don't be surprised if you see only birds during your hike, of which the park has recorded 227 species to date.

Having an urban center this close to a nature park has its drawbacks: a new highway, Corredor Norte, cuts right through the park's eastern edge, and other busy streets run by its borders. You're never far from the roar of the road.

There are about four kilometers (2.5 miles) of trails spread among three main loops. Not surprisingly, the most strenuous one, **La Cienaguita**, also offers the best chance of seeing animals. It takes about two hours to walk. It's an interpretive trail; the visitor's center sells an informative booklet about it for $2. The **Mono Tití Road** is, as the name suggests, a rocky road. Mountain biking is allowed on it, which would be great if there were a place to rent mountain bikes. It's named for the tití monkey (Geoffroy's tamarin) that lucky visitors may see while hiking the trail. The easiest trail is **Los Momótides**, across an extremely busy road—be careful crossing the street. It's short and level, designed for people in a hurry or who have difficulty walking, and is a nice little walk.

Details: The entrance to the park is on Avenida Juan Pablo II in the Curundu district of Panama City. Trails are open 6 a.m.–6 p.m. every day. There is no fee, but donations are encouraged. The visitor's center offers a free brochure, but ask for the glossy color trail guide (50 cents), which has a much-needed map. The visitor's center is open 8 a.m.–4 p.m. weekdays and 8 a.m.–1 p.m. Saturday. Guided tours in English and Spanish are available for $6, but you have to call at least a day or two in advance. Call 507/232-5552 or 507/232-5516.

OTHER SIGHTS

Casco Viejo—The "Old Part," also known as Casco Antiguo or the San Felipe district, is the most colorful part of Panama City. UNESCO admired its unusual blend of architectural styles, most notably its ornate Spanish- and French-influenced buildings, and declared Casco Viejo a World Heritage Site in 1997. It's a city within the city, and one from a different age. It's a great place for a walking tour. You can wander down narrow brick streets, sip an espresso at an outdoor café, visit old churches, and gaze up at wrought-iron balconies spilling over with bright tropical plants.

Casco Viejo has always had a romantic look, but for decades the romance has been of the tropical-decadence, paint-peeling-from-rotting-walls variety. Now, though, it's in the midst of a tasteful and large-scale restoration that's giving the old buildings new luster. Elegant bars and sidewalk cafés are opening, and historic hotels that had deteriorated into flophouses are being resurrected. In some places the district now resembles New Orleans's French Quarter. Unfortunately, the renovation is coming at the cost of booting out the poorer residents who've lived here for ages.

Please note: Even with the makeover, Casco Viejo is not the safest part of Panama City. There's no reason to be overly concerned, but use common sense. Don't come dripping jewelry and dressed in expensive clothes, do try not to look too much like a confused gringo tourist, and don't wander around at night. A good way to explore the area is to come with a knowledgeable guide or taxi driver who can drop you in different areas to explore on foot. Safety aside, you'll probably save time this way, as the streets are confusing and it's easy to get lost.

Below are a few highlights of the neighborhood.

At the southwest tip of Casco Viejo is the **Plaza de Francia** (French Plaza), which has seen a great deal of history. You can still walk along part of the old seawall that protected the city from the Pacific Ocean's 5.5-meter (18-foot) tides. There's a good view of the Panama City skyline, and the breeze is great on a hot day. The marble plaques along the wall tell part of the story, in Spanish, of the failed French effort to build a sea-level canal in Panama. The area housed a fort until the beginning of the 20th century, and the *bóvedas* (vaults) in the seawall were used as jails. You'll still hear gruesome stories about other jail cells in the seawall, where prisoners were left at low tide to drown when the tide rose, but no such cells have ever been found. What you will find is one of Panama's most attractive restaurants, **Restaurante Las Bóvedas** (see Food, below).

If you head up Avenida A for a couple of blocks (away from the water), you'll see the ruins of the **Iglesia de Santo Domingo**. The nearly flat arch (Arco Chato) in this church is very famous. Since it was built without a keystone and has almost no curve, it should be a very precarious structure, yet it has stood for more than 200 years. One of the reasons a transoceanic canal was built in Panama is that engineers concluded from the intact arch that Panama was not subject to the kinds of devastating earthquakes that afflict its Central American neighbors.

Next to the church is the **Museo de Arte Religioso Colonial**. It's a tiny place with miscellaneous religious artifacts from the 17th and

18th centuries. If you're in a hurry you can easily give this place a miss. The museum is open from 9 a.m. to 4:15 p.m. Tuesday through Saturday, closed Sunday and Monday. Admission is 75 cents for adults, 25 cents for children.

Continuing up Avenida A until you come to Calle 9 you'll find the **Iglesia de San José**. The church's massive **Golden Altar** is a prime tourist attraction. Legend has it that the altar was saved from the rapacious Welsh pirate Henry Morgan during the sacking of the original Panama City when a quick-thinking priest had it painted black, hiding its true value.

In the center of Casco Viejo is the **Plaza de la Independencia**, where Panama declared its independence from Colombia in 1903. Construction began on the **Cathedral** here in 1688, but it took more than 100 years to complete. The towers are inlaid with mother of pearl from the Perlas Islands.

El Museo del Canal Interoceánico, 507/211-1995 or 507/211-1649, to your left as you face the cathedral, is housed in what was once the headquarters of the French canal effort. It's worth a visit, but be

Renovated buildings in Casco Viejo

43

William Friar

Casco Viejo, Panama City, a UNESCO World Heritage Site

prepared for some frustration if you don't speak Spanish. There's not a word of English in the whole place, which is a problem for gringos since the "exhibits" consist more of text than anything else. The museum claims to have English-speaking guides, but you have to call ahead of time to arrange this service. There's no fee, but a small tip is always welcome. The displays tell the story of both the French and American efforts to build the canal, throwing in a little bit of pre-Columbian and Spanish colonial history at the beginning. There's a bit of anti-American propaganda, and most of what's written about the canal from the 1960s on should be taken with a big chunk of salt. You can do the whole place in under an hour. It's open 9:30 a.m. to 5 p.m. Tuesday through Sunday, is closed Monday. Admission is $2 for adults, 75 cents for children. There's a pleasant indoor/outdoor café, **La Petite France,** on the premises that's open 11 a.m. 'til midnight.

The **Teatro Nacional**, on Avenida B between Calles 3 and 4, is worth a brief visit to get a glimpse of its Old World elegance. The place was intimate and well preserved until the rains of 2000 caused serious damage. The ceiling was covered with faded but still colorful frescos of cavorting naked ladies, painted by Roberto Lewis, a well-known Panamanian artist. Leaks in the roof destroyed about a quarter of these frescos, and the roof partially collapsed. Repairs were expected to be completed by mid-2001.

Café de Asís, a good place to stop for a drink, is a block away from the theater on **Plaza Simón Bolívar**. Outdoor tables appear in the evening so you can enjoy the soft tropical breeze. The plaza is dedicated to the legendary figure who is considered the father of Latin America's independence from Spain. In 1826 Bolívar called a congress near here to discuss forming a union of Latin American states. Bolívar himself did not attend and the congress didn't succeed, but the park and the statue of Bolívar commemorate the effort.

The presidential palace, the **Palacio de las Garzas** (Palace of the Herons) is at Avenida E. Alfaro and Calle 5 Este, overlooking Panama Bay. It's a lovely place that houses the presidential office and residence. You can't go in, but through the gate you can see, wandering around a fountain, the herons that give the palace its name. As this was written there was talk of moving the presidencia to the old Administrator's House on Ancon Hill, which has been the residence of the chief executive of the Panama Canal since construction days.

Near Casco Viejo—As long as you're in the neighborhood you may want to check out Panama City's **Mercado Público** (public market), which is close to Casco Viejo at the intersection of Avenida E. Alfaro and Calle 13 Este. As part of the renovation of Casco Viejo, there's been talk of moving the market to the El Chorrillo barrio, and there's a slight chance the move may have happened by the time you read this. There's not a whole lot to see in the market, but it'll give you a flavor of daily commercial life in this old part of town. The meat section is on the ground floor, and if you're not already a vegetarian this dirty, non-refrigerated place may convert you. Fruits and veggies are on the second floor. The market opens at 2 a.m.

In front of the market, up Calle 13 Este, is the crowded shopping area of **Salsipuedes** (a contraction of "get out if you can"). Again, this is mostly of interest for those into people-watching. The area is crammed with little stalls selling clothes, lottery tickets, and bric-a-brac. To the right as you face away from the public market is a small **Chinatown** (make a right at Calle Juan Mendoza), which frankly has little to interest tourists.

Mi Pueblito (aka Los Pueblitos)—This is a charming, if idealized, re-creation of a typical Panamanian town on the Azuero Peninsula, Panama's heartland. (Though Mi Pueblito re-creates a bygone era, you can still find a few real towns that resemble it; see Chapter 6, Pacific Islands and Beaches, for details.) The architecture is Spanish colonial, which is especially noticeable in the red tile roofs and whitewashed walls, the mission-style church, and the central plaza and fountain. The builders have included lots of small, loving touches, from the lesson plan on the blackboard of the schoolhouse to the telegraph office that looks as though the operator has just left for a siesta. There's even a rustic outhouse behind the buildings.

Mi Pueblito includes a small *pollera* museum, where a *pollera*-wearing semi-bilingual docent is on hand to give you a detailed description of this lovely traditional dress and, if you're lucky, an utterly wacky theory of Christopher Columbus's ethnic background.

There is also a folkloric dance school where you can sometimes see small children learning the steps to traditional Panamanian dances. Performances by grown-ups are sometimes given, though the schedule was up in the air at the time of writing. Call 507/228-7154, 507/228-2361, or 507/228-7178 for information.

The Mi Pueblito complex has recently been expanded to recognize the traditional dwellings of some of the other peoples that make up modern Panama. These are directly across the street from the Spanish colonial village. The first site you'll come to honors the West Indian immigrants who provided most of the labor force for the building of the Panama Canal. The brightly painted two-story wooden buildings are an extremely fanciful take on what the laborers' accommodations were really like. A walk through a little forest takes you to more accurate re-creations of the way three indigenous peoples—the Kuna, Emberá-Wounaan, and Guaymi—lived, and in many cases still do. The houses of all three are made of similar materials, but it's interesting to compare the quite different style of huts they favor.

Souvenirs are on sale at shops throughout the complex. There are three simple open-air restaurants—in Mi Pueblito proper, the West Indian village, and the Kuna village—specializing in seafood and offering a few "native" dishes. Prices range from inexpensive to moderate. The complex also offers a good view of Panama Bay and the Pacific entrance to the Panama Canal, as well as an eavesdropper's peek into the ramshackle apartment buildings of El Chorrillo, a nearby barrio.

Details: Mi Pueblito is near the base of Ancon Hill, just off the westbound side of Avenida de Los Martires. It's a quick right turn off this busy road, and easy to miss because there are no signs. Taxi drivers should know where it is. The complex is open 10 a.m.–10 p.m. Tuesday–Sunday. Admission is 50 cents. There's an out-of-date and minimally informative Spanish-only brochure. Most of the signs in the complex are in Spanish.

Museo Antropológico Reina Torres de Araúz—Panama's anthropology museum, housed in a massive building that was once the terminal of the Panama Railroad, was reopened in 2000 after several years of renovation. It's considered Panama's finest, but bear in mind this is not a country known for the quality of its museums. At the time this was written, only one exhibit had been opened to the public. This consisted of 16 carved stone figures and fragments from the Barriles culture, believed to be Panama's earliest major civilization. It grew up around Volcán Barú in western Panama before 700 B.C. and came to a sudden end with the eruption of Barú in A.D. 600. These figures came from a ceremonial center that dates from around 60 B.C. Even though the exhibit is modest and little is known about this culture, you may find it worth a visit. Other exhibits should be open by the time you read this. Shortly after the grand reopening, guides were friendly and eager to show visitors around the place.

The pollera, *the hand-embroidered national dress of Panama*

Clea Efthimiadis

47

Details: *The museum is located on Plaza Cinco de Mayo, which is near the pedestrian section of Avenida Central. Hours are 10 a.m.–4 p.m. Tuesday–Sunday. The museum is closed on Mondays. Admission is $2. Call 507/212-3079.*

Panama La Vieja (Old Panama)—These extensive ruins are all that's left of the original Panama City, the first Spanish city on the Pacific Ocean. It was founded on August 15, 1519 by the notorious conquistador Pedro Arias de Ávila, better known as Pedrarias, and burned down by the equally notorious Welsh pirate Henry Morgan in 1671. After that disaster, the Spanish moved Panama City to a more defensible site a few kilometers southwest, in the area now known as Casco Viejo.

Since most of Panama La Vieja was made of wood, only the partial remains of a relatively few stone buildings were left standing. Two of the best-preserved structures are near the main entrance. The first is the tower of the **cathedral**, which is largely intact. It's one of Panama's national symbols and was built between 1619 and 1626. The other, a bit farther in, is the **Casa Alarcón**, also known as the Casa del Obispo (bishop's house). There are other ruins worth exploring, but try not to wander too far away—the more distant ruins border a dodgy neighborhood.

A restoration is in progress, and there are new signs in English and Spanish explaining the ruins. During the restoration archeologists have turned up Spanish pots, plates, and utensils dating from the 16th and 17th centuries as well as a much older Indian cemetery with bones dating from 50 B.C. You can see examples of all these items in the small **museum** next to the ruins. Descriptions are in Spanish only. Ask the guide, who speaks English, to let you get a quick look at the lab on the premises, where other artifacts are being restored. The museum's main attraction is a scale model that depicts the city in 1671, the year it was destroyed. A cassette tour of the model is included in the price of admission. It consists of the guide slipping a tape, in English or Spanish, into a boom box and switching lights on and off at the appropriate time.

You can buy handicrafts from all over Panama at shops in the same building that houses the museum and in a separate building next door. El Trapiche Panama Vieja, a restaurant on the grounds that served traditional Panamanian food, had changed hands and was being remodeled at the time of my most recent visit. It looked as though it were going to be called **Rincón Típico** and serve similar food.

Details: Panama La Vieja is on the eastern outskirts of Panama City, an easy drive away along Vía Cincuentenario. There is no charge to explore the ruins. Admission to the museum is $1.50. It's open 9 a.m.–4 p.m. Monday–Saturday and 9 a.m.–1 p.m. Sunday. There's an IPAT information booth next to the museum entrance, but you'll probably have a better chance turning up lost pieces of eight than finding anyone actually working there. A booklet

Old Panama, ruins of the first Spanish city on the Pacific

William Friar

with a map and history of Panama La Vieja is available at the museum entrance for $2.50.

GUIDES AND OUTFITTERS

Most of Panama's tour operators have their headquarters in Panama City, and nearly all offer city tours of different kinds. See Appendix B for details.

Taxi drivers often double as tour guides. Don't expect a scholarly lecture on what you're seeing, but it can be a reasonable way to cover a lot of ground. Agree on a price ahead of time.

If you're planning to go snorkeling during your stay in Panama, you should know that most of the gear available on Panama's beaches and islands is mediocre at best. If you haven't brought your own, consider buying it in Panama City. Your best bet is **Scubapanama**, 507/261-3841 or 507/261-4064, fax 507/261-9586, Panama's largest dive operator. You can also rent snorkel gear from them for $8 a day.

LODGING

There is a massive oversupply of hotel rooms in Panama City, which doesn't stop gleaming new hotels from popping up seemingly every day. Locals love to speculate on where all that money is coming from.

The hotel glut doesn't necessarily mean you'll be able to strike a great bargain, but it's worth asking if your hotel of choice has a promotional deal going. Moderate to expensive hotels typically offer corporate rates that are significantly, sometimes drastically, below their standard "rack" rate. It never hurts to ask about the corporate rate, which you may get without having to produce so much as a business card. You can also sometimes get better deals by going through travel agencies or tour operators.

Except where noted, the hotels listed below are centrally located, within easy walking distance of good restaurants and tourist services. You can find cheaper rooms that are clean and very basic, but they tend to be located in inconvenient, unattractive, or dangerous neighborhoods. If you want to go el cheapo, the best supply of budget hotels in a reasonably okay neighborhood can be found in La Exposición, within a couple-block radius of the Gran Hotel Soloy. (This is also the departure point for the Panaline buses to Costa Rica.) See below for that hotel's address.

All the hotels listed below have air-conditioning and hot water. Most have TV sets, often with multiple cable channels. For luxury hotels, prices quoted are for standard rooms. These hotels all have more expensive options for those who can't burn through their money fast enough. As elsewhere in the book, prices don't include the 10 percent room tax unless specified.

Upper-End Economy

Tower House Suites, 507/269-2244 or 507/269-2526, fax 507/269-2869, towerh@sinfo.net, www.towersuite.com, is on Calle 51 near Restaurante-Bar Las Tinajas. It's a great find. Not only is it the best deal among the "apart-hotels," it's also more appealing than some conventional hotels that charge twice as much. Rooms are immaculate and tastefully decorated. Some have a view of Panama Bay. The standard accommodations are "junior suites" that include sitting areas and small fridges; suites with fully stocked kitchenettes are the same price. There's a pool, laundry room, and attractive restaurant (I haven't yet tried it). Fax and Internet services are available. The place was recently redecorated in cheerful good taste, so cross your fingers that prices don't rise to match the quality. Rates are $45 single or double occupancy, $30 for stays of a month or more.

The **Gran Hotel Soloy & Casino,** at Avenida Perú and Calle 30, 507/227-1133, fax 507/227-0884, soloy@sinfo.net, is not really all that gran, but it has a few things going for it. For one thing, the Panaline bus from Costa Rica stops here, making this an ideal place to collapse after that marathon bus ride. There's a rooftop disco, Bar Mai Tai, that may be appealing. Ditto for the small rooftop pool with its big rooftop view of Panama Bay and the city skyline. Rooms are clean and basic, with mattresses that have seen better days. You can't have an aversion to red plaid if you stay here. There's a casino on the premises, if you care about such things. Rates are $45 for one, $53 for two people.

Hotel Marbella, behind the Hotel Granada on Calle D near Calle Eusebio A. Morales, 507/223-2220, fax 507/263-3622, is generally considered one of the better economy hotels. It's a clean, modern, five-story place located on a pleasant residential street but close to a lot of urban action. However, I find the rooms dark and austere, and most look out on blank walls. Rates are $35 single, $40 double occupancy.

Hotel Costa del Sol, at the corner of Vía España and Avenida Federico Boyd, 507/223-7111, fax 507/223-6636, offers Motel 6-quality rooms with extremely bright bedspreads and curtains. All rooms are equipped with kitchenettes in the closets. In the old days the U.S. military used the place as temporary lodging for enlisted personnel. There's a pool on the roof. This place is pricey for what you get. Rates are $51 single, $54 double occupancy.

If all you want is a clean, basic room not too far from the action, the 58-room **Hotel California,** on Via España and Calle 43, 507/263-7736, fax 507/264-6144, will do nicely. The rooms are pleasant enough but they're small, and the management hasn't yet discovered the concept of smoke-free accommodations. Also, the hotel has the misfortune of being located on loud, crowded Vía España without being conveniently close to anything. (If you stay here, try to get a room at the back of the building.) But the price is certainly appealing. Rates are $23 single or double occupancy.

Las Vegas Hotel Suites, on Avenida Eusebio A. Morales and Calle 55, 507/269-0722 or 507/223-0047, lasvegas@pan.gbm.net, www.lasvegaspanama.com, would be a good option if the rooms weren't so aged. The place is an old former apartment building, and it shows: the furnishings are cheap and date from the early 1970s at the latest. All accommodations include a mini-fridge and kitchenette (some have a bizarre only-in-the-'70s contraption: a combination mini-fridge and stove). But the place is clean and has several things going for it. These include an Internet computer on the premises (the first 5 to 10 minutes are free, after which you're charged $5 for a half-hour; note that this is more than three times the going rate at local Internet cafés), and fax service (25 cents to receive, $5 plus toll to send). You can also get room service from the trendy Caffé Pomodoro, which is in the same complex, as is the new and pricey Wine Bar. Some of the suites are much nicer than others for the same price. Studios are $55 for one person, $60 for two. The significantly larger suites are only $5 more. Corporate rates knock about $20 off the price, and they're given to just about anyone who stays longer than a night. Children under 12 stay free.

Mid-Range

The 180-room **Hotel Granada,** 507/269-1068, 507/265-1962, or 507/265-1963, 800/RIANDE-1 from the U.S., fax 507/263-7197, granada@sinfo.net, is a long-established hotel that enjoys a solid reputation. It's part of the Riande chain, which also owns Hotel Continental (and the Riande Aeropuerto near Tocumen International Airport). It's located on Calle Eusebio A. Morales, near Vía España in El Cangrejo district. Rooms are pleasant, clean, and modern, though they're on the small side and showing slight signs of wear. There's a swimming pool, casino, and cafeteria. Rates are $110 for one, $120 for two people, including an "American breakfast." Corporate rates are $77 for one, $88 for two.

Hotel Ejecutivo, on Avenida Aquilino de la Guardia between Calle 51 and Calle 52, 507/265-8011 or 507/264-3989, fax 507/269-1944, has long been a favorite with Latin American businessmen.

Rooms are similar to what you'd expect at a Best Western–style hotel: clean, pleasant enough, but nothing fancy. All come equipped with refrigerator, TV, coffeepot, desk, and balcony. The hotel is centrally located just down from Vía España and some rooms have terrific views of the lights of the city and Panama Bay. There's no formal restaurant on the premises but the 24-hour cafeteria offers big portions at low prices. There's a tiny pool that wasn't working last time I checked. Guests are allowed to use the health spa at the nearby Hotel El Panamá. For reservations from the United States call 305/866-5058 or 972/714-0585. Rates are $100 single or double occupancy, $65 corporate rate. Special deals are often available; be sure to ask.

Aparthotel Torres de Alba, next to the Las Vegas Hotel Suites on Calle Eusebio A. Morales, 507/269-7770, fax 507/269-3924, alba@sinfo.net, www.torresdealba.com, offers what are essentially small modern apartments, each of which has a bedroom, sitting room, fax machine, full kitchen, and washer and dryer. The place consists of twin 13-story towers and is mainly aimed at short-term residents. But even tourists who don't need all that stuff might consider the place, especially those staying five days or more; it's simple but quite nice. There's a small gym and a pool that's borderline big enough for lap swimmers. Rates are $95 for one or two people, $85 for stays of five nights or more. Corporate rates are $10 less. A third person is $5 per night.

Plaza Paitilla Inn, on Vía Italia in Punta Paitilla, 507/269-1122 or 507/269-1069, fax 507/223-1470, ppinn@ns.sinfo.net, was originally a Holiday Inn. It's showing signs of age but is still a pleasant enough place and a decent deal for what you get. Many of the 252 rooms have a good view of Panama Bay from their balconies. (By the way, if you look carefully, you'll see a note on the balcony's sliding glass door that reads, "The balcony area was designed for ornamental purposes only. We recommend it not be used." Such notices are so extremely rare in Panama, even when desperately needed, that you'd be wise to take this one seriously.) There's a casino and pool. Historical note: This hotel was one of the tallest buildings in Panama City well into the 1980s. Take a look and you'll notice that today it's dwarfed by dozens of enormous neighbors. Rates are $80 single or double occupancy, including tax, a welcome cocktail, and a minimally acceptable buffet breakfast.

Sevilla Suites Apart-Hotel, 507/213-0016, fax 507/223-6344, sevillasuites@candleonda.net, a little farther down Avenida Eusebio A. Morales from the Las Vegas Hotel Suites, was brand new in 2000: finishing touches were being added in late February. Rooms are smaller and darker than those at the Torres de Alba, but the furnishings are quite nice. Accommodations lie closer to the hotel end of the apartment-hotel spectrum, but all the suites have mini-kitchens and some have terraces. There's a small gym and pool. Two of Panama's best restaurants, Restaurante 1985 and Rincón Suiza, are right across the street. Rates run $55 to $80.

Hotel Suites Central Park, on Vía España across from the Hotel California, 507/223-3100, fax 507/223-9630, beswescp@pty.com, www.suitescentralpark.com, is a somewhat austere Best Western hotel offering nothing but suites. They're not fancy, but they're spacious. Each has a sitting room with a dining table, desk, and mini-fridge. The hotel has a small pool. Rates are $85 for single, $90 for double occupancy, including breakfast. (These are corporate rates. Regular prices start at $135, but the cheaper rate is readily offered.)

The **Suites Ambassador Apart-Hotel**, 507/263-7274 or 507/263-6068, fax 507/264-7872, ambassad@sinfo.net, www.suitesambassador.com, is right next door to Hotel Marbella and has some of the same pluses and minuses (on a pleasant and centrally located street, but in the shadow of neighboring buildings). The suites are fairly modern and each has a bedroom, sitting room, and kitchen. Service can be unhelpful and less than friendly. Rates are $70 for a studio, $5 more for a suite.

Luxury

Pretty much the top of the line to date is the **Bristol,** on Avenida Aquilino de la Guardia just down from the Hotel Ejecutivo, 507/265-7844, fax 507/265-7829, from the U.S. 888/767-3966, www.rosewood-hotels.com. From the outside it's a modest salmon-colored building that's easy to miss, but inside it's a boutique hotel that's part of the Rosewood Hotels & Resorts chain. Everything is luxurious here, from the 24-hour butler service to the personalized local business cards you're presented upon check-in. Standard rooms are "deluxe," and they truly are. All the rooms are lovely and tastefully done. The furnishings are elegant, with local touches such as *mola* pillows and lamp bases made from Guaymi sandstone figurines. The restaurant and bar are attractive and the food is good. Note that this isn't a huge resort. If you want a pool and several restaurants to choose from, try the Caesar Park or Miramar Intercontinental; this place is more low-key. Service is so intensely attentive you may feel stalked, which is not to say you won't also find it inept at times. Rates start at $225 for single or double occupancy and go straight up from there.

The **Hotel Miramar Intercontinental,** 507/214-1000, fax 507/214-1004, panama@interconti.com, www.interconti.com, dominates the middle of Avenida Balboa and has great views of the Pacific and the Panama City skyline. It's a 206-room luxury hotel that's part of the Intercontinental chain and comes with the works: two restaurants, a private marina where you can charter boats, a largish pool, a health spa, several bars, etc. The standard rooms are quite nice, naturally, but not as fancy as one might expect given what this place charges. The best things about the hotel are its views and attractive pool. The place also gets good marks for service. Gossip item: Mick Jagger spent the night in a suite here in February 2000, which got Panama City residents quite excited. Rates start at $240 for a standard room; corporate rates are $185.

Hotel Caesar Park, on Vía Israel and Calle 77 across the street from the Atlapa Convention Center, 507/270-0477 or 507/226-2693, panres@caesarpark.com, part of the Westin chain, is a huge luxury hotel with four restaurants, a casino, athletic club, pool, sauna, and so on. *Note:* Large tropical birds are kept on the premises, including a toucan in a painfully small cage. Though the hotel is generally considered one of the top three in Panama City (the Bristol and Miramar Intercontinental are the other two), its standard rooms are arguably not quite as nice as its rivals'. Also, the hotel is on the outskirts of town, quite a hike from everything but the convention center, the ruins of Panama la Vieja, and the international airport. Rates start at $195 for single or double occupancy. Cabañas by the pool are the same price. Corporate rates are $150.

The new **Panama Marriott Hotel**, on Calle 52 at Calle Ricardo Arias, 507/210-9100, fax 507/210-9110, is quite an elegant place with 296 rooms, a small pool, and a cafeteria but no formal restaurant. Ask for a corner room; they're the largest of the standard rooms. Rates are $160 for one or two people, $20 more for a third person in the room. Weekend packages including a Friday and Saturday night stay are $109 per night for up to two people, including a buffet breakfast each day. Corporate rates are also available.

The eight-story **Radisson Royal Panama Hotel**, 507/265-3636, fax 507/265-3550, in the U.S. 800/333-3333, radisson@sinfo.net, is next to the World Trade Center on Calle 53 and Avenida 5B Sur. It's another in a seemingly endless parade of new hotels catering to the upscale business crowd. The rooms are, of course, attractive and comfortable, but the suites are a considerable step up in quality. There's a pool, gym, sauna, and lighted tennis court. It's a good location for businesspeople, but it's not the most scenic part of town. Le Bistrot, one of Panama's better restaurants, is right across the street. Rates are $175 single or double occupancy; corporate rates are $140.

Hotel Continental, 507/263-9999 or 507/263-5143, in the U.S. 800/RIANDE-1, riande@sinfo.net, right on busy Vía España, is another old Panama City landmark, but it's benefited from a tasteful remodeling that has made it an upscale business hotel. It's part of the Riande chain, which also owns the Hotel Granada. All the rooms are nice, but some are bigger and more elegantly appointed than others; ask to see several. The hotel has a restaurant, cafeteria, small pool and casino. Rates are $140 for one, $150 for two people; corporate rates plummet to $85 for one or two people, including American breakfast. You can probably make a deal here.

The **Hotel El Panamá**, on Vía España next to Iglesia del Carmen, the large church, 507/223-1660 or 507/269-5000, fax 507/223-6080, reservas@elpanama.com, www.elpanama.com, was once Panama's premier hotel. It has 340 rooms, including some cabañas by the large, attractive pool. The hotel has changed hands several times over the years, but no matter how many times it's made over one thing remains constant: the service is lousy. Because of its international name recognition it still draws a lot of guests, many of whom compete to see who can be louder and more obnoxious. On the weekends especially, the place is bedlam. For the money you can do far better elsewhere. Rates are $80 for one, $160 for two people.

The new **Holiday Inn Hotel and Suites**, 507/206-5555 or 507/206-5556, fax 507/206-5557, holidayinn-panama@sinfo.net, between the Hotel El Panamá and Iglesia del Carmen on Avenida Manuel E. Bautista, is among the more upscale specimens of the chain: standard rooms are spacious, well-appointed, and have mini-bars. However, the whole place had a strong, unpleasant chemical smell a month after it opened in early 2000. Presumably, this will fade in time. There's a small pool and gym, a computer room that offers Internet access, and a sports bar. Rates are $175 for single or double occupancy.

FOOD

The restaurants are among the best things about Panama City. It's easy to find excellent food, gracious service, and pleasant surroundings, not to mention a surprisingly wide array of cuisine. For the higher-end restaurants, expect to pay what you would for a similar place in the United States. It's also quite possible to stuff yourself on tasty, simple food for about $2 if ambiance means nothing to you. However, the list below doesn't include such basic places on the assumption that visitors to Panama will get more than their fill of them during their travels around the country. Below is just a sample of the city's culinary treats.

Golosinas, on Calle Ricardo Arias near Calle 50 in the "Area Bancaria" (banking district), 507/269-6237 or 507/269-2028, has long been considered one of the finest restaurants in Panama City, and you'll get no argument here. The food is delicious and the service is excellent. The atmosphere is pleasant, too. It's a quiet oasis that attracts the local beautiful people. The décor tends toward the floral but is quite cozy and romantic, with candles everywhere. The inventive menu might be described as eclectic continental. Italian dishes, seafood, and assorted meats are particularly well represented. Main courses are $10 to $19. Try the guabina (a delicate-flavored local fish) in champagne sauce and capers ($15). The crabcakes in cranberry chutney ($6.25) are a light and unusual appetizer. My one quibble about the place is that hot dishes aren't always quite as hot as they should be, which stands out only because everything else is done right. There's a patio dining area that's inviting on dry-season nights.

57

You'll find a happy meeting of Chinese and Japanese food at **Nobu**, at the corner of Calle 49 Este and Calle Uruguay in the Bella Vista district, 507/265-1311 or 507/265-1312. The restaurant concentrates on seafood, but other offerings include duck, chicken, meat, and noodle dishes. Corvina is prepared seven unusual ways, ranging in price from $7.50 to $13.75. The corvina in hot sauce, green onions, and mushrooms spices up this delicate fish without burying its flavor. Interestingly enough, the sushi and sashimi come from imported fish. The atmosphere leans toward casual elegance and the service is friendly and attentive.

Another good place for seafood is **Siete Mares**, at Calle Guatemala near Vía Argentina, 507/264-0144. It's a cozy, tranquil place and the service is good. An unusual house specialty is fried ceviche ($6), a light and tangy appetizer. Most main dishes are in the $10-to-$14 range. The fish is so tasty you won't need to order anything fancier than corvina *a la plancha* (grilled corvina; $9.50). The décor is a tad peculiar—for instance, the chairs are on rollers and there are no windows. The place resembles a cross between a plush conference room and a cocktail lounge. There's also a piano bar. The environmentally conscious won't be pleased to see tortoise-shell as a wall ornament.

Le Bistrot, 507/264-5587 or 507/269-4025, tucked away in a nondescript office building across from the World Trade Center in Marbella, is a 20-year-old Panama institution. Its décor may remind you of Siete Mares (chairs on rollers, etc.), which makes sense since they're both owned by the same folks. It's a good place for a romantic dinner, as the banquettes and mood lighting offer lots of privacy. Food tends toward the usual array of seafood, fish, and meats, but it's quite well prepared. Main dishes start at around $10. The calamari *a la plancha* (grilled squid; $5) is a bit oily but delicious. Also try the *langostinos a la thermidor* (jumbo shrimp thermidor; $14.50) or the very tender *filete a la pimienta* (pepper steak; $13). Give in to the *flan de queso* (cheesecake flan; $2.50).

Restaurante 1985 on Calle Eusebio A. Morales near Vía Venetto in El Cangrejo, 507/263-8541 or 507/263-8571, is one of Panama's best restaurants, and one of its most expensive. It specializes in French cuisine and seafood, with entrees going for $14 to $28. It's a good place for a serious splurge. If you chicken out at the last minute, **Rincón Suizo**, in the same building, 507/263-8310, offers good Swiss food at more moderate prices.

Tre Scalini, on Calle 52 in Bella Vista, 507/269-9951 or 507/269-9952, offers good Italian food and warm, friendly service in a cozy faux-Italian atmosphere. Most dishes are around $9. It's a favorite standby for many a Panama City dweller. There's a second Tre Scalini in the El Dorado district, 507/260-0052 or 507/236-5303, if you happen to find yourself out that way.

Caffé Pomodoro, in the Las Vegas Hotel Suites complex at the corner of Avenida Eusebio A. Morales and Calle 55, 507/269-5936, was one of the hottest restaurants in Panama City as this was written, for reasons that escape me. The pasta here is pretty good and the atmosphere is pleasant, but it sure inspires a lot of affection for an outdoor café with plastic chairs that's wedged in the shadow of several unattractive high-rises. Still, it's a good place to go if you want to get a glimpse of the local scene. With the opening of an overpriced wine bar next door (called, creatively enough, Wine Bar), Pomodoro will probably stay hot for some time to come.

Restaurante Las Bóvedas (The Vaults), on Plaza Francia in Casco Viejo, 507/228-8068, is worth visiting for the ambiance at least as much as for the food. It's built right into the historic stone vaults of the old city's seawall, so you're dining in what was once a dungeon. A recent redecoration has made the place slightly less cozy but a little more elegant. Main dishes start at $12 and go up to $22 for Alaskan king crab. The *filete* "Las Bóvedas" is pretty good and comes with a choice of four sauces. Monday through Saturday evenings a guitarist adds to the ambiance; Friday and Saturday from 9 p.m. to 1 a.m. there's live jazz in the back room. The house drink is caipirinha, a potent Brazilian concoction.

Restaurante-Bar Tinajas, on Calle 51 near Avenida Federico Boyd, 507/263-7890 or 507/269-3840, is an unabashed tourist restaurant. It's worth checking out for its folkloric dance performances at 9 p.m. on Thursday, Friday, and Saturday. The cover for the show is $5 per person, and you must make reservations. The cuisine is Panamanian, with main dishes in the $6.50-to-$12 range. The restaurant is decorated with touches meant to remind you of a traditional town on the Azuero Peninsula.

Restaurante Mercado del Mariscos, 507/212-0071, is just upstairs from the city fish market, which is at the west end of Avenida Balboa. It boasts that it has the "best and freshest fish and seafood in Panama," and one would hope so, given its downstairs neighbor. (The fish market is modern and clean, so you shouldn't have to worry about a fishy smell wafting upstairs.) It's certainly reasonably priced; most items run $5.50 to $7. Offerings include ceviche ($2), seafood soup ($2.50), corvina ($4.95), jumbo shrimp ($8), and octopus in garlic sauce ($6.25). An all-day "executive menu" includes salad, fish, soup, rice, and plantains for $4.50. If you don't see anything on the menu you like you can buy your own fish downstairs and have them cook it for you here. The restaurant is a Spartan place with little atmosphere, but there's a partial view of the bay and the Panama City skyline. The waitresses are friendly and speak a little English. It's open from 11 a.m. to midnight (more or less).

If you're just looking for a simple place for breakfast or a snack, try **Cafeteria Manolo**, Vía Argentina at Avenida 2B Norte, 507/264-3965. There's a second Manolo's in El Cangrejo, but this is the cozier original. It has an unpretentious coffee-shop atmosphere that attracts both locals and resident foreigners. The people-watching can be fun, and Vía Argentina is a nice place to hang out. Pancakes are $2.75, and no other breakfast costs more than $4.25. Hamburgers, sandwiches, and salads are less than $5. Other items include ceviche ($4.90), shrimp cocktail ($4.90), and Italian antipasto ($6.50). *Churros*, a sugary fried pastry shaped like a hot-dog, are popular here.

La Cascada, on Avenida Balboa and Calle 25, 507/262-1297, is worth visiting purely for its only-in-Panama vibe. It's a rather bizarre place, which you'll notice even before you're handed the tome of a menu. (Fans of Dr. Bronner's soap will detect a kindred spirit in its text.) It's an outdoor place decorated with what looks like leftover Elk's Club furnishings and lawn ornaments circa 1958. To call a waitress, you flip on a light switch at the table that also lights up a console by the cashier. The food? Oh yeah, the food: think Sizzler on an off night. But you can't beat the portion size; food here is measured by the pound. A typical "high-end" offering is a huge platter of fried steak, breaded shrimp, salad, rolls, and pretty tasty French fries for $9.25.

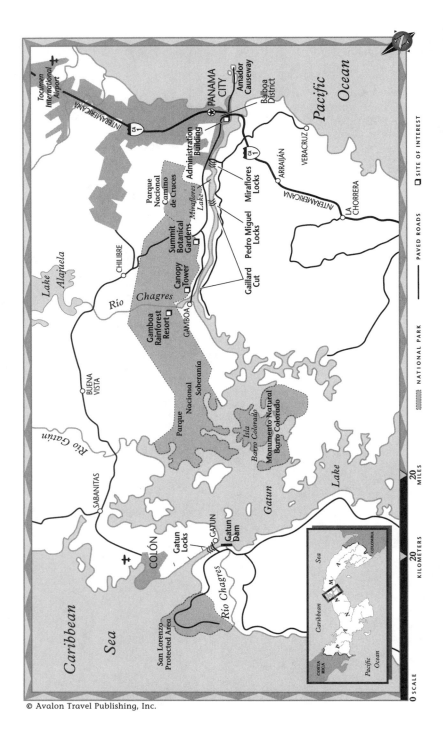

Caribbean Sea

San Lorenzo Protected Area

COLÓN

Gatun Locks

Gatun Dam

GATUN

Río Chagres

Río Gatún

SABANITAS

BUENA VISTA

Parque Nacional Soberanía

Gamboa Rainforest Resort

GAMBOA

Isla Barro Colorado

Monumento Natural Barro Colorado

Gatun Lake

Lake Alajuela

CHILIBRE

Río Chagres

Canopy Tower

Summit Botanical Gardens

Parque Nacional Camino de Cruces

Gaillard Cut

Miraflores Lake

Pedro Miguel Locks

Miraflores Locks

ARRAIJÁN

VERACRUZ

LA CHORRERA

INTERAMERICANA

CA 1

Administration Building

PANAMA CITY

Balboa District

Amador Causeway

Pacific Ocean

Tocumen International Airport

INTERAMERICANA

CA 1

SCALE

0   20   KILOMETERS

0   20   MILES

NATIONAL PARK   PAVED ROADS   SITE OF INTEREST

Costa Rica   Caribbean Sea   Colombia   Panama   Pacific Ocean

© Avalon Travel Publishing, Inc.

CHAPTER 4

Panama Canal and Environs

The Panama Canal was being hailed as a wonder of the world even before it opened for business on August 15, 1914. It still stands as one of the most awe-inspiring of all human endeavors. If you come all the way to Panama without visiting the canal, you're cheating yourself—not to mention inviting puzzled looks from your friends and relatives when you return home.

The canal itself is so impressive it's easy to overlook nature's equally astonishing handiwork on its banks and in its waters. Parque Nacional Soberanía is one of the most accessible tropical forests in the world. It has an astonishing amount of wildlife, especially considering that its trails start just a half-hour drive from Panama City. Gatun Lake, one of the largest manmade lakes in the world, has caimans and crocodiles that can sometimes be spotted during a boat trip on its fish-filled waters. And you don't have to venture far up the powerful Chagres River, source of water for the canal and Panama City, to feel you've entered another world.

LAY OF THE LAND

The Panama Canal, built across the isthmus of Panama at one of its narrowest and lowest points, is 80 kilometers (50 miles) long, extending from the city of Colón on the Caribbean Sea to Panama City on the Pacific Ocean. To the bafflement of many a visitor, the Caribbean entrance is northwest of the Pacific entrance.

All the attractions described here run along the east bank of the canal and are easily accessible from Panama City. (For information on Gatun Locks and other destinations near Colón, see Chapter 9, The Central Caribbean.)

What was once the Canal Zone ran the length of the canal, extending eight kilometers (five miles) on either side of it. The U.S. civilian townsites and military bases near the Pacific Ocean are being engulfed by Panama City, though some of the forested lands in the former Canal Zone have been set aside as protected areas.

A FEW FACTS ABOUT THE PANAMA CANAL

The Panama Canal is a trivia buff's dreams. The mind-boggling engineering details and the canal's colorful history make for an endless list of unusual factoids. Here are just a few:

- *If all the rock and dirt dug from the canal were piled into box-cars, the resulting train would circle the earth four times at the equator.*
- *The highest canal toll to date was paid by the cruise ship* Rhapsody of the Seas *on April 15, 1998. It paid $165,235.58 to transit.*
- *The adventurer Richard Halliburton paid the lowest toll, 36 cents, to swim the canal in 1928. (No one else has ever been allowed to swim the entire canal; it's too dangerous.)*
- *The widest ships allowed to transit the canal are the USS* New Jersey *and her sister ships. They have a beam of 108 feet (32.9 meters). The lock chambers are 110 feet (33.5 meters) wide.*

NATURE AND ADVENTURE ACTIVITIES

There is good hiking in the national parks near the canal, and scenic boating and fishing on Gatun Lake and the Chagres River. It's easy to charter a boat with an outboard motor or to rent kayaks and pedal boats. Even scuba diving is possible in the lake for those feeling adventurous; see the Gatun Lake sight description, below.

FLORA AND FAUNA

Some of the best bird-watching in the country is found close to the

- *The longest ship to transit was the* San Juan Prospector, *a bulk/oil carrier. It's 973 feet (297 meters) long. Each lock chamber is 1,000 feet (305 meters) in length.*
- *The average transit takes 8 to 10 hours.*
- *The fastest transit time, 2 hours and 41 minutes, was set by the U.S. Navy hydrofoil* Pegasus.
- *Ninety-two percent of the world's ocean-going ships can still transit the canal.*
- *No pumps are used to raise and lower ships in the locks; it's all done by gravity.*
- *The United States is the major user of the canal.*
- *Grain is the most common cargo shipped through the canal.*
- *The builders of the Panama Canal included 20,000 Barbadians and just 357 Panamanians.*
- *The record for the most transits on a single day, 65, was set on February 29, 1968.*
- *A ship traveling from New York to San Francisco saves 12,674 kilometers (7,872 miles) by using the canal instead of going around the tip of South America.*

banks of the Panama Canal. There's also a surprisingly decent chance of coming across largish mammals, including three species of monkeys (white-faced capuchins, Geoffroy's tamarins, and howlers), sloths, kinkajous, coatimundis, and capybaras (the largest rodent in the world) in the extensive moist tropical forests still standing here. Even jaguars are not unheard of, but the chances of spotting one are extremely slim. You may see a green iguana or two and, if you're lucky—or unlucky, depending on your point of view— perhaps even a snake.

Gatun Lake is home to caimans, crocodiles, tons of peacock bass, and much more. In the middle of the lake is Barro Colorado Island, a world-famous biological reserve; see the sight description below for details on some of its flora and fauna.

VISITOR INFORMATION

There's an ANAM station near the trailheads to Parque Nacional Soberanía where you can buy hiking and camping permits. The Panama Canal Authority's Orientation Service provides free guided tours of Miraflores Locks. See the Parque Nacional Soberanía and Miraflores Locks sight entries for details, and the Getting There section for directions.

The Smithsonian Tropical Research Institute is based in Panama and has its headquarters, the Earl S. Tupper Research and Conference Center, in Panama City. It's a large building located on Roosevelt Avenue in the Ancon district of the city, across Avenida de las Martires from the Legislative Palace. It has a small research library (open 9 a.m. to 5 p.m. Monday, Wednesday, Thursday, and Friday; 8 a.m. to 5 p.m. Tuesday; 9 a.m. to noon Sunday) and bookstore (10 a.m. to 4:30 p.m. weekdays) that are worth a visit if you want detailed information on Panama's flora and fauna. They are open to the public, but you have to have an ID to get into the center. Call 507/212-8000 for more information.

There are a couple of good places in the Balboa district of Panama City (formerly a townsite in the Canal Zone) to buy handicrafts. The first is the Centro de Artesanías Internacional, behind the YMCA on Balboa Road. It houses different kiosks selling handicrafts from all over Panama and other parts of Latin America. It's open 9 a.m. to 5 p.m. Monday through Saturday and 10 a.m. to 6 p.m. Sunday. Farther up the same road as you head toward downtown Panama City you'll see the Centro Municipal de Artesanías Panameñas on the right. It's run by Kunas and has a wider choice of *molas* than the Centro de Artesanías. You can probably strike a better bargain here, since they see less business. The Kuna women sewing *molas* and wearing *mola* blouses aren't doing it for show. That's really how they dress and what they do. The center is open 8 a.m. to 6 p.m. daily.

GETTING THERE

Most of the attractions described in this chapter are reachable by the same road, Gaillard Highway, so directions to these destinations are listed here.

From Panama City, head west on Gaillard Highway, which borders the canal for part of the way. The entrance to Miraflores Locks will be on your left less than 10 kilometers (6 miles) from the Balboa district which is at the Pacific entrance to the canal. Pedro Miguel Locks are about five kilometers (3 miles) farther on. Just beyond Pedro Miguel is the beginning of Gaillard Cut, now sometimes referred to by its original name, Culebra Cut.

Passing Pedro Miguel, you'll summit a small hill, then cross under a narrow underpass, a railroad bridge with "1929" carved into it. The ANAM office that sells hiking and camping permits is located right at the fork. If you stay straight you'll head into Madden Forest, a part of Parque Nacional Soberanía. Here's where you'll find the Camino de Cruces (Las Cruces Trail). If you make a left at the fork you'll stay on Gaillard Highway and come to Summit Botanical Gardens, Plantation Road, the Canopy Tower, and Sendero El Charco, in that order. Right before the one-way bridge over the Chagres River is the public marina, where you can hire boats to explore the Chagres and Gatun Lake. Crossing over the bridge (caution: be sure to stop if the red light is on) you'll come to the town of Gamboa, which is where you'll find Pipeline Road, the launch to Barro Colorado Island, and the Gamboa Rainforest

Resort. The road is good the entire way, and the most distant location is just a 45-minute drive from Panama City.

Panama City taxis charge around $20 one-way to the Gamboa area. You can get buses to Miraflores Locks and all the Gamboa-area destinations at the SACA Bus Terminal, 507/212-3420, which serves the canal area. It's located a block from the Legislative Palace in the Calidonia district of Panama City. Look for the orange-and-white buses. Gamboa-bound buses will get you within reasonable walking distance of every attraction listed above except for the Camino de Cruces. See the Parque Nacional Soberanía entry, below, for information on that trail.

Buses to Gamboa (65 cents) leave every half-hour from 4:45 to 8:00 a.m., then every hour until 11 p.m. The ride takes about 45 minutes. On Sunday the bus leaves once an hour from 6 a.m. to 3 p.m., with the last two buses at 4:30 and 6:30 p.m. If you want to go only as far as Miraflores Locks (35 cents), you can also take a Paraiso-bound bus.

Buses to the Amador Causeway (Calzada de Amador) leave "frequently," especially on the weekends, from about 5:40 a.m. to 8 p.m. The fare is 30 cents.

Note: Schedules from this terminal are particularly subject to change. To avoid being stuck at this congested place for a couple of unpleasant hours, call ahead to confirm departure times and show up early.

The Panama Railroad, which has a history nearly as rich as that of the canal, was allowed to fall apart a few years after its handover to Panama's military government in the 1980s. It is now being rebuilt by the Kansas City Southern Railway and is expected to begin some service by early 2001; however it will be used mainly to transport cargo. Whether it will eventually offer passenger service was up in the air at the time of writing.

NATURE AND ADVENTURE SIGHTS

Amador Causeway (Calzada de Amador)—Try to find time to go for a walk or run along the causeway. It's a beautiful breakwater that extends more than three kilometers (around two miles) into the

Pacific, calming the waters at the entrance of the Panama Canal and preventing that entrance from silting up. It was built from spoil dug from the canal and connects three islands: Naos, Perico, and Flamenco. In the old Canal Zone days, it was a major lover's lane and hang out spot for high school kids.

For the foreseeable future it's going to be the center of a different kind of action: tons of construction. A cruise-ship port, resort complex, and lots of other big-ticket tourist facilities are in the works in this area and around the former military base, Fort Amador, that leads to it.

Because of all this hubbub, being accurate about what you'll encounter when you visit is tough. But chances look good for the causeway's simpler pleasures still being available. It's especially pleasant to visit the causeway in the morning and evening, when the weather is cool and the light is gorgeous. On one side you can see the Bridge of the Americas and ships gliding in and out of the Pacific entrance to the canal. On the other you can see Panama Bay and the ever-growing Panama City skyline.

Be sure to stop at **El Centro de Exhibiciones Marinas (Marine Exhibition Center)**, a Smithsonian-run operation toward the end of the causeway that's very nicely designed. Exhibits set up along a beach-side path explain the extensive natural and human history of the area and touch on that of Panama in general. There's a small outdoor aquarium and an air-conditioned observation building. Free telescopes are set up along the path for you to check out the surrounding area and the ships at anchor waiting to transit the canal. At the end of the path are a few hundred square meters (less than a tenth of an acre) of **dry forest**, once common all along the Pacific coast of Central America but now mostly wiped out since it's easy for farmers to burn. It's amazing what you may find in this little patch of forest. There are lots of iguanas, and the last time I was there I saw a shaggy three-toed sloth walking upside down along a branch just 15 meters (less than 50 feet) above my head.

Note: You may see people splashing around in the little beaches along the causeway, but I don't advise you join them. Way back in high school I participated in a beach-cleanup day here that netted all kinds of disgusting stuff, including hospital waste, that had washed up from Panama City. No way would I ever set foot in the waters on that side. We used to play in the beach on the other side of the causeway when I was a kid, but that's when there was a shark net to discourage hopeful scavengers following ships toward the canal. The net rotted away years ago, after the demise of the Zone. Your call.

Details: *The causeway is at the end of Fort Amador, a former U.S. military base. The last couple of times I visited Panama, every trip to the causeway was an adventure in dodging trucks and watching out for unmarked ditches. Presuming there's still construction going on when you visit, you should be very careful if you drive. Taxis from Panama City charge around $8 to take you to its end. For buses from Panama City, see the Getting There section, above. There are a couple of simple open-air restaurants toward the end of the causeway that, with luck, will still be there when you visit. There may also be places to rent bikes and inline skates once the dust settles.*

El Centro de Exhibiciones Marinas is located on Punta Culebra toward the end of the causeway. At the public beach on the first island, Naos, make a right when the road forks. There should be large signs. It's open 1–5 p.m. Tuesday–Saturday and 10 a.m.–5 p.m. Saturday and Sunday. In the dry season, from about mid-January to the end of March, it's open 10 a.m.–6 p.m. Tuesday–Sunday. Special guided tours can be arranged. Call 507/212-8000, ext. 2366. Admission is $1.

Barro Colorado Island—BCI, as it's commonly known, is one of the world's most famous biological reserves. Part of what makes it exceptional is that it's been left alone so long: it was declared a protected area in 1923, when such reserves in the neotropics were almost unheard of. Since then its flora and fauna have been more intensely studied than that of any other tropical area of comparable size. The island is administered by the Smithsonian Tropical Research Institute (STRI), which is based in Panama.

Barro Colorado Island was actually a hill until 1914, when the damming of the Chagres River to create Gatun Lake made the hill an island. The flooding of the lake left only 15 square kilometers (about six square miles) of tropical forest on the island, but they contain 480 species of trees (more than in all of Europe), 70 species of bats, 384 species of birds, 30 species of frogs, 47 species of snakes, and on and on. Just accounting for the insects on the island is an

William Friar

Barro Colorado Island

overwhelming task. Take ants, for instance: more than 200 species have been identified so far.

Day visitors, as opposed to research scientists, are allowed on only one trail, an interpretive loop that takes two to three hours to walk at an easy clip. It's fairly flat most of the way, but it does get muddy at times. There's a short side trail off the main loop that's well worth taking. It leads to the aptly named "Big Tree," a kapok *(Ceiba pentandra)* so huge other trees are growing on its branches.

You will almost certainly take the hike with a guide, as it's rare for visitors to be allowed on the trails without one. But consider buying *A Day on Barro Colorado Island* (Smithsonian), by Marina Wong and Jorge Ventocilla, anyway. It contains a trail guide and information on the island's flora and fauna that will help you get much more out of your visit. It's available for $7 at the little bookshop at STRI's main office in Panama City (see Details, below).

Note: BCI has the kind of wildlife many visitors come to the tropics to see, including tapirs, coatimundis, sloths, ocelots, anteaters, collared peccaries, and three species of monkeys. A jaguar made a brief appearance as recently as 1993. It swam over from the mainland, hung out for four months, then vanished. But as STRI personnel will be the first to tell you, day visitors expecting a jungle crawling with creatures will likely be disappointed. You may see almost no animal life during a short visit to BCI. Your chances will drop to near zero if you get stuck with a guide who insists on shouting nonstop, as a certain someone I know did. You actually have a better chance of seeing wildlife at the Canopy Tower, and day trips there are about the same price and much less hassle to arrange than visits to BCI. (See the following sight entry.)

The only mammals you're likely to encounter on a brief visit to BCI are agoutis and howler monkeys. It's actually hard not to stumble upon howlers. A 1977 census found 65 troops on the island, each with about 19 monkeys. Do the math. Their numbers haven't changed much since.

Details: Access to the island is strictly controlled. Visitors must arrange a tour through STRI or an STRI-approved tour operator, and the few spaces available are often booked a year in advance. Cancellations are not uncommon, however, so even if you can't plan that far ahead it's worth checking with STRI to see if any last-minute spaces have opened up. Some tour operators offer trips to Barro Colorado Nature Monument, which includes the surrounding mainland as well as the island itself. Make sure the tour actually goes to the island if that's important to you.

The Smithsonian offers tours on Tuesday, Saturday, and Sunday. The cost is $28 per person and includes a morning hike and lunch. The fee must be paid at least two weeks in advance (U.S. checks are accepted). You can also pay in cash at the Earl S. Tupper Research and Conference Center, STRI's headquarters. You will not be admitted to the center without ID. See the Visitor Information section, above, for details on the center. For reservations, contact 507/227-6022, 507/212-8026, or 507/212-8100, fax 507/212-8148, hernandm@tivoli.si.edu, www.stri.org. Ask for Meylin Hernandez, Orelis Arosemena or María Leone.

The launch to the island leaves from Gamboa, about a 45-minute drive from Panama City, at 7:15 a.m. on Tuesday and 8 a.m. on Saturday and Sunday. You have to arrange your own transportation to Gamboa. See the Getting There section, above, for information on taxis and buses. STRI will give you an information sheet with directions and all the other details you'll need.

Canopy Tower—This is a special place. It's an old U.S. 1 radar tower that has been cleverly transformed into a six-room hotel and wildlife observation platform high above the floor of a protected forest, Parque Nacional Soberanía. You can look out the window of your room right into the forest or climb up two more flights of stairs and actually look down on the canopy. In the middle distance you can see ships cruising through the Panama Canal and watch the widening of Gaillard Cut. In the far distance you can see the Pacific Ocean and the high-rises of Panama City. All this is just a half-hour drive from the city.

The six rooms are on the third floor. All are simple but cheerful and comfortable, with teak louvered doors and other touches that soften the utilitarian feel of the structure (the teak comes from a commercial plantation belonging to the hotel's owner). Each room sleeps two and has mosquito nets, ceiling fans, and a good hot-water bathroom. One of the rooms is quite large and has a private balcony with a hammock swing.

One flight up is the dining and living room, which offers a near 360-degree view. The living room has couches, hammocks, observation chairs, a telescope, and a small library. You can continue up to the roof, which is a great place to watch the sun rise and set over the forest and listen to the roar of howler monkeys.

The place is not cheap: a night here costs $145 per person double occupancy, including tax and the $3 admission to the national park. If you're alone, it'll cost you $200. (The larger room, the Blue Cotinga Suite, costs $175 single/$250 double occupancy.) Discounts are sometimes available, but in any case you get a lot for your money, including two daily guided hikes into the national park on a well-maintained trail, three meals, and all the booze you can drink. The food here is good, concentrating on simple but tasty local dishes. You can get a partial discount if you don't want all meals.

The best way to get the full experience is to arrive at around 5 p.m., which gives you time to check out the sunset and evening forest activity while enjoying a drink and appetizer in the tower. After dinner there's a two-hour guided hike into the forest, which starts with a walk down the one-mile tower road. The road can be deceptively slippery, so watch your step. Those not up to the walk down the hill and back, which some may find strenuous and steamy, can take the "rainfomobile" shuttle. The hike through the park is along the wide, flat Plantation Road. At sunrise the next morning you watch the forest action from the roof then go on the morning hike, also along **Plantation Road**. If it gets too hot, there's a lovely little waterfall 1.5 hours into the park where you can go for a splash. Then it's back for a shower and lunch. Checkout is around 3 p.m., which gives you nearly a full 24 hours at this remarkable place.

The tower also offers a variety of day tours if you don't want to spend the night. You can come for a long breakfast (6 to 10 a.m.) or lunch (11 a.m. to 3 p.m.) and view wildlife from the tower for $25. Dinner (5 to 9 p.m.) is $35, including drinks. A two-hour guided hike in the forest is $15. The tower also has a booklet identifying 46 numbered trees in the park if you want to go for a self-guided hike.

You're likely to see more wildlife while lounging in the tower than you would on many long hikes in remote areas. Within five minutes of my first visit I saw a tití monkey (Geoffrey's tamarin) and a host of other creatures. By the end of my second visit, I had seen a kinkajou, a dozen coatimundi moms and babies, a sloth, an unidentified snake, and innumerable birds (short-tailed hawk, three toucans in a single tree, dusky-capped flycatcher, white-whiskered puffbird, white-shouldered tanager, blue-crowned manakin, etc., etc., etc.). At last count, bird-watchers had identified 255 species of birds just from the tower and the road into the park. *Note:* The reason so many mammals hang out here is that the staff leaves food out for them. This may bother those who believe ecotourism means being strictly hands-off in one's interaction with wildlife.

Details: You have to call ahead to make reservations, even for day trips. Specify whether you need an English-speaking guide. Weekday discounts are sometimes offered; be sure to ask.

*The Canopy Tower is 25 kilometers (about 15 miles) from Panama City, about a half-hour drive. See the Getting There section for information on buses and taxis. If you're driving, take the left fork off Gaillard Highway after the railroad bridge and follow the road toward Gamboa. The well-marked turnoff to the Canopy Tower will be on your right 1.6 kilometers (1 mile) past Summit Botanical Gardens. There's a gate across the entrance to the tower road that you may have to open (and be sure to close). Go up the one-way, well-maintained road 1.7 kilometers (1.1 miles) to the tower. **Note:** The tower is far from being handicapped-accessible. Access to the tower is by stairs—five dozen of them*

Contact information: 507/264-5720, cell 507/612-9176, or tel/fax 507/263-2784, fax in the U.S. 800/854-2597, stay@canopytower.com, www.canopytower.com.

Gamboa Rainforest Resort—Some think this new, massive undertaking will put Panama tourism on the map. Others think it will be a spectacular experiment in search of a clientele—luxury-resort ecotourists—that may not materialize. Either way, it's quite a place. Spread over its 137 hectares are a slice of tropical forest with an aerial tram running through its canopy, a model Emberá village, a full-service spa, a 100-room hotel, an entire neighborhood of one- and two-bedroom "villas" converted from old Canal Zone housing, a huge swimming pool, two restaurants, an orchid nursery, a snake house, an amphibian exhibit, several aquariums, a butterfly house, a marina, and on and on. It's a peculiar mixture of an ecotourism resort, luxury spa, and theme park.

The location couldn't be better: the resort was built right on the banks of the Chagres, one of Panama's most important rivers, and is only a stroll away from Gatun Lake, where you can see ships transiting the Panama Canal. It's bordered by Parque Nacional Soberanía, the major trails of which are just a few kilometers away, as is the Canopy Tower.

There are two basic kinds of accommodations. The first are in the main hotel overlooking the Chagres River. The hotel hadn't opened when I last visited but a sample "deluxe river view" room was on the order of what you'd find in a decent Best Western, though it did have a balcony and hammock overlooking the river. These were going to go for a whopping $350 a night, plus tax. The most basic room will cost $300. For that amount, you could stay in the most luxurious hotel in Panama City and have plenty left over to hire a personal tour guide to usher you around this area, which is open to the public. However, these are just the initial "rack" rates, and prices may settle down once the whole place is up and running. If you're interested in staying here, you should contact the hotel or a travel agency to see if the rates have become more reasonable or if any special packages are available.

The price for the one-bedroom "villas" is a comparative bargain at $200. Whereas the rooms in the hotel are generic, these have

Kayaking in Gamboa Rainforest Resort

John Neubauer

character. They consist of renovated wooden buildings dating from the 1930s that actually housed Panama Canal employees and their families in the old Canal Zone days. The renovation was done in simple, cheerful good taste, from the rattan furniture to the historic canal clippings and sketches on the walls. All have sitting rooms and kitchenettes with microwaves, mini-fridges, and coffeemakers. They don't have a view of the river, but they're surrounded by trees. Why these are the "budget" accommodations is one of those mysteries of life in Panama.

The **aerial tram** will likely be one of the star attractions of the resort. It's sort of like an enclosed ski lift that takes passengers up about 80 meters (87 yards) to a hill, passing through the canopy of a small secondary forest along the way. Passengers can get off at the top and climb a 25-meter (82-foot) observation tower that will give them a great view of the canal, the Chagres, and the surrounding forest. The trip takes about an hour, not including the stop at the observation platform. I took a test run in the late morning, while loud construction was still going on and the forest was just beginning to recover from the disruption of installing the thing. Not surprisingly, I didn't see any animals. But during earlier testing the staff claimed to have seen monkeys, peccaries, coatimundis, toucans, caimans, and anteaters from the tram. As usual, your best bet for seeing wildlife is to visit in the early morning or evening. A price for the ride hadn't been set when I visited, but given the trend at this place don't expect any bargains.

The resort will offer everything from bicycle rentals to helicopter rides, though prices for these were also in flux at the time of writing. See the Guides and Outfitters section below for a few of the offerings.

One bit of trivia worth mentioning: To the credit of the resort's builders, the plans for the main hotel were changed—apparently at considerable expense—to save an enormous tree growing on the site.

Details: The Gamboa Rainforest Resort is located at the entrance to the town of Gamboa. See the Getting There section for directions and transportation options to Gamboa. If you drive, make a right turn immediately after crossing the one-way bridge over the Chagres River. For reservations and information contact 507/214-1690/-1691/-1692, fax 507/214-1694, in Gamboa 507/276-6812, in the U.S. 877/800-1690, www.gamboaresort .com, gamboaresort@sinfo.net. Rates are $200 for a one-bedroom and $270 for a two-bedroom apartment, $300 to $1,000 for accommodations in the main hotel.

Gatun Lake—Once the largest manmade lake in the world, at 422 square kilometers (163 square miles) Gatun Lake is still a plenty impressive body of water. It was formed by damming the Chagres River near its mouth, at Gatun, and is an integral part of the Panama Canal. Transiting ships still follow the submerged river bed of the Chagres, since it's the deepest part of the lake. It's long been a popular spot with boaters, water-skiers, fisherfolk, and even scuba divers. The diving here is unusual, to say the least. A Belgian locomotive and 40 train cars abandoned during construction days are at the bottom of the lake, as are submerged trees and remnants of old towns. Not surprisingly, however, the water is murky and in some places choked with vegetation. Divers often find the experience of poking around down there rather spooky. If a ship passes nearby while you're exploring the train, the chugging makes it's easy to imagine a ghost has somehow stoked the ancient engine back to life.

These days, the only recreation I'd recommend on the lake is a boat ride or a fishing trip. Caimans have always shared the lake with people, but these days there are apparently a lot more of the critters. An acquaintance whose idea of a fun family outing used to be playing catch-and-release with caimans—we're not talking a wimp here—told me recently she would not even go water-skiing in the lake today. "It's infested," she said. The lake also has crocodiles. A friend of a friend who lives in Gamboa, a town right on the lake, took his dog for a walk not long ago and watched in horror as a crocodile lunged out of the water and ate it.

In other words, I advise you to stay in the boat. The fishing here is terrific—the peacock bass population, accidentally introduced decades ago, is so out of control fishermen are actually encouraged to catch them to restore some kind of ecological balance. It's not uncommon for an angler who knows the good spots to catch dozens of fish an hour.

Details: You can charter a small, basic fishing boat from the public marina just outside the town of Gamboa. You'll see the entrance to the marina on your right shortly before you come to the one-way bridge across the Chagres River. (See the Getting There section for information on taxis and buses to Gamboa.) You should stop by the marina at least a day before you want to go and work out a deal with one of the captains hanging around the dock. If you want to go fishing, you need to be on the lake just before dawn; by mid-morning the fish stop biting. A morning of fishing from about 5:30 a.m. to noon costs $40 for two or three people, $50 for four. Bait (about 100 minnows) is another $5. You can also just go for an exploratory cruise around Gatun Lake and/or the Chagres River. The price depends on how far you want to go.

Parque Nacional Soberanía—This is a true tropical forest, and it's one of the most accessible in the world. Its 22,000 hectares extend along the east bank of the Panama Canal, ending at Gatun Lake near the town of Limón. The wildlife is amazing, especially considering how close the park is to population centers. Among its inhabitants are 525 species of birds, 105 species of mammals, 55 species of amphibians, and 79 species of reptiles.

All of its well-maintained trails are a short drive from Pa ____ City, making it quite feasible to go for a morning hike during which you may encounter such tourist-pleasing critters as sloths, coatimundis, toucans, and kinkajous, then be back in the heart of the city in time for lunch at a fancy restaurant. There are also two very different kinds of ecotourist resorts bordering the park if you'd like to stay overnight in comfortable surroundings. (See the Canopy Tower and Gamboa Rainforest Resort entries, above.)

A section of the famous **Camino de Cruces (Las Cruces Trail)**, which has a history dating back to the 16th century, runs through the park. To reach it by car, continue straight when the road forks just past the railroad overpass with "1929" carved in it. The road, Madden Road (don't expect a street sign), will pass through a forest which, sadly, is often strewn with litter. You'll see a parking area and picnic tables on your left after 6.3 kilometers (3.9 miles). The trailhead is well-marked. You can hike this trail for about five or six hours to the Chagres and even camp along it if you like. For just a glimpse of this storied trail, walk at least five minutes along it and you'll come to a section where the ancient paving stones that once lined the trail have been restored. In the dry season, you may have to brush aside dead leaves to find them. (Use your boot to do this, not your hand, as there are still some poisonous snakes in the forest.)

If you make the left turn toward Gamboa instead of continuing straight, the first major trail you'll come to will be the wide, flat **Plantation Road**. It's a right turn off the highway; follow the Canopy Tower signs. The entrance to the trail will be on your left at the base of the road leading to the Canopy Tower. See that entry (above) for more information on the trail.

Farther along the main road you'll come to **Sendero El Charco (Pond Trail)**, also on the right. This is a very short (844 meters, about a half-mile) trail that you can easily skip. A little waterfall near the entrance sure looked a lot bigger and nicer when I was a kid. A barbecue area on the premises attracts hordes of families on the weekends.

The best trail for viewing bird life is **Pipeline Road (Camino del Oleoducto)**. To get there, cross over the one-way bridge leading into Gamboa. Continue straight. After about three kilometers (about two miles) the road will fork; take the left fork onto the gravel road. The swampy area to your right, just before you get to Pipeline Road, is worth checking out on the way back from an early-morning birding trip. At around 8 to 9 a.m., as the forest warms up, you have an excellent chance of spotting capybaras, the world's largest rodents, on the far side of the clearing. A couple of kilometers past this area you'll see a "Parque Nacional Soberanía" sign indicating you've reached Camino del Oleoducto. Make a right here and park.

For the first six kilometers or so (less than four miles) the forest is mostly second-growth. You'll see dozens of birds if you arrive early. There's also a reasonable chance of finding anteaters, howler monkeys, white-faced capuchins, Geoffroy's tamarin, green iguanas, agoutis, coatimundis, or two- and three-toed sloths. Serious birders will want to continue on past this area into old-growth forest, where there's a possibility of seeing such rare specimens as yellow-eared toucanets, crimson-bellied woodpeckers, sirystes, and other gorgeous birds that will impress even those who don't know a russet antshrike from a slaty-winged foliage-gleaner. If you are unbelievably lucky, you might see an endangered harpy eagle. (But don't count on it.) Pipeline Road continues for many kilometers, but the bridges over streams are not well-maintained these days. One was out in early 2000, but it supposedly was going to be repaired soon. This kind of problem could curtail a long hike. *Note:* You must get here by dawn to see this famous birding road in all its feathered glory. It's worth the loss of sleep.

Details: Hiking and camping permits are available at the ANAM office at the edge of the park, conveniently located before you reach any of the trails. It's on Gaillard Highway at the fork just past the narrow overpass; you can't miss the huge Parque Nacional Soberanía sign. The office is officially open 8 a.m.–4 p.m. weekdays, but the staff live in the little house behind the office so there should always be someone there to take your money. Entrance fee is $3, which allows you onto all the trails for the day. The camping fee is another $5. If you're planning an early morning hike, probably no one would mind too much if you paid on your way back. Ask about the conditions of the trails before venturing out, especially Pipeline Road. For bus and taxi information from Panama City, see the Getting There section. Note that the Camino de Cruces is quite a hike from the other trails; Gamboa-bound buses will drop you only as far as the fork to Gamboa, after which you'll have to hoof it for *six kilometers (3.7 miles) unless you can flag down a ride. You're probably better off taking a taxi from Panama City or going with a tour group to this trail.*

Summit Botanical Gardens—This place is worth a quick side trip on the way to or from the Canopy Tower or Gamboa Tropical Rainforest Resort. It was created by the Panama Canal Company in 1923 for the study of tropical plants and was turned over to the Panama government in 1985. It has deteriorated in recent years, but some efforts are being made to fix the place up. At last count there were 4,000 plants representing 366 species still growing in the gardens.

There's also a small zoo that contains tapirs, caimans, jaguars, and other large animals. Their cages are antiquated, which will be disturbing to many visitors.

The harpy eagle compound, Summit's showcase, is more encouraging. The harpy eagle is the world's most powerful bird of prey; it can grow up to a meter (about 39 inches) high from bill to tail. Sadly, it's also endangered. The bird is indigenous to Panama, and a major purpose of the compound is to try to get the birds to reproduce in captivity. The specimens here are magnificent, with thick plumage, fearsome hooked bills, and steely talons. They look like stoic high chiefs.

There's an audiovisual display at the compound that's supposed to be open from 8:30 a.m. to 12:15 p.m. and 1 to 3 p.m., but it was closed when I got there at 11 a.m. Your best bet is to arrive on a weekend or holiday. Even if the display is closed, however, you can still see the eagles in their huge cage.

Details: *Summit is open 8 a.m.–4 p.m. daily. Admission is $1. Retirees and children younger than 12 are admitted free. Ask for a brochure/map at the gate. It's in Spanish and something resembling English. See the Getting There section for taxi and bus information from Panama City. The gardens are a half-hour drive from Panama City along Gaillard Highway. If you drive yourself, take the left fork of Gaillard Highway after the railroad bridge; the gardens will be on your right. For more information call 507/232-4854.*

OTHER SIGHTS

The Administration Building and Administrator's House—The agency that runs the Panama Canal, now known as the Panama Canal Authority, is headquartered in an imposing building on the side of Ancon Hill. Called the Administration Building, it's worth visiting for a couple of reasons.

First, there are dramatic **murals** inside the building's rotunda that depict the construction of the canal. These were painted by William B. Van Ingen, a New York artist who also created murals for the Library of Congress and the U.S. Mint in Philadelphia. They were installed in January 1915 and underwent a restoration in 1993. The four major panels of the mural show excavation at Gaillard Cut and the construction of Miraflores Locks, the Gatun Dam spillway, and a set of lock gates. They give a sense of what a staggering task the building of the canal was.

Second, there's a sweeping view of part of the former Canal Zone from the back of the building. In the foreground you can see what was once Balboa Elementary School on the left and Balboa High School on the right. The long, palm-lined promenade is the Prado; each of the two sections, if you include the sidewalks, has the exact length and width of a lock chamber (1,000 by 110 feet, or about 305 by 33.5 meters). In the distance you can see the Bridge of the Americas and Sosa Hill.

If you continue up the main road, which will curve left, you'll see the **Administrator's House**, a wooden mansion set in a well-tended garden. During construction days this was the home of the canal's chief engineer. It originally sat overlooking what is now Gaillard Cut, allowing the chief engineers (first John F. Stevens, then George W. Goethals) to keep an eye on the excavation even when they were home. In 1914 it was taken apart and moved by flatcars to its present location. It has been the home of the canal's chief executive ever since. As this was written, rumors were circulating that it may eventually become the new presidential palace.

Details: The Administration Building is on the side of Ancon Hill in Balboa Heights, a short drive from downtown Panama City. It's hard to miss. A taxi ride from Panama City costs about $2. Ask the driver to take you to "el edificio de administración, en Balboa." If that doesn't work, *tell him it's "cerca de McDonald's" (close to McDonald's, alas). Visitors are free to explore the rotunda any time of the day or night, but they're prohibited from visiting other parts of the building without an appointment. The guard at the door will sign you in. The Administrator's House is a short drive or an easy, pleasant walk farther up the road. Visitors are not allowed inside the house.*

Miraflores Locks, Pedro Miguel Locks, and Gaillard Cut— Miraflores Locks, completed in May of 1913, stand at the Pacific entrance to the Panama Canal. They link the Pacific Ocean with the manmade Miraflores Lake, raising and lowering ships 16.5 meters (54 feet) in two impressive steps. Of the canal's three sets of locks, these are the easiest to reach from Panama City and the best equipped to handle visitors.

There is a comfortable covered observation platform right above the lock chambers that offers a good view of transiting ships. Panama Canal Authority guides are on hand to give nuts-and-bolts commentary in English and Spanish throughout the day, every day of the week. The visitors' center has a topographic model of the canal that leads you through a mock transit with the help of a slide show and recorded narration in English or Spanish; it's well worth checking out. The presentation is held repeatedly throughout the day, depending on demand. Brief documentaries on the canal are also screened in the center through special arrangement.

Pedro Miguel Locks, about a 10-minute drive farther down Gaillard Highway from Miraflores, raise and lower ships in one 9.5-meter (31-foot) step, linking Miraflores Lake and Gaillard Cut. These locks are not open to the public, but there's a little rest stop just beyond them that gives a good view of the action. You can also see the beginning of Gaillard Cut (aka Culebra Cut), where the canal was dug right through the Continental Divide. It's a dramatic sight, though the widening of the cut is making it a bit less so by pushing back and lowering the rocky peaks through which the waterway runs. Construction at the cut makes it hard to get close enough for a good look these days. The best way to see it is from the canal itself, during a transit (see below).

For information on Gatun Locks see Chapter 9, The Central Caribbean.

Details: *Miraflores Locks are about a 20-minute drive from Panama City, located just off Gaillard Highway. The road continues on to Gamboa, so if you're heading out that way you should consider making a visit to the locks as a side trip. Taxis from Panama City cost about $7. Taxis often hang out at the locks, and you can probably get a slightly cheaper ride back into the city. If you don't see any cabs, ask your driver to wait and take you back (agree on a price for this ahead of time). You can also catch a Gamboa- or Paraiso-bound bus from Panama City for 35 cents, but you'll have to walk the one kilometer (0.6 miles) from the highway to the locks, then back again to catch the return bus. See the Getting There section for details. Tell the driver you want to get off at Miraflores Locks or "las esclusas de Miraflores." The locks are open to visitors 9 a.m.–5 p.m. daily. Call 507/276-8325, 507/276-3187, or 507/272-5463 to find out when a ship is transiting or to reserve a showing of one of the films.*

Panama Canal Transit—A transit of the Panama Canal is unforgettable, and fortunately you don't have to buy an entire cruise to have the experience. One local company, Argo Tours, offers canal transits every Saturday. Most of these are partial transits that take you through Miraflores and Pedro Miguel Locks and Gaillard Cut before turning around. One Saturday a month the company offers a complete ocean-to-ocean transit, which takes you through Gatun Locks as well. Transits are on either the 29-meter (95-foot) *Islamorada* or the 36-meter (118-foot) *Fantasia del Mar*. Either vessel will give you the dramatic experience of being deep down in the lock chambers. You're sometimes so close to the walls that you can reach out and touch them.

Details: *All tours leave from Balboa's Pier 18 Saturdays at 7:30 a.m. Taxi fare to the pier from Panama City should be about $4. Partial transits end back at Balboa around 3 to 4:30 p.m. Return times depend on the amount of canal traffic; don't count on an exact return time. Full transits last until evening, after which you're driven back from the Caribbean side of the canal by bus. It's a long day. Rates for partial transits are $90 for adults, $45 for children 12 and younger. Prices include breakfast, lunch, and snacks. Complete transits cost $135 and include breakfast, lunch, dinner, and the bus ride back to Panama City. On the one Saturday a month complete transits are offered there are no partial transits. Contact Argo Tours, 507/228-4348 or 507/228-6069, fax 507/228-1234, www.bigditch.com for reservations and more information.*

GUIDES AND OUTFITTERS

Just about every tour company in Panama City offers a variety of tours of the canal and canal areas. See Appendix B for a few possibilities.

Professional, informative explanations of the workings of the Panama Canal are offered every day at Miraflores Locks by **Panama Canal Authority guides.** The service is free and available in English and Spanish. See the Miraflores Locks sight, above, for details.

You don't have to be a guest at the **Gamboa Rainforest Resort** to use its activities center. Here you can rent kayaks ($10/hour), pedal boats ($12/hour), bicycles ($10/two hours), and other toys. The center is open every day from 8 a.m. to 6 p.m. *Note:* The resort had not fully opened as this was written, so prices, hours, and equipment may have changed by the time you read this. Call 507/232-4855 or 507/314-9000 for current information. You can also charter fishing boats here, but expect to pay a fortune. At the time of writing, the hotel is advertising a two-person fishing day trip on the Chagres River for $280. This is seven times what you'd pay to char-

Courtesy of Panama Canal Commission

A ship navigates the Canal.

ter a more rustic boat and gear at the nearby public marina, even though these boats have access to the same fishing spots. See the Gatun Lake sight, above, for details.

CAMPING AND LODGING

Camping is possible in Parque Nacional Soberanía. See that sight listing, above, for details. You can also spend the night in far more comfortable surroundings next to the park; see the Canopy Tower and Gamboa Rainforest Resort entries, above, for details.

FOOD

There are few restaurants worth mentioning in the Panama Canal area, though their numbers are slowly increasing. This isn't a big problem, since any point along the Pacific side of the canal is only a short drive from Panama City.

The food at the Gamboa Rainforest Resort's first restaurant, **Restaurante Gamboa Grill**, 507/276-6812, is surprisingly poor. It's the only place in Panama I've ever had bad corvina: it tasted like a packet of stale Italian spices. Enough people had complained about the food in the months following the restaurant's opening that it may have improved by the time you visit. Other offerings include attempts at variations on traditional Panamanian fare, such as a sancocho (a hearty stew) made with duck instead of chicken. Fixed-price menus that include an appetizer, main dish, dessert, and a drink cost $18. Sunday champagne brunch (11 a.m. to 5 p.m.) is $25. As with the resort itself, the location is terrific. The restaurant is an attractive, open-walled wooden terrace that juts out into the Chagres River, which is crawling with wildlife. The last time I was there I saw an iguana and a small turtle sunbathing on the same log, peacock bass and tilapia nosing about in the shallows, and little blue herons and jacanas hunting for food among the floating vegetation. See the Gamboa Rainforest Resort sight, above, for directions to the restaurant.

Niko's Café, 507/228-8888, at the end of the Prado next to Steven's Circle in Balboa, is one of a chain of successful cafeterias scattered throughout Panama City that offer simple, tasty food at rock-bottom prices. This one is located in the heart of the old Canal Zone, between what was once the high-school football stadium and the employees' commissary, built on the site of a bowling alley. Reflecting its location, the cafeteria has great panoramic black-and-white photos of the Canal Zone, U.S. military bases, and parts of Panama dating from the 1920s and 1930s. Much to the amazement of old Zonians, the seal of the Canal Zone is above the counter. Nothing on the menu is over $4, which will buy you piles of local food. Most breakfast items are under $2. Ditto for sandwiches, soups, individual pizzas, and desserts. It's open from 7 a.m. to 11 p.m. every day.

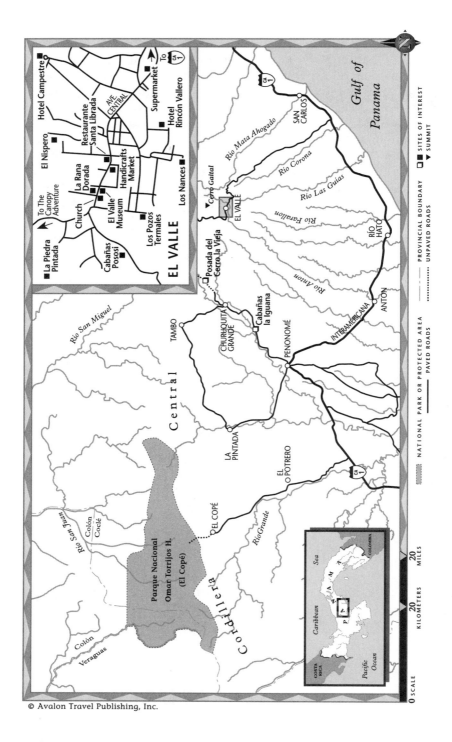

EL VALLE

Hotel Campestre
To CA 1
Supermarket
Hotel Rincón Vallero
AVE. CENTRAL
Restaurante Santa Librada
El Níspero
La Rana Dorada
Handicrafts Market
Los Nances
To The Canopy Adventure
Church
El Valle Museum
Los Pozos Termales
La Piedra Pintada
Cabañas Pososi

Gulf of Panama

Río Mata Ahogado
SAN CARLOS
CA 1
Cerro Gaital
Río Corona
EL VALLE
Río Las Guías
Río Farallón
RÍO HATO
Río San Miguel
Posada del Cerro la Vieja
Cabañas la Iguana
Río Antón
ANTÓN
TAMBO
CHURUQUITA GRANDE
PENONOMÉ
INTERAMERICANA
Central
LA PINTADA
EL POTRERO
CA 1
Colón Coclé
EL COPÉ
Río Grande
Río San Juan
Parque Nacional Omar Torrijos H. (El Copé)
Cordillera
Colón
Veraguas

SITES OF INTEREST
SUMMIT
PROVINCIAL BOUNDARY
UNPAVED ROADS
NATIONAL PARK OR PROTECTED AREA
PAVED ROADS

COSTA RICA
Caribbean Sea
PANAMA
COLOMBIA
Pacific Ocean

0 SCALE
20 KILOMETERS
20 MILES

© Avalon Travel Publishing, Inc.

CHAPTER 5

The Central Highlands

You don't have to travel far from Panama City to find cool, lush highlands filled with forests and waterfalls. Attractive and accessible spots are within a couple of hours' drive of Panama City. More-isolated spots are not much farther away, and their beauty makes it worth the trouble to get there. All are dotted along the Cordillera Central, the mountain range that separates the Pacific and Caribbean sides of the isthmus.

The most popular of these spots is El Valle de Anton, and most of the chapter is devoted to this pretty little town and its surroundings. A few other noteworthy points west of El Valle are listed at the end of the chapter.

EL VALLE DE ANTON

When the steamy heat of Panama City is too much even for locals, they head to the hills of El Valle de Anton, which everyone simply calls El Valle. It's a pleasant little town nestled in the valley of a huge extinct volcano. The valley floor is about 600 meters (about 2,000 feet) above sea level, high enough to make this area significantly cooler and fresher than the lowlands. This is one of the few places in Panama where you'll find houses with fireplaces.

Note: As attractive as the area is, if you're short on time and planning to head to the wilder and even more beautiful western highlands, you won't miss too much by skipping El Valle.

LAY OF THE LAND

El Valle proper lies along the flat valley floor, and most of the sights are within town or on gentle slopes not far away. That makes it easy to get almost anywhere on foot or by bicycle, a pleasant way to get around given the mild climate and the flower-lined streets. Watch out for monster potholes.

The first thing you'll see as you enter El Valle is a *supermercado* (supermarket), with a gas station to your right. This and the handicrafts market in the center of town are common landmarks, and most of the directions in this section will use them as starting points. A single main road, sometimes called Avenida Central or Avenida Principal but not marked in any case, runs through the town from the *supermercado* past the handicrafts market, ending in a fork at the west end of town.

Several of El Valle's biggest attractions—El Macho waterfall, the Canopy Adventure, and the petroglyphs of la Piedra Pintada—are a few minutes' drive past this fork. Another waterfall, Las Mozas, is also nearby, but the road is virtually impassable and you'll probably be just as happy with the far more accessible El Macho.

You'll hear talk of La India Dormida (the sleeping Indian girl) during your stay. This refers to the silhouette some see along a section of the hilltops ringing the valley. Given the correct angle and enough imagination, you may see it too.

NATURE AND ADVENTURE ACTIVITIES

If you want to get the old heart pounding, try the unusual Canopy Adventure ride (see below for details). Other popular nature activities in El Valle include hiking, horseback riding, and splashing around under waterfalls.

FLORA AND FAUNA

El Valle is famous for its endangered golden frogs and its square trees. Even though the area is heavily settled you may still see wildlife in the protected forests. There's also a small zoo with indigenous and non-native species.

VISITOR INFORMATION

There's a new IPAT kiosk at the west end of the handicrafts market. As usual, the staff is pleasant, speaks only Spanish, and has minimal information to offer. You may be able to get a decent map here showing the major points of interest. The kiosk is open from around 8:30 a.m. to 4:30 p.m. Wednesday through Sunday; closed Monday and Tuesday.

You can find taxis near the handicrafts market or ask your hotel to track one down for you. A dollar and a half should get you just about anywhere in town, though you'll usually find it just as easy to walk.

If you come early in the week, especially Monday or Tuesday, you're likely to have El Valle all to yourself. This is nice in some ways, but you may find the place a bit too sleepy. If you want to see the handicrafts market in full swing you have to come on a Sunday.

There are no banks or ATMs in El Valle.

GETTING THERE

El Valle is 120 kilometers (about 75 miles) from Panama City, a drive that takes a little under two hours. If you're driving yourself, head west on the Interamerican Highway for 95 kilometers (60 miles, about an hour and 10 minutes). The turnoff to El Valle will be on your right. It's not well-marked; look for a small sign on the right. If you get to Playa Corona you've gone too far.

Turn right and follow the winding two-lane road over the hills and into the valley. The road leads straight into El Valle, about 25 kilometers (15 miles) from the highway. It's a lovely drive, with a craggy ring of lush, forested hills before you and a good view of the Pacific behind. This road used to have more craters than the moon but is now in great shape, though it floods in heavy rains. Watch out for tire-eating roads in the town itself.

Buses to El Valle from Panama City leave every 35 minutes from 7 a.m. to 6:30 p.m. every day except Sunday, when they run from 6:45 a.m. to 9 p.m. The fare is $3.50.

NATURE AND ADVENTURE SIGHTS IN EL VALLE DE ANTON

Canopy Adventure—This is a lot of fun, as long as you're not too uncomfortable with heights. The Canopy Adventure is sort of a cross between a nature hike and a thrill ride. The hike part comes at the beginning, when you head uphill through steamy forest on a trail that's steep and slick at times. The hike takes about an hour.

William Friar

Canopy Adventure, El Valle

You're hiking through protected private land that borders a forest reserve, so you have a good chance of seeing some wildlife. When I was there, among other critters I spotted a sloth hunting for fruit high up in the canopy; a giant blue morpho butterfly; and a *sapo* coral, a fearsome, bug-eyed frog bigger than a softball.

The guides, who speak only Spanish, may point out the *espíritu santo* ("holy ghost," a white orchid that is Panama's national flower), birds of paradise, rubber trees, medicinal plants, the plant whose fibers are used to weave Panama hats, and so on. They will also be pleased to disturb an army-ant colony for you. You may decide this is rude, but don't worry about the ants gobbling you up—that's a myth. Their bites do sting, though, and their jaws are so fierce that indigenous people use them as sutures.

Now for the really fun part. Up ahead you'll see a steel cable attached to a series of enormous trees in the middle of the forest. It's attached toward the top of the trees, to be specific. You, in turn, will be attached to the cable by harness and pulley. The cable is strung at a gentle downward angle, so you go flying back down to the trailhead in five stages. Even better, you cross over the lovely **Chorro El Macho** waterfall on the way down. You're about 30 meters (about 100 feet) above the base of the falls at the beginning of the ride.

You zip through the trees under your own power. You have to brake yourself by grabbing firmly—but not too firmly—to the cable (the guides give you a heavy-duty glove for the purpose). The first run is the most dramatic, when you're also the most nervous about slamming into a tree.

Each part of the ride lasts only a few seconds, but you get plenty of time to enjoy the vertiginous view while standing on tiny platforms in the trees, waiting for your guide to strap you onto the next section of cable.

Note: Pay close attention to the instructions the guides give you. This can be tricky if you don't speak Spanish. The key things to remember are (1) Keep your gloved brake hand *behind* the pulley; (2) rest your brake hand lightly on the cable at all times to keep yourself from spinning around; (3) keep your legs up when you near the end of the run; and (4) if you brake too hard and stop mid-run, turn yourself around and pull hand-over-hand to the end of the run and the next platform.

So should you do it? On the one hand, two things Panama is not known for are maintenance and consumer safety. And the tropics have a way of eating away at everything in the forest. On the other hand, the ride is owned by the same guy who owns the Canopy Tower near the Panama Canal, and his operations enjoy a good reputation. Also consider that the guides are doing the ride with you—one goes before you and the other after. My guides, Danilo Rodriguez and Alexi Sanchez, were as cautious as they were friendly, and it's certainly in their best interest to make sure the thing is safe.

Don't attempt it if you're not in at least fair shape, as the hike is a bit strenuous and you have to have a decent grip and sturdy legs to stop yourself. The weight limit for the ride is around 90 kilograms (just under 200 pounds). Small children are not allowed on the ride.

At the entrance to the adventure there's a photo of Mariel Hemingway, who strapped herself into the harness a few years back while in Panama shooting a documentary. The unstated message seems to be if it was safe enough for her, it's safe enough for you. Your call. If you lose your nerve, you can just hike through the forest and around the waterfall. During the week you can also go for a dip in the pool beneath the falls.

Details: *The Canopy Adventure is three kilometers (1.8 miles) past the handicrafts market (heading west) on the main road. Follow the blue signs reading "El Macho." At the west end of town, the road forks after a bridge. Take the right fork, which is Calle El Macho. The ride's office, a thatched-roof hut, will be on your left. The ride costs $40. For $95 the Canopy Adventure will provide transportation to and from Panama City, lunch, and a tour of El Valle in addition to the ride. Part of the proceeds go to maintaining the nature preserve. Contact information: 507/264-5720, cell 507/612-9176, or tel/fax 507/263-2784, www.canopytower.com/adventure.*

You will get muddy, but wear long pants to protect your legs. Also, wear sturdy, closed shoes with decent traction. The guides will offer you water and insect repellent.

The hours are 8 a.m.–4 p.m. weekdays, 8 a.m.–5 or 6 p.m. weekends and holidays. Sunday is the busiest day, so show up before 10 a.m. to avoid long lines. Allow two hours for the whole thing.

If you just want to tour the park, the admission fee is $2 for adults, 75 cents for children. The pools under the falls are closed on the weekends, when the crowds can get too big to manage.

El Níspero—Even if you have qualms about zoos, you might want to visit this one. For one thing, it's your best bet for seeing Panama's endangered **golden frogs** (*Atelopus zeteki*). There are dozens of the little guys here. It's hard to believe something this color could exist in nature. Their caged-in pond is not well marked, but at the time of this writing it was next to the coyote cage.

Other indigenous creatures here include the capybara, the world's largest rodent—it can grow up to a meter (about 39 inches) long and weigh up to 45 kilograms (about 100 pounds); several species of monkeys, including Geoffroy's tamarin and white-faced capuchin; sleepy-looking sloths; and two species of felines, the margay and ocelot.

Be sure also to check out the huge cage with three onion domes. It hosts tropical birds in a whole crayon-box worth of tropical colors. Specimens include the scarlet macaw, red-lored amazon, and great curassow.

The zoo also has a greenhouse stuffed with orchids, extensive gardens, and a fish-filled wishing well.

Details: Heading into El Valle, continue 1.4 kilometers (0.9 miles) from the supermercado just as you enter town. Take a right turn at the sign that reads El Níspero. Follow the winding road 1.1 kilometers (0.7 miles). The road is rough but you don't need a four-wheel-drive vehicle. The zoo is on the left.

There's no guide, but Wednesday through Sunday you can try imposing on one of the caretakers. Ask for Machilo at the gate. A small tip would probably be appreciated but is not necessary. He speaks only Spanish. Entrance fee is $2 for adults, $1 for children. It's open 7 a.m.–5 p.m. daily.

La Piedra Pintada—That's Spanish for "painted rock." No one is sure what all the squiggly hieroglyphics carved (not painted) into the face of this boulder mean, or even who made them. Maybe it's just the doodling of the gods. But the boulder is easy to get to and thus worth a visit. It's just a five-minute walk up a trail that follows a pretty little stream.

Details: Drive west on the main road past the handicrafts market and out of town. Take a left after the bridge. Make the first real right, then follow the road until it ends at a cul-de-sac at a small church. (The whole way is well marked.) Small boys will mysteriously appear, eager to show you the rock—for a fee, of course. Being surrounded by a swarm of tykes can be intimidating, but you shouldn't have a problem. As soon as you choose one the others will back off. He'll probably be pleased with 50 cents. Another lad will probably offer to watch the car for you. If you value your paint job, you might want to promise him the same amount. Don't pay either one until you return. By the way, they're not leading you astray if they steer you left rather than straight up, as the misleading sign would have you go.

Los Pozos Termales (thermal pools)—You can easily give these a miss. We're talking three small pools with cloudy, greenish water. The temperature is supposedly 36°C (97°F), which you'll note is below body temperature. There's an unappealing picnic site on the grounds. For the thermal-pool obsessionist only.

Details: From the handicrafts market, head west on the main road for 0.6 km. Take a left and head straight down for another kilometer (0.6 miles). Admission is 50 cents for adults, 25 cents for kids. The only pool you might dare stick your feet in charges another $1 for adults, 50 cents for children. Open 8 a.m.–noon and 1–5 p.m. daily.

Square Trees—El Valle is as famous for its square trees as it is for its golden frogs. A good place to see the trees is behind the Hotel Campestre. There's a grove up in the forest, though for the most part they look like pretty ordinary, if sinewy, trees. There's one convincing specimen, though. It's next to the tree with the sign nailed into it—a sign that warns you not to damage the trees by writing on them.

Details: See the Lodging section for information on getting to the Hotel Campestre. As you face the hotel, walk past the swimming pool on the right of the building toward the little yellow building at the back of the grounds. Pass it on the right. The trees are a five- to 10-minute walk up a forest trail marked with arrows. You'll see a sign in English and Spanish when you've arrived. The trail is muddy in the rainy season.

OTHER SIGHTS IN EL VALLE DE ANTON

Handicrafts Market—Some visitors come to El Valle just for this market. Here you'll find souvenirs from many parts of Panama, in addition to fresh fruit, vegetables, and plants. This is a good place to buy Panama hats. Note that these are not the elegant, tightly woven hats that most people think of—those "Panama hats" are actually Ecuadorian, though you can find some hats of that style in Panama. But what most Panamanians think of as Panama hats are more coarsely woven, usually of white and black fibers. Prices range from $8 to $25. You should expect to pay about $20 for a decent one. Other items to consider include soapstone figures, which range in price from $2 to $15. The limiting factor isn't the price but the weight you have to lug around. Tightly woven baskets made by the indigenous peoples of the Darién are also sold here.

Details: The handicrafts market is 1.7 kilometers (1.1 miles) down the main road as you enter El Valle. You can't miss it—it's smack in the center of town. The market operates on a limited scale during the week, but it's in full swing on Sundays, when it's the hub of activity for the entire surrounding region. There are also a few souvenir kiosks directly across the street. If you're not in town on Sunday, there are some newer souvenir shops to the east of the market.

Museum—El Valle has an extremely bare-bones little museum that is hardly worth a visit. If you do go, you'll mostly find a few traditional tools of valley life, ranging from a wooden *trapiche*—a press for crushing sugarcane—to a decidedly non-indigenous sewing machine from someone's attic. Other exhibits include a chunk of a petroglyph and a brief, unenlightening description in English and Spanish of the geological history of El Valle. There are also a few old clay pots and figures with almost no explanation of what they are.

Details: The museum is right behind the town church, which in turn is just west of the handicrafts market. It's open only on Sunday, 10 a.m.–2 p.m. Admission is 25 cents.

GUIDES AND OUTFITTERS

You can rent horses at **Kiosco Samy**, 507/983-6628, at the fork in the road one kilometer (0.6 miles) up Calle El Hato, the road to Hotel Campestre. It's hard to miss—there's a colorful mural of a horse on the side of the kiosk and a big sign that says "Horseback Riding." The price is $3.50 an hour, which includes a Spanish-speaking guide. They're open from 8 a.m. to 6 p.m. every day. You can request a destination or just take their advice; many trails lead up through the wooded hills.

Jaque Mate, 507/983-6347, a little general store on the same road, rents bicycles for $3 an hour. Heading up toward Hotel Campestre, you'll see it on your left before you get to Kiosco Samy. The store is open 7 a.m. to 7 p.m. seven days a week.

Manfred Koch, the owner of **Hotel y Restaurante Los Capitanes**, 507/983-6080, fax 507/983-6505, will arrange horseback riding, a trip to the Canopy Adventure, tour guides, and bike rentals at no cost. He'll do this even if you're not staying at the hotel, which is either great PR or a real spirit of generosity.

Rincón Vallero, 507/983-6175, can arrange tours, horseback riding, and bike rentals for its guests.

CAMPING

You can pitch a tent next to a river on land belonging to the owners of **Cabañas Potosi**, 507/983-6181 (El Valle) and 507/226-3914 (Panama). See Lodging, below. The site, which is undeveloped, is across the street from the cabañas. Theoretically this will cost you a whopping $20, but if manager Patria Greco likes your looks you can probably haggle her down.

Manfred Koch, the owner of **Hotel y Restaurante Los Capitanes,** 507/983-6080, fax 507/983-6505, capitanes@cwp.net.pa, had plans to build a thatched-roof hut up in the mountains and run camping trips up to it. These would be by horseback, and Koch would provide the hammocks and barbecue. Contact him ahead of time to see whether this got off the ground.

LODGING

Hotel options used to be quite limited in El Valle, as much of the potential clientele own vacation homes here. But three pleasant places have sprung up in recent years. They're listed below, followed by old stalwarts. There may be more options by the time you visit. Rates at some places go up in the high season, which runs approximately from November to March.

The **Hotel Rincón Vallero,** tel/fax 507/983-6175, is a lovely new hotel surrounded by flowering trees. (For reservations from Panama City, contact 507/226-6432 or 507/226-7554, fax 507/226-6567, ericpaz @sinfo.net.) A human-made waterfall and fish-filled stream runs through an enclosed patio, which contains the dining room and lobby. All rooms have color TVs, air-conditioning, and hot water. Most of the rooms are in cabins set around a garden with an artificial duck and fish pond. There are 14 rooms. The "junior suites"— really just largish rooms—are probably the best value. The standard rooms are cheaper but are on the small side and rather dark. The hotel is too close to the hills to offer a view. Directions to the hotel are well-marked. As you enter El Valle, make a left turn off the main road 0.2 kilometers (220 yards) past the *supermercado*. Follow the road 0.6 kilometers (about 650 yards), then make a left. Follow that road another 0.2 kilometers (220 yards). The hotel is on the left. Rates run $60 to $95; $75 to $125 in the dry season.

Hotel y Restaurante Los Capitanes, 507/983-6080, fax 507/983-6505, capitanes@cwp.net.pa, is my favorite place to stay in El Valle. This is also a new place, set on lovingly tended grounds in the heart of the valley. There's not much else around it, so you get sweeping views of the mountains ringing the valley. It's a spotless, peaceful place that gives you room to breathe. It's run by a retired German sea captain (hence the name of the place) named Manfred Koch. Be sure to chat with him—he has lots of interesting tales. The cheapest rooms are in a long, one-story building next to the main hotel. They're pretty simple and a bit dark, but they're wheelchair accessible, which is almost unheard of anywhere in Panama. The rooms in the tower are nicer. The family suites upstairs have lofts and balconies and are a good deal for what you get. *Note:* If you're in Panama around Oktoberfest, this is the place to be. To get to Los Capitanes, head down the main road into town 0.8 kilometers (0.5 miles) past the *supermercado*. Turn right at the big anchor. (There should also be a sign.) You'll soon see the hotel on your left. Rates are $50 to $65 during the week, $50 to $85 on the weekend. The hotel also offers weekend packages.

The nine rooms at **La Rana Dorada**, 507/983-6606, fax 507/983-6670, are simple, clean, and pleasant, but don't expect anything fancy. The place is right across the street from the town church and museum, at the west end of town just down the street from the handicrafts market (see Other Sights, above). There's a partial view of the hills from the front porch, but none from the rooms. Don't expect to sleep in on Sunday mornings, as the church bells will be a-clanging. The place is run by a Panamanian woman and her English partner. Rates are $40 for a double room, $10 less if you don't need hot water (you probably will).

If you're looking for an unusual B&B experience, try **Los Nances**, 507/983-6126. The place is owned by an elderly couple of the same name, who offer four to six rooms (depends on demand) in their house in the hills above town. The husband is retired form the U.S. Air Force; the wife came to Panama in 1930 (she calls herself "an old Vallero"—valley resident). Each of the four rooms normally rented out has a kitchenette with a refrigerator, stove, and TV. All have a soul-soothing view of the valley. The best room in the house is large, with a queen-sized sofa bed and a stunning view. Ask for "the room with a view." A couple of the rooms are on the dank side. As this is a residence, you have to call for directions. It's not far from the Rincón Vallero, on a rough road that's just barely navigable without a four-wheel-drive. Rates run $50 to $65 for two people, including breakfast.

Cabañas Potosi, 507/983-6181 (El Valle), 507/226-3914 (Panama), is run by a friendly doña named Patria Greco. The place offers four cabañas and one room in the family house, all set on two well-tended hectares just west of town. The rooms are plain and very simple, but they have high ceilings and porches with a good view of the hills. Try the mattresses before agreeing on a room. The location is pretty isolated and quiet, but be warned you'll be sharing the grounds with some roosters. The place is a bit musty, like many things in El Valle. It's located about one kilometer (0.6. miles) west of town on the main road. At the end of town, take the first two lefts you come to. The cabañas will be on your right. Rates are $40 per room, each of which has a double and single bed. Doña Greco can arrange meals for an extra charge. (Camping is also possible; see Camping, above.)

The grand old lady of El Valle is **Hotel Campestre**, 507/983-6146, fax 507/983-6460, and like most such places in Panama she's feeling her age. I don't recommend you stay here, but since many tour operators do you should know what may await you. The hotel, which has 30 rooms, looks rather grand from a distance, like a wooden safari lodge with extensive grounds. It's on a hill at the end of Calle El Hato, a right turn off the main road shortly after you enter town. The best thing about it is an enormous fireplace in the lobby. Close up it's dingy and tired. The rooms are drab and overpriced and need new mattresses. The swimming pool is fed by an artificial waterfall that gushes forth water so opaque you'll enter at your own risk. The hotel is trying to position itself as eco-conscious, but it's off to a shaky start. For many years the place was well-known for its golden-frog pond, but the last time I visited all but two of the endangered frogs had died; the hotel was planning to get more. It was also building larger cages to house its beautiful birds (parrot, cockatoo, pheasant, etc.). In the meantime, though, they were being kept in cat carriers in a filthy hotel room. Rates are $50 to $60 double occupancy.

FOOD

El Valle isn't exactly overrun with fine restaurants. With one exception, hotels are your best bet. See the Lodging section for directions on how to get to every place but Restaurante Santa Librada.

Hotel Los Capitanes, 507/983-6080, offers good food in a pleasant environment, a small open-air octagonal restaurant separate from the hotel. You'll find German food here along with more typical Panamanian fare. The German owner prepares his own homemade sauerkraut. ("Even the Germans like it, and that is something.") Dishes range from about $4 to $10. A full American breakfast will cost you $5. There's also a bar.

You should stop by **Rincón Vallero**, 507/983-6175, for a meal even if you're not staying there. It's very pleasant to eat on its enclosed patio, which has an artificial waterfall and fish stream running through it. Fortunately, the food is good, too. You can make a meal just on the appetizers, which run about $4. Try the *plato típico*, which consists of favorite Panamanian finger food: *patacones, carimañolas, chorizos,* and *bollas*—all basically fried death, but tasty and worth experiencing at least once if you haven't been served the stuff a zillion times already. Also go for the fried ceviche ($4.50), which is a rarity in Panama and quite delicious. Meat, chicken, and fish dishes go for around $8 to $9. Fancier seafood is $10 to $12.

La Rana Dorada, 507/983-6606, offers the usual assortment of meat, chicken, and seafood (when fresh). Prices range from $4.50 to $7. You can get a tasty but somewhat greasy plate of chicken, rice, and beans for $6.50. They sometimes do barbecue here.

If you don't mind a simple place that doesn't pretend to be otherwise, **Restaurante Santa Librada**, 507/983-6376, is the spot for eating decent local food and hanging with decent local folk It's certainly cheap: You can get a full breakfast for under $3. Seafood and grilled meats top out at less than $8. The big bowl of *sancocho de gallina* (chicken stew; $2) has a nice flavor but is a little light on the chicken and veggies. The papaya *batido* (shake), however, is killer. The restaurant is on the right as you head into town, down the main road about 1.5 kilometers (0.9 miles) from the first *supermercado*. There's a second branch near the handicrafts market.

The **Hotel Campestre**, 507/983-6146, has a large, austere restaurant with standard dishes ranging in price from $3.50 to $9.50.

HIGHLANDS WEST OF EL VALLE

There are a couple of other highland locales in this part of Panama worth visiting. The most impressive of these is also the most inacces-

William Friar

The view from La Posada del Cerro La Vieja

sible: Parque Nacional Omar Torrijos H., commonly referred to simply as El Copé. If you're looking for something cushier and more accessible, there's also a mountain inn, La Posada de Cerro La Vieja, that's a good base for exploring the surrounding highlands.

LAY OF THE LAND

There's nothing for nature tourists in Penonomé, the provincial capital of Coclé, but it's a hub for snagging buses and taxis to the more scenic places listed below. It's also a place to re-provision, if needed.

Penonomé is in the middle of wide expanses of flat, humid lowland, with the Interamerican Highway running right through it. Visible off to the distant north are the tantalizingly lush highlands. La Posada del Cerro La Vieja is in the highlands northeast of Penonomé. Access to Parque Nacional Omar Torrijos H. is farther west along the highway, as are the cultural sights of the central provinces.

NATURE AND ADVENTURE ACTIVITIES

Hiking, horseback riding, and bird-watching are the main things to do around here.

FLORA AND FAUNA

The highlands here run along the Continental Divide, which means you get to experience both Pacific and Caribbean flora and fauna. The highland areas closer to Penonomé are much more densely settled and thus have less plant- and wildlife, but some reforestation programs are underway. In the lowlands west of Penonomé you may encounter birds of prey such as the white-tailed hawk. Near the lowland rivers you'll probably have little trouble spotting herons and other water-loving fowl.

VISITOR INFORMATION

There's an ANAM administrative station in El Copé, a small town below the national park, that's theoretically open from 8 a.m. to 3 p.m. There's also a ranger station at the entrance to the park.

GETTING THERE

Penonomé is 143 kilometers (89 miles) west of Panama City on the Interamerican Highway. If you're driving, it'll take you about an hour and a half. Buses to Penonomé leave from Panama City every 20 minutes from 4:55 a.m. to 9:15 p.m. The one-way fare is $3.70. The trip takes about two hours.

Parque Nacional Omar Torrijos H. (El Copé) is another 55 mostly tough kilometers (about 34 miles) west and north of Penonomé by four-wheel-drive vehicle. This trip could take you 1.5 hours if the road is bad, which it often is. You can catch a bus from Penonomé to the town of El Copé, which will get you most of the way there. Buses from Panama City to El Copé run from 6 a.m. to 6 p.m., once an hour. The trip takes about 3.5 hours and costs $5. See the sight description below for details on getting to the park from the town of El Copé.

La Posada del Cerro La Vieja is 28 kilometers (17.4 miles) northeast of Penonomé and is relatively easy to get to, but you'll still need a four-wheel-drive if you're not coming by bus or taxi.

NATURE AND ADVENTURE SIGHTS WEST OF EL VALLE

Parque Nacional Omar Torrijos H. (El Copé)—This hard-to-reach park consists of more than 25,000 hectares of forested highlands stretching down the Pacific and Caribbean sides of the Continental Divide. Its full name is Parque Nacional General de División Omar Torrijos Herrera, but most people know it simply as El Copé, and that's how it'll be referred to here.

The park was created to honor the late military dictator Omar Torrijos, who died in a mysterious plane crash in these mountains on July 31, 1981. Supposedly some charred remains of the plane are still intact on Cerro Marta, a peak you'll see to the right as you enter the park, but you'd have to be a major bushwhacking mountain-climber to prove it.

Because this park is hard to get to, it's filled with thousands of acres of primary forest you're likely to have to yourself. It's a beautiful place with sweeping vistas, as long as it's not too foggy. Even when it is, the morning mist rising off the mountains is quite dramatic.

El Copé is about as far east as the bird life of the western highlands venture, so if you're a bird nut and you're not heading west this is a place for you. If you're not an experienced bird-watcher or guided by one, however, you may not spot many species. El Copé is well known as a place to see hummingbirds, especially the snowcap and green thorntail. The rare bare-necked umbrellabird—which looks as though it's wearing a thatch roof—has been spotted here in the last few years. Its call sounds like the roar of a bull.

All the feline species of Panama are still found in the park, but chances are slim you'll bump into any. Ditto for Baird's tapirs, white-lipped peccaries, and collared peccaries.

William Friar

A cabaña at La Posada del Cerro La Vieja

Yes, there are venomous snakes here, but as is true throughout the tropics you're unlikely to see one and extremely unlikely to be bothered by one. That said, in the interest of full disclosure you should know that the day before I visited, a U.S. Peace Corps volunteer nearly stepped on a deadly bushmaster while cutting a trail. The volunteer also once found an eyelash-palm pit viper coiled in the cyclone-fence wall of the shelter that serves as visitor quarters here. These are cute little devils, but also venomous. And during one hike, a group of experienced hikers ahead of me thought they came across a coral snake. In other words, watch where you step and sleep. And let someone else go first.

There are several good, wide **trails** that start from the entrance to the park. Facing into the park, with the visitor shelter and park sign to your right, you'll see two trails. The one to the left heads straight up to the top of a mountain with views of both oceans (about a half-hour's walk). The one to the right heads down toward the Caribbean slope (endless). The latter trail is rocky and rutted, and you'll have to cross several streams. Be prepared for ankle-deep mud. An hour into it there's a far more rugged, strenuous trail that leads you back to the shelter. The umbrellabird has been spotted here (as have venomous snakes). Do not take this trail without a guide: you will get lost. It takes about an hour to get back to the shelter. There is also a half-kilometer (0.3-mile) interpretive trail that starts behind the shelter.

If you're planning to **camp**, you may want to stay in this shelter, a large, rustic structure with a concrete floor and a cyclone fence for walls. Get the key from the forest ranger. There's a wooden, windowless loft if you want to escape the cool night breeze. Miraculously, there's also running water and a flush toilet. Just 128 paces behind the shelter is a large thatch-roofed, open-air hut on a ridge with an awe-inspiring view of mountains, the valley, and the Caribbean. You can also sleep here.

Note: This area gets rain and fog year-round and is quite a bit cooler than the lowlands, so bring warm, waterproof clothes. You'd be surprised how easy it is to get hypothermia even in this relatively mild climate.

Details: *The turnoff to El Copé is 20 kilometers (12.4 miles) west of Penonomé. At the time of writing the highway was being widened and there was no sign marking the turn. Turn right when you see the Accel station* *and a building marked "Casa Río Grande." From here it's a 33-kilometer (20-mile) drive into the mountains, a trip that takes over an hour. The last eight kilometers (about 5 miles) are horrendous; even a four-wheel-drive vehicle might not make it. If you're coming by public transportation, take the El Copé bus ($1.50) and switch at the little town of El Copé to the Barrigón bus (40 cents). The destinations will be painted on the windshield. From Barrigón you can hike uphill into the park, which takes about an hour, or hire the Navas family to drive you up. (See Guides and Outfitters, below.) You'll see the ranger station on the left. The park fee is $3. If you don't see the ranger on the way in, he'll collect the fee on the way out.*

El Caño Irrigation Channel—This site isn't actually in the highlands, but it's so close to the turnoff to El Copé that it's worth a visit, especially if you had unsuccessful bird-watching up in the park. This old irrigation channel heads north five kilometers (3.1 miles) from the Interamerican Highway to the Río Grande. You can see lots of birds all along the channel, including such elegant specimens as the tropical kingbird, kingfishers, fork-tailed flycatcher, mourning dove, little blue heron, and tons of egrets. Even if you're not particularly into birds you'll probably be impressed. The road ends at the Río Grande, where you can have a picnic if you packed a lunch. This would be a great area to bike if there were a nearby bike-rental place, which there isn't.

Details: The irrigation road is a right turn off the Interamerican Highway as you head west. It's five minutes past the turnoff to El Copé. There may be a sign when you visit, but there wasn't one the last time I did. Look for a huge white sign on the left side of the road; the irrigation road will be on the right. Head straight down the road and start looking for birds. When you come to a fork, head right. The road will narrow and become overgrown with brush, but keep going. The road dead-ends at the Río Grande.

Posada del Cerro La Vieja—This mountain inn was started in 1992 as a simple spa resort, but the beauty of its surroundings gives guilty campers an excuse for doing a little self-pampering. If your time is limited and you're heading to the western highlands you can give this place a miss, but it has several things to recommend it. For reservations call 507/223-4553 or 507/223-4079, fax 507/264-4960, in Panama City or contact info@posadacerrolavieja.com. The web site is www.posadacerrolavieja.com. The number at the posada is 507/983-8900.

The posada is perched atop a 470-meter (1,541-foot) ridge with a terrific view of a huge forested valley and the green peak of the 520-meter (1700-foot) high Cerro La Vieja (Old Lady Mountain), which looks close enough to touch. The breezes here blow strong and cool, but when they stop it can be as hot and humid as the lowlands. The land around here is settled by farmers—on the drive up you'll get a real flavor of Panamanian country life—but the posada is attempting to bring back native vegetation on its 250 hectares (618 acres).

The posada's owner, Alfonso Jaén C., also owns the tourist restaurant Las Tinajas in Panama City. He takes understandable pride in the posada. If he's there when you visit, ask him to give you a tour of the herb garden, where he grows bayberry (bay rum), cilantro, rosemary, marjoram, peppermint, and other fragrant plants. Herbs from the garden are mixed with clay brought from Ocú, on the Azuero Peninsula, and the concoction is used for therapeutic clay treatments ($14, or $25 with a massage).

There are 23 rooms, all with hot water, and some are definitely nicer than others. The best are in the new pair of modern two-story cabañas perched right on the edge of the ridge. The day after I visited, one of these was scheduled to host the president of Panama. Ask for Chihibalí or El Turega; the rooms on the top floor are best of all, but all have balconies and hammocks. Package deals are the norm here, with a room and three meals going for $56.

Details: The posada is 28 kilometers (17.4 miles) northeast of Penonomé on the Chiguiri Arriba road. At the time I visited, the upper stretch was impassable except by four-wheel-drive vehicle. The drive takes about 45 minutes. You can catch a bus from the handicrafts market in Penonomé during daylight hours ($1.50). Look for the "Chiguiri Arriba" bus. You can also come by taxi from Penonomé, which will cost you $20–$30 depending on the condition of the road and the driver's mood.

Cabañas La Iguana (Alberque Ecológico La Iguana)—If you don't feel like driving all the way up to La Posada del Cerro La Vieja, you can consider staying at this place, which is much closer to Penonomé. For reservations call 507/224-9737 (Panama City). The local number is tel/fax 507/983-8056.

Officially this place is called Alberque Ecológico (ecological shelter) La Iguana, even though the signs say Cabañas La Iguana. It offers eight airy, pleasant rooms set on 100 hectares of land, 50 of which are part of a reforestation project, with five **trails** running through it. There's a river with three waterfalls a half-hour hike away. You can hire a guide for $10. One thing you should know before considering this place is that it has a small zoo where animals ranging from ocelots to toucans are kept in painfully small cages. There are a couple of swimming pools on the grounds. Rooms are cold-water only. **Camping** is also possible on the grounds; make them an offer ($10 per tent will probably do it). Rates are $30 to $50 per room.

Details: The cabañas are 14 kilometers (8.7 miles) from Penonomé on the Chiguiri Arriba road, which continues up to the posada. This stretch of the road is in good shape. The bus from Penonomé costs 75 cents. Look for the "Chiguiri Arriba" and be sure to tell the driver where you want to get off. A taxi from Penonomé should cost you $5.

GUIDES AND OUTFITTERS

As noted above, there is a ranger station at El Copé. If you can find the ranger, he may be able to guide you; a tip would probably be much appreciated.

Santos Navas and his daughter, **Nuris**, can give you a lift in their pickup the last few brutal kilometers from the tiny settlement of Barrigón to the park entrance. Call 507/983-9130, or look for the house with the sign that says Alberque Navas in Barrigón. It'll be on your right as you face uphill. It'll cost you $10 one-way; you can arrange a time for them to pick you up. Be sure to ask them about progress at La Rica, far into the park. They own 100 hectares of primary forest there, and were trying to start an ecotourist lodge when I visited.

Posada La Vieja (reservations, 507/223-4553 or 507/223-4079, fax 507/264-4960, in Panama City; info@posadacerrolavieja.com, www.posadacerrolavieja.com; at the posada, 507/983-8900) offers many different excursions for its guests. It can arrange hiking or mule-riding trips to, among other places, **Cascada El Tavidal,** a 30-meter (98-foot) waterfall, and nearby petroglyphs; to the top of Cerro Congal, a peak from which you can see both oceans on a clear day; and to **Vaquilla,** where there's a campsite by a river. The latter hike supposedly takes about 1.5 hours (I didn't have time to check it out myself), and I was told the campsite consists of a riverside wooden hut that can hold up to 28 people. There's a kitchen and running water but no electricity. A camping excursion that includes one night at the posada and one night at the Vaquilla camp site costs $125 per person including mules, guides, and all meals.

For other excursions, mule rentals cost $15 for a half-day. Guided day hikes cost $15 per person. Do not attempt any of these hikes without a guide.

If you're feeling ambitious, the posada also offers a five-day, four-night trek to the Caribbean. You'll spend the first night at the lodge, then head north by mule and riverboat, camping out in hammocks at night. Total one-way cost (you can get a bus back from the coast) including mules, guides, all meals, and the boat is $472 per person. This is a demanding trip. Far less grueling is a day hike or mule ride to or from El Valle. The trip plus two nights at the posada and all meals costs $150 per person. Add another $75 if you want to spend a night at Hotel Rincón Vallero in El Valle.

See the Cabañas La Iguana sight listing, above, for information on hiring guides there.

CAMPING AND LODGING

See Sights and Guides and Outfitters sections, above.

FOOD

The food at **Posada del Cerro la Vieja,** 507/983-8900, is simple but tasty; and cheap—soup, salad, an entree, dessert, and coffee will cost you $7.50. The restaurant has a spectacular view of the valley and Cerro La Vieja.

The restaurant at **Cabañas Iguana** is open from 10 a.m. to 6 p.m. It's an attractive, open-air place that has traditional Panamanian folkloric designs carved into the floor. It offers the usual fare at prices ranging from $2 to $7.

PANAMA'S HEARTLAND

Because this book focuses on adventure and nature travel, unfortunately it must skip over some historically and culturally important parts of Panama with little to offer outdoorsy types. This is especially true of the areas on and near the Azuero Peninsula, which many Panamanians consider their heartland. It's a region large enough to be shared by three provinces: Los Santos, Herrera, and Veraguas.

Slash-and-burn agriculture and logging have been more extensive here than in any other part of Panama, and the inevitable result has been both dramatic and sad. Deforestation has turned some parts of this region into barren desert.

There are still some lovely spots, especially in Veraguas, but most of these are extremely hard to get to. That's why they're still lovely; the accessible lowland areas are now mostly farm country. This book, therefore, concentrates on the more intact and reasonably accessible sights in the highlands and coastal parts of the region. (For the latter, see Chapter 6, Pacific Islands and Beaches.)

But if you get tired of hiking in the hills or hanging out on beaches, you may want to explore the Azuero Peninsula and the area east and west of it more thoroughly. This is where many Panamanian traditions were started and are kept alive. The pollera, *the Panama hat, various handicrafts, and popular folkloric dances originated here. Points of interest include the little town of San Francisco, which has a well-preserved 18th-century church, and Las Tablas, worth visiting at Carnaval since it has the country's biggest and most colorful celebration. Tour operators can help you explore the area. (See Appendix B for operators.) You can also try getting information from IPAT offices in the area or in Panama City.*

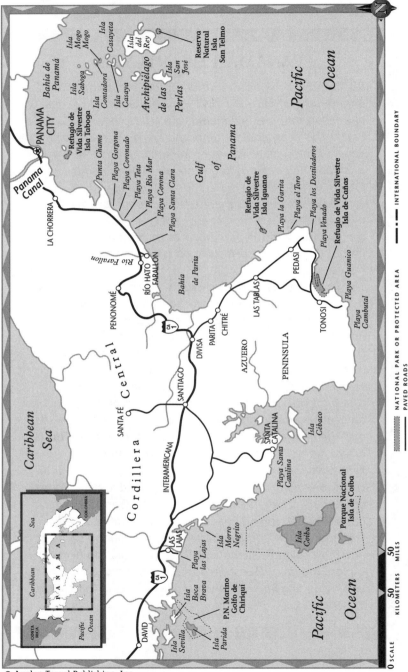

© Avalon Travel Publishing, Inc.

CHAPTER 6

Pacific Islands and Beaches

If you can't find a tropical paradise to your liking along Panama's endless Pacific coast or among its hundreds of Pacific islands, you're just not trying.

Want cushy accommodations on a sandy spot a short jaunt from the capital? The Pacific's got it. Or if you'd prefer a primal paradise so remote you feel you're the first person to set foot on it, Panama's Pacific side can provide that too. There's a beach and an island for every taste and every budget.

LAY OF THE LAND

The coastal beaches described in this chapter start less than an hour's drive from Panama City and stretch west for hundreds of kilometers. The closest islands are an hour's ferry ride or a few minutes in a small plane away. The most remote will take you a full day to reach by car and boat.

This chapter is organized somewhat differently from most of the others in this book. Each stretch of beach or island group is treated as a unit, with accommodations, food, and guides in each area described separately. Beaches and islands closest to Panama

113

City are described first, with those closest to the Costa Rican border toward the end.

LET'S BE CAREFUL OUT THERE

There are few things as relaxing as lazing or romping on Panama's beaches. But keeping a couple of safety tips in mind can make sure your fun isn't suddenly spoiled.

Beware of rip currents*: Rip currents are generally created when surf gets trapped on its way back out to sea, often by a sandbar. Pressure builds up until a concentrated stream of water flows back out in a narrow channel, sometimes at impressive speed. Be on the lookout for patches of muddy, dark, or disturbed water, which can indicate a rip. If you feel yourself being pulled out to sea, don't panic and don't try to fight against the current—it's stronger than you are. Instead, swim at a sharp angle to it, parallel to the shore. Rip currents are typically narrow and you can swim out of the channel fairly quickly. Stay calm and conserve your strength. Once you escape the rip current you can swim back to shore.*

Watch out for the sun*: Remember that Panama is just eight degrees north of the equator. Don't be fooled by mild or cloudy days. Even if you don't feel you're getting burned, ultraviolet rays are frying you. Always wear sunscreen. You have to be especially careful when you're on the water, as you're getting reflected rays as well. (Ever had a chin burn?) Sunglasses and a hat are also a good idea. Pale northerners have been known to get a nasty sunburn after just a half hour out in the noonday sun. Try to stay in the shade between noon and about 3 p.m.*

Dave G. Houser

Snorkeling at Isla San José in the Perlas Islands

NATURE AND ADVENTURE ACTIVITIES

Swimming, surfing, diving, snorkeling, windsurfing—just about any water sport you can think of is possible off the Pacific coast.

FLORA AND FAUNA

The Pacific side of Panama is completely different from the Caribbean side. For one thing, where the Caribbean tides average 30 centimeters (about 11 inches), the Pacific's massive tides range from about 3.5 to 5.5 meters (about 11.5 to 18 feet).

And the creatures you find in those waters are dramatically different as well. The Pacific is home to very big fish. While the Caribbean is the place to find crystalline waters, bright tropical fish, and corals, the iffier waters of the Pacific are where you'll find white-tip and hammerhead sharks, dolphins, orcas, hump-back whales, marlin, manta rays, amberjack, moray eels, and on

115

and on. Obviously, some of these are easier to find than others. But even when the visibility is limited or your luck isn't the best, you're likely to encounter stunning sea life that'll make the diving or snorkeling trip worthwhile, particularly around Coiba and the Perlas Islands.

Other wildlife highlights include the massive sea turtle haven on Isla de Cañas, off the southern edge of the Azuero Peninsula; the last stand in Panama of the flamboyant scarlet macaw, on Isla Coiba and the southwestern tip of the Azuero; and colonies of brown pelicans and other majestic seabirds, especially on the southern side of Isla Taboga and its southern neighbor, Isla Urabá, and in some parts of the Perlas Islands.

VISITOR INFORMATION

See the individual sections listed below for sources of visitor information in each region.

The beaches and islands around the Azuero Peninsula and points west can be a long haul away from Panama City. If you need to break your trip for the night, consider Santiago, about midway between Panama City and Costa Rica. It's a mostly unattractive and crowded town, but it does have an IPAT office and a few other facilities that may be of use. The IPAT office is in the Plaza Palermo shopping center on the right side of Avenida Central as you come into the city.

There are also a few decent hotels along the Interamerican Highway past the turnoff to Santiago. The best of the lot is **Hotel Camino Real,** 507/958-7950-51-52-53-55, fax 507/958-7954, on the right side of the Interamerican Highway as you head west, just past the turnoff to downtown Santiago. It's next to a small mall and offers 40 rooms, a bar, and a restaurant. It's nothing fancy, but the rooms are clean and modern with hot showers and cable TV. There's even a weight room. The restaurant is open for breakfast, lunch, and dinner. You'll see Mexican food on the menu that may be very tempting, but I found the offerings were served cold and bland. You're better off sticking with the usuals. Rates start at $30 for one or two people.

GETTING THERE

See the Details section of each sight.

NATURE AND ADVENTURE SIGHTS

▣ *Isla Taboga*

Taboga is the most easily accessible island from Panama City. It's just 12 nautical miles away, a trip that takes about an hour by ferry.

The **ferry ride** over is half the fun of a Taboga trip. It takes you past the Pacific entrance to the Panama Canal, under the Bridge of the Americas, and along the Causeway. You can occasionally see dolphins on the way over, and if you're very, very lucky you may spot a Sei or humpback whale.

An awful lot of history has passed through Taboga since the Spaniards first came calling in the early 16th century. The current town was founded in 1524, and the simple white **church** on its high street claims to be the second oldest in the western hemisphere. Francisco de Pizarro is said to have stopped by Taboga on his way to destroy the Inca Empire. Besides the conquistadors, its visitors have included pirates, 49ers, and workers on both the French and American canals. Canal workers recovered from their illnesses at a convalescent hospital that has long since disappeared.

Taboga is home to a full-time population and attracts many weekend visitors. It's an appealing place but inspires an affection somewhat out of proportion to its charms, especially for those who like deserted, pristine shores. Beaches here are okay, if a bit rocky, but they can get relatively crowded on dry-season weekends, and some trash does wash up from Panama City. The main beaches are on either side of the floating pier, where all the ferries arrive. The more attractive one, **Playa La Restinga**, is in front of the Hotel Taboga. If you head right as you leave the pier, you'll walk along a ocean path shaded by tamarind trees. The path ends at the grounds to the hotel. You can either pay $5 to use the facilities (see Guides and Outfitters, below), or take a right turn down to the public entrance to the beach. Remember: All beaches in Panama are pub-

117

lic. Avoid the stretch of beach on the far left side of the Hotel Taboga as you face the ocean; the smell of sewage will tell you why. At low tide you can walk across a sandbar from Playa La Restinga to the neighboring islet of **El Morro**. (*Note:* The sandbar disappears at high tide.) A new resort is supposedly going to be built on this tiny isle, but at the time of writing it was pretty junked up.

The town itself is quite attractive and worth exploring. There are two main roads, a high street and a low street, which are easy to walk on since there are few cars on the island. Both roads are to the left of the pier as you leave the ferry. When the jasmine, oleander, bougainvillea, and hibiscus are in bloom, you'll understand why Taboga is called "the Island of Flowers." Houses tend to be well-maintained and quaint. When Paul Gauguin first left Europe for the tropics he was so taken with Taboga that he tried to buy land here. However, he was broke and ended up having to help dig the Panama Canal instead, a job that he detested. He never could afford Taboga's prices and soon sailed on. He eventually found Tahiti, and the rest is art history. There's a plaque commemorating his stay, from May to July 1887, on the high street one block uphill from the Hotel Chu. It's by some picturesque Spanish ruins which in turn are next to a lovely garden filled with a rainbow of flowering plants.

Taboga is a hilly island that lends itself to hikes on which you're likely to come across old grave sites, abandoned U.S. military bunkers, and the overgrown remains of Spanish fortifications, in addition to a bit of wildlife. You can take a moderately strenuous walk to the top of **Cerro de la Cruz**, which, as the name implies, is topped by a cross. You can get a good view of the ocean from here. The south side of the island, together with neighboring Isla Urabá, is part of a national wildlife refuge that protects the nesting area of an important brown pelican colony. A water festival in honor of the Virgin of El Carmen is celebrated on Taboga every July 16.

Neither of the island's two hotels, not to mention their restaurants, is anything special. Since you can explore Taboga's attractions in a day, you may not want to bother spending the night. But it is a good place for a day trip, especially for those with limited time who need a quick island fix.

Details: The port is an easy drive or about a $4 taxi ride from downtown Panama City. Two long-established ferry services run between Taboga and Pier 18 in the Balboa district of Panama City. The trip takes about an hour. It's a good idea to make reservations on holidays and dry-season weekends. The fare is $4 one way, $8 round-trip.

Argo Tours' Islamorada and Fantasia del Mar make the trip over at 8:30 a.m. and 2 p.m. weekdays, returning at 10 a.m. and 3:30 p.m. On Saturday, Sunday, and holidays the schedule is 8:30 a.m., 11:30 a.m., and 4 p.m. to Taboga, returning at 10 a.m., 2:30 p.m., and 5:30 p.m. Contact 507/228-4348 or 507/228-6069, fax 507/228-1234, pcanal@panama.phoenix.net, www.big-ditch.com.

The Calypso Queen makes one trip a day at 8:30 a.m. Tuesday–Friday, returning at 4 p.m. On Saturday, Sunday, and holidays the ferry leaves Balboa at 7:45 a.m., 10:30 a.m., and 4:30 p.m., returning at 9 a.m., 3 p.m., and 5:45 p.m. It does not run on Monday. Call 507/232-5736 or 507/264-6096, fax 507/223-0116.

The boat ride is part of the Taboga experience, but if you're in a hurry you can try a new service, Expreso del Pacifico. For the same price charged by the slower ferries it offers a big speedboat and claims to make the trip in 20 minutes, but the first—and last—time I tried it the trip took 35 minutes. I can't recommend these guys because when the wind picks up just a little bit it's a wet, wild ride. Neither the captain nor crew inspired much confidence, and there was one life jacket for every dozen passengers. But if you're looking for an adrenaline rush, you can take your chances. They make the trip four times during the week and five times on weekends. Call 507/261-0350 or 507/229-1639, fax 507/229-3962, for reservations and details. Their office numbers at Pier 18 are 507/232-6687 and 507/232-7524.

GUIDES AND OUTFITTERS

A $5 entrance fee to the grounds of the **Hotel Taboga**, 507/264-6096 (Panama City reservations), 507/250-2122 (Taboga), earns you $5 in play money to spend on food or facilities (pool, towels, hammocks, etc.) at the hotel. Use of the changing rooms, bathroom, and showers is included with the entrance fee. Lockers are $1. There's a pleasant garden on the grounds, but macaws and toucans are kept in painfully small cages. The hotel offers a boat tour of the island for $25 for or up to four people. You can rent a kayak for $7 an hour.

Scubapanama, 507/261-3841 or 507/261-4064 (Panama City office), supposedly has a dive master on the island on the weekends, but you should call the Panama City office ahead of time to make arrangements just in case. The tiny dive shop is on the grounds of the Hotel Taboga, just past the entrance. Look for the Scubataboga sign. Scuba gear rents for $20 a day during the week and $25 on the weekend. The first tank is $8 and refills are $4.50. As usual, you must present a certification card and credit card to rent scuba gear. A snorkel, mask, and fins go for $10 a day.

LODGING

Hotel Chu, 507/250-2035, about a 10-minute walk along the ocean-front road (left as you leave the pier), is housed in two old Caribbean-style wooden buildings. The place has character and clean but extremely basic rooms. Don't expect more than a mattress and four walls. If you stay here, go for rooms in the main building, which juts out over the water. All have a balcony and shared bathrooms. There's an open-air restaurant on the ground floor veranda and an open-air bar below it. Rates run $18 for one, $22 for two people. Cash only.

Hotel Taboga, 507/264-6096 (Panama City reservations) or 507/250-2122 (Taboga), is down the path on your right as you get off the boat. It offers 54 basic but okay rooms with air-conditioning. The place is overpriced for what you get. Rates run $60 to $70 per room.

FOOD

The two hotels have the only real restaurants on the island, and neither is about to win any culinary awards. If you're just coming for the day, consider packing a lunch.

The restaurant at **Hotel Chu**, 507/250-2035, offers some Chinese dishes as well as the usual local fare. The food is cheap and the location is pleasant: it's a breezy open-air veranda right on the water. You can look out at the Pacific, Panama City, and ships waiting to transit the canal while you wait and wait for your food. (Service can be glacially slow.)

You have a choice of eating cafeteria-style or from the menu at the **Hotel Taboga**, 507/250-2122. If you've paid for day use of the facilities, your $5 credit will just about cover a drink and a plate of greasy chow mein or other less-than-enticing items from the cafeteria's steam table.

🖼 *"The Beach": Beaches within Two Hours of Panama City*

Wide, sandy, and accessible beaches start a little under an hour's drive from Panama City and stretch west for 50 kilometers (31 miles). This strip of coast is where most people who live in and around Panama City, at least those who can afford it, go for a weekend at the beach.

It wasn't that long ago there was little along the coast but small beach cottages and fishing boats. The area has undergone major development in the last couple of decades, however, and now the most popular beaches have the odd condo tower looming over them. On the most popular beaches, you sometimes have to contend with weekend Jet Skiers, dune-buggy riders, and boom-box blarers, though some efforts are being made to control these nuisances. But it's still quite possible to find clean, secluded spots without another soul on the beach for as far as you can see, especially if you come during the week.

Note: If only pure white sand makes you happy, you may be disappointed by these beaches. The sand mostly comes in shades of brown, gray, and even black. But if you can get beyond your postcard preconceptions of a tropical beach, you'll find these quite inviting. They're wide, long, and sandy, and the water is warm.

The beaches below are listed in order of their distance from Panama City, with the closest described first.

The turnoff to **Punta Chame** is about 70 kilometers (44 miles) from Panama City, a drive that takes a little under an hour. Don't confuse the turnoff to Punta Chame with the town of Chame, a few kilometers farther along the Interamerican Highway. From the turnoff it's another 25 kilometers (15.5 miles) to the beach. This place seems poised for a major development push, but at the time of writing it was still mostly off the beaten track. It's a popular windsurfing spot, and you can rent sailboards here. (See Guides and Outfitters, below.) There are prettier beaches farther west, and that, combined with its relatively remote location and the lack of decent accommodations at the time of writing, makes this place a good bet only for avid windsurfers. If you do go, notice the signs around the Motel Chame warning you not to swim at low tide. They're supposedly there because of the danger of stepping on a stingray.

The next beach area is **Playa Gorgona**, about six kilometers (four miles) past the Punta Chame turnoff. There are three places to stay in Gorgona, none of which I recommend. Again, there are better hotels and nicer beaches farther west.

Playa Coronado, about 10 kilometers (6.2 miles) past the Punta Chame turnoff, is the most developed beach in Panama. It has condo towers, housing developments, several simple restaurants, and a major resort hotel (see Lodging, below). Every centimeter of beachfront property has been built on. However, even here you stand a good chance of not having to deal with crowds. On my most recent visit, at 11:30 a.m. on a dry season Saturday, I counted two dozen people on the beach as far as the eye could see. Note that the sand here is blackish.

The turnoff to Coronado is well marked. There's a guardhouse at the entrance to the area, and on the weekends access is controlled. Just telling the guard you're going to the Coronado Hotel and Resort or Club Gaviota will do; you don't have to produce evidence of a reservation. It's a nuisance, especially since all beaches in Panama are open to the public, but it does keep the crowds down.

The 15 kilometers (about nine miles) of beach between Coronado and Corona are relatively undeveloped and have few facilities. The area is most popular with surfers. **Playa Río Mar**, the turnoff to which is just past the town of San Carlos, has the most famous break and the best facilities; see Lodging, below. The bottom is rocky here and you'll need booties. (Non-surfers will not find the beach very attractive.) Another popular surfer spot is **Playa Teta**, a couple of kilometers east (about a mile or so, to the left as you face the ocean). Waves are on the small side at both spots, especially Teta.

You can skip the last beach, **Playa Corona**, along this stretch of coast. The beach is rocky with black sand, and the one hotel and camping spot, Hotel Playa Corona, is run-down.

The poorly marked turnoff to **Playa Santa Clara** is 13 kilometers (about 8 miles) past Corona. It's about a 1.5-hour drive from Panama City, and it has it all: pleasant places to stay, a few decent places to eat, a beautiful beach, and not too many people. During the week, the only signs of life you may see are a few fishing boats motoring by in the distance. The short road from the highway to the beach has lots of potholes but is drivable if you're careful.

A large resort, the Royal Decameron Costa Blanca Beach and Resort, 507/214-3435 or 507/993-2416, was opening for business as this book went to press. It is in the **Río Hato/Farallón** area, a couple of kilometers (about a mile or so) farther west along the Interamerican Highway. It offers all-inclusive package deals for the beach- and disco-set. If this sounds appealing, contact your travel agent for current offers. Historical footnote: Río Hato was an army base during the Noriega regime, and it was attacked by the United States during the "Just Cause" invasion of 1989. When I last visited, a few bullet-ridden walls of Army buildings, their crude militaristic murals still visible, had not yet been knocked down. They'll probably be long gone by the time you visit. There's an **IPAT office**, 507/993-3241, fax 507/993-3200, by the turnoff to Farallón on the west side of the airstrip. It's open 8:30 a.m. to 4:30 p.m. weekdays.

Details: All these beaches are well-served by buses from Panama City. Try to travel in the morning, when service is more frequent and it's easier to find your way around. You'll have a hard time getting transportation to more remote areas after dark. You don't have to take a bus that has your destination on the windshield; any bus heading west along the Interamerican Highway that goes at least as far as your stop will drop you off.

Renting a car is also a reasonable option. The road from Panama City is good the whole way, if a bit dangerous. Speeding is a problem on the Interamerican Highway, so drive defensively. The drive is especially exciting lately, as major construction is underway to widen the road all along the Interamerican highway. Be on the alert for road signs that suddenly direct you to cross over the divided highway and head down what you might reasonably think is the wrong side of the road. It's nerve-wracking, to say the least. It's not a good idea to drive at night. There's a toll booth about 30 kilometers (19 miles) from Panama City (50 cents).

At the time of writing, buses left from the Terminal de Autobuses al Interior in Curundu, but by the time you visit they will probably have been moved to the new Gran Terminal Nacional de Transportes, which was being built in nearby Albrook.

Directions for getting to various beaches by bus follow:

To get to Punta Chame, take a bus that goes at least as far as Bejuco ($2.15), about a kilometer (0.6 miles) past the Punta Chame turnoff. Get off at Bejuco, a small settlement on the Interamerican Highway, and take either a "bus" (really a pickup truck, 50 cents) or a taxi (asking $15, but you should bargain) to Punta Chame. The pickup-buses are by the Texaco station; the taxis are a little farther west, near an underpass. The bus service runs from 6 a.m. to about 7:30 p.m. From Bejuco it's a 25-kilometer (15-mile) ride on a decent road.

Buses run constantly between Panama City and Coronado ($2.30). From the turnoff you can take a taxi to the beach or your hotel for a couple of dollars.

Buses heading toward El Valle or Santa Clara can drop you off at the Río Mar turnoff ($2.70), but you may have to hike the couple of kilometers (about a mile or so) to the beach.

San Carlos ($2.70) is the only sizable town along the stretch of highway between Coronado and Corona. It's about at the midpoint of the surfing beaches along this part of the coast. There's little of tourist interest in the town, but if you're an intrepid surfer you could use it as your base for some exploring.

The bus ride to Santa Clara ($2.95) takes around two hours. Any bus heading to Río Hato, Antón, Penonomé, or points farther west can drop you there. A taxi at the crossroads can take you to your hotel or the beach for a couple of dollars, or you can just hike in the two kilometers (1.2 miles).

GUIDES AND OUTFITTERS

Panama finally has a place where you can rent sailboards, and it's right on Punta Chame, Panama's most popular windsurfing spot.

Punta Chame Windsurf, cell 507/612-7490 or 507/613-1662, is next door to Motel Punta Chame (see Lodging). Board rental is $25 for two hours or $50 for the day. The shop also offers a mini-course ($25, one hour) or full basic course ($100, five hours).

Coronado Hotel and Resort, 507/240-4444, corogolf@sinfo.net, www.coronadoresort.com, rents bicycles for $5 an hour and horses for a whopping $25 an hour. You can also rent Jet Skis if that's your idea of peace-shattering fun.

Restaurante/Balneario Santa Clara, 507/993-2123, can get you a horse for $3 an hour on the weekends. You can also rent a boat any day of the week for $30. Trips last "until the gas runs out."

Also in Santa Clara, the **XS Memories** hotel/RV resort, 507/993-3096, xsmemories@hotmail.com, www.xsmemories.com, rents bikes for $6 a day. The owners were planning to develop bike paths in the woods behind their place and were also talking about offering a variety of nature tours in the area and beyond.

You can rent horses directly from campesinos (country folk) all along this stretch of coast, especially on the weekends. If you have trouble finding a likely candidate, ask for help at your hotel. You shouldn't have to pay more than a few dollars an hour. Please be considerate about where you ride; horses can muck up the beach for sunbathers.

CAMPING

Campers considering sleeping on the beach along this strip of coast should be careful. As usual, you should sleep in a tent as a precaution against vampire bats, which carry rabies. Locals may also warn you about *maleantes* (thugs). Given that there are several guarded, inexpensive places with good facilities on or near the beach, you're better off pitching your tent there than on a secluded stretch of beach. The spots listed below are in Santa Clara.

You can camp at **Restaurante/Balneario Santa Clara**, 507/993-2123, for $5 per rancho—a little thatch-roofed hut right on the beach. The price includes use of clean bathrooms and outdoor showers, and there's a guard on duty at night. This place is right between Cabañas Las Sirenas and Cabañas Las Veraneras; see

Lodging, below, for directions. The restaurant is little more than a large thatch-hut on the beach. The food isn't memorable, but it'll do in a pinch and the location is cool. The place specializes in seafood and pizzas. *Pulpo a ajillo* (octopus in garlic sauce), $7.50, is chewy but tasty. Everything but lobster is $7.50 or less. You'd better be in the mood to eat early, as the last order has to be in by 6 p.m. You'd be wise to come by ahead of time to make sure the cook's around and has what you want. Place your order for a specific time then go for a swim. The restaurant opens at 11 a.m.

Cabañas Las Veraneras, 507/993-2123, right next door, will let you camp for $10 per person, which includes use of all facilities. The site is not as nice as that at Balneario Santa Clara, though, and it's next to the mouth of a slow-moving river that looks like a great mosquito breeding ground.

XS Memories, 507/993-3096, xsmemories@hotmail.com, www.xsmemories.com, is a secure and comfortable place to pitch a tent or park the RV. The cost to camp is $2 per person or $4 per tent. Campers should note, however, that the site is a couple of kilo-meters (about a mile or so) from the ocean, on the other side of the Interamerican Highway from the Santa Clara turnoff. Motor homes can hook up here for $6 to $10 a day, a price that includes water, electricity, septic service, and access to a small shop for repairs. You're also welcome to use the pool, shower, and all other facilities. See Lodging, below, for more details.

LODGING/FOOD

The places listed below were your best bet for rooms near or on the beach at the time of writing. Most of them have restaurants; for one more food sugges-tion, see the Camping section. There are lots of other simple places to eat along the side of the road on your way to or from the beaches. If you've got your own car, you might consider doing what local tourists do: pack a cooler and fend for yourself. Many of the places listed below have kitchen facilities. The most popular beach areas have small grocery stores where you can pick up basic supplies.

Motel Punta Chame, 507/240-5498, near the tip of Punta Chame, is a rather shabby, gloomy place and I can't recommend it, especially since it isn't even cheap. But if you're a windsurfer who needs a roof over your head, at the time of writing this place was pretty much your only option. Accommodations range from four rooms in a trailer with fake wood paneling to an ultra-cheapo one-room place with a hot plate, sink, fridge, and dining area in an apartment complex near the motel proper. The best bet is probably one of the two rooms in a stand-alone building on the motel grounds. They're basic and cold-water only, but a step up from the trailer. The motel has a little restaurant/bar that serves food 7 a.m. to 9 p.m. in the dry season, until 8 p.m. in the rainy season. Rates are $40 for a trailer room, $50 for a regular room, and $60 for the one-room apartment (maximum of six people). Expect to pay a few dollars more on holidays.

Coronado Hotel and Resort, 507/264-2724 (Panama City reservations), 507/240-4444 (Coronado), fax 507/223-8513, corogolf@sinfo .net, www.coronadoresort.com, a short drive past the Coronado guard house, is the biggest resort hotel outside of Panama City. It has a health spa, 18-hole golf course, three tennis courts, a basketball court, a disco, two restaurants, a large swimming pool, etc. Semi-private hot tubs are dotted all over the hotel's extensive grounds. Its 77 rooms (they're all suites) are modern and cheerful, ranging in size from large to gigantic. The least expensive are the garden suites, which have a sitting room, minibar, and TV. If you're into the resort scene, you should know that one drawback about this place is it's not actually on the beach. A frequent shuttle bus runs you between the hotel and its private "beach club" on the water two kilometers (1.2 miles) away. The resort has two restaurants. The first, La Terraza, is a casual open-air place near the pool. The food is nothing special, but the atmosphere is pleasant. It offers sandwiches, pasta, steaks, seafood, a few veggie dishes, etc. Most items cost around $5 to $10. There's also a more formal air-conditioned restaurant upstairs with tablecloths and such and a small but fancy menu. Main dishes are $11 to $25 except for pasta, which costs about $8.50. If you're not staying at the hotel, you'll have a minor hassle to eat at either of these places, but they'll probably let you. Rates start at $165 for one, $175 for two people in the garden suites. Package deals are sometimes available.

A simpler and cheaper option in Coronado is the **Club Gaviota**, 507/224-9053 or 507/224-9056 (Panama City reservations), 507/240-4526 (Coronado). It's located to the right of the white condo towers on Paseo George Smith (aka Paseo Lajas); ask for directions at the guard house. It offers two small, very simple rooms with cold water and cable TV. The rooms are just okay, but the grounds are quite attractive and secluded. The place has two swimming pools set in a well-tended, flower-filled garden on a rise overlooking the ocean. There's a bar on the premises and a new restaurant that should be completed by the time you visit. Two caveats: Day trippers from Panama City are shipped in by the busload on the weekend, and the stagnant mouth of the Río Lajas cuts you off from the beach right below the place (there's a path to the beach just uphill from the club). Rates are $48 for the single, $60 for the double.

The 20 rooms at **Hotel Playa Río Mar**, 507/223-0192 (Panama City) or 507/240-8027 (Río Mar), near the end of the road leading to the beach, are just a tad too shabby to recommend. However, the open-air restaurant and the grounds make this a pleasant place to stop at least for a drink (I haven't tried the food here yet). The hotel is set on a ridge overlooking the ocean, and there's an attractive pool surrounded by flowers. If you're a surfer and can deal with basic accommodations you might want to consider this place, at least during the week. The rooms don't have hot water, but some have a sea view. Rates are $33 per couple during the week, which climbs to an absurd $97 on the weekend. If you're planning a weekend trip, call ahead and try to talk them down. Prices include tax.

Santa Clara's **Cabañas Las Sirenas**, 507/223-5374, 507/263-7577, 507/263-8771, fax 507/263-7860, pesantez@sinfo.net, is my favorite place to stay on my favorite beach. (*Note:* The above contact numbers are for Pesantez Tours in Panama City, which books the place.) To get there, head down the paved main road from the Santa Clara turnoff and follow the "Las Sirenas" signs, which will lead you onto a dirt road. Both roads are potholed but drivable. Las Sirenas is just beginning to get a slightly weathered look, but it's still well-functioning and tastefully designed. It's not luxurious but it offers quite comfortable and large beach cottages. The cabañas above the beach all have sitting rooms, fully stocked kitchens, barbecue areas, patios with a hammocks, and a view of the ocean. The cottages on the beach are similarly equipped. I prefer these because they're more private and the porch looks out on the beach a few steps away. Only the bedrooms are air-conditioned. The grounds are home to peacocks and all kinds of flowering trees. The one thing this place lacks is a restaurant. Rates run $80 per cottage.

Restaurante y Cabañas Las Veraneras, 507/230-1415 (Panama City), fax 507/230-5397, tel/fax 507/993-3313 in Santa Clara, is a newer place with 14 cabañas. It's just to the right of Las Sirenas as you face the beach; the road is well marked. It offers a range of accommodations, some quite pleasant. My favorites are the three quaint split-level cabins with thatch roofs on a bluff overlooking the ocean. They're a bit rustic and don't have air-conditioning or hot water, but they do have a private bathroom and a balcony overlooking the ocean. Each goes for $50 and can sleep five. (Management calls these "*tipo campestre,*" or country style, for reservation purposes.) There are four slightly fancier rooms with basic outdoor kitchens for the same price. These are set back from the ocean, but they do have a view. There's also a far less charming little house for $65 that can sleep 10. It's air-conditioned and has hot water, but it's set right on a stagnant river and I don't recommend it. There's also a "bungalow," a very rustic cabin right on the beach and above a public restroom, for $40. Camping is possible here; see the Camping section, above. The large open-air restaurant, right on the beach, is open for breakfast, lunch, and dinner. It serves seafood, meats, and chicken for $4 to $9. Don't expect anything fancy, but the food is edible. Fresh fruit juice is only $1. You can get a full lunch or dinner for $5. Rates run $40 to $65.

XS Memories, 507/993-3096, xsmemories@hotmail.com, www.xsmemories.com, is a hotel/RV haven located just across the Interamerican Highway from the Santa Clara turnoff. The turnoff is well marked. It's a tidy little place with a pool set on well-tended grounds. It's run by a friendly couple from Las Vegas and offers three handicap-accessible cabins, each with air-conditioning and hot water. One of the cabins has a kitchenette. Rooms are simple but clean and cheerful. There's a restaurant and sports bar with a big-screen TV tuned to the States-side game of the day. The restaurant concentrates on simple, hearty American fare. Most dishes are $6 or less. It's open for breakfast, lunch, and dinner. The place also

has the distinction of being the only full-service motor-home facility in Panama. There's also a small campsite; see Camping, above. Note that there's a small zoo on the premises. Rates run $50 to $60, slightly more during holidays. The three rooms book up quickly—reservations are a must.

Perlas Archipelago

Ninety named islands and more than 130 unnamed islets make up this archipelago, which begins just 15 minutes by plane or a couple of hours by fast boat from Panama City. "Perlas" is Spanish for pearls, and pearls are what first brought these beautiful islands international fame. When Vasco Nuñez de Balboa crossed the Darién looking for the "South Sea," one of his motives was to find and conquer the islands he had heard were overflowing with the precious little oyster by-products. The conquistadors eventually brought back a treasure that presumably made the king of Spain quite happy. In the process they wiped out the islands' indigenous population.

You'll find lush forests on the islands, lovely sandy beaches on their shores, and healthy coral reefs a short swim away. The latter attract a wealth of brilliant small fish and impressive larger creatures, including sea turtles, manta rays, white-tipped reef sharks, and moray eels. The Perlas are considered one of the best spots in the country for divers to encounter big fish.

By far the most developed and visited of the islands is **Contadora**, named for its role as the counting-house island for the Spanish pearl trade. Wealthy Panamanians have beach homes here, and the island has also hosted, among others, the exiled Shah of Iran in 1979. Here's where you'll find nearly all the accommodations, places to eat, and tour operations in the archipelago. It's a small island—just 1.2 square kilometers (about 0.5 square miles). You can easily explore just about all of it on foot in a couple of hours. It has several nice beaches, including one, Playa de las Suecas (Swedish Women's Beach), where you can sunbathe nude. There is good snorkeling, sometimes very good snorkeling, among the coral just off Playa de las Suecas, Playa Galeón, and Playa Ejecutiva. There's even decent snorkeling off Contadora's most touristed beach, Playa Larga. There's very little else to do on the island, though Hotel Contadora has a nine-hole golf course and tennis courts if you're so inclined.

The islands listed below are just a sampling of what else the archipelago has to offer. Usually visitors use Contadora as a base for exploring the other islands.

Pacheca, immediately north of Contadora, is also known as Isla de Los Pájaros (Bird Island) because it's a sanctuary for magnificent frigate birds, brown pelicans, and cormorants, among other seabirds. **Mogo Mogo**, less than five kilometers (3.1 miles) south of Contadora, is a picturesque island with nice beaches. The one time I snorkeled here there wasn't too much to see, but supposedly there are extensive coral fields off a part of the island I didn't visit. **Casaya**, about three kilometers (1.9 miles) farther south, still has a small village of pearl divers. You can shop for pearls here, but don't expect any great treasures. **Isla del Rey** is, at nearly 240 square kilometers (about 94 square miles), the giant of the islands. To its south is **San Telmo**, a private nature reserve owned by the nonprofit environmental group ANCON. It's home to a large brown pelican colony as well as to boobies, cormorants, and the magnificent frigate birds. The forest on the island is endangered moist premontane. A Japanese submarine, abandoned during World War II, still lies grounded on one of its beaches. As this was written, plans to open up San Telmo to ecotourism were on hold. If you're interested in visiting, contact Ancon Expeditions to find out if that's changed. See Appendix B for contact information.

Details: Aeroperlas, 507/315-7500, 507/315-7580, iflyap@aeroperlas.com, flies between Panama City and Contadora once every weekday morning and evening and four times on Saturday and Sunday. Aviatur, 507/315-0307, fax 507/315-0316, also has daily flights to Contadora. The fare for either airline is $24 one-way, $48 round-trip. The flight takes 15 minutes. At the time of writing, two speedboat companies were running a ferry service over to Contadora from Pier 18 in the Balboa district of Panama City. Expresso del Pacifico, 507/261-0350, fax 507/229-1639, makes the trip Friday–Monday, leaving at 7 a.m. and returning at 4 p.m. It claimed to make the trip in under two hours. Aquaexpress, 507/226-9823, fax 507/270-1241, also has one morning trip over and one afternoon trip back on those days; the schedule varies by day. Round-trip fare with either *operation is $40. I have personal experience only with Expreso del Pacifico. After one wild ride over to Taboga Island on a boat sorely lacking in life jackets, I would never make the much longer trip over to Contadora with them. Bear in mind that neither company has very large boats, and you're going to be on open seas that can get quite rough. It's your call whether you think a small plane is safer.*

GUIDES AND OUTFITTERS

Captain Morgan's Diving Center, 507/250-4029, cell 507/634-4193, fax 507/250-4043, can take you to 18 scuba-diving spots within a 45-minute boat ride from Contadora. Most are only 10 minutes away. The diving in the Perlas is terrific, especially if you're fond of big fish: You have a quite good chance of spotting white-tipped reef sharks, manta rays, and moray eels. Among the many other critters you may come across are angelfish, parrotfish, grunts, snappers, amberjack, sergeant majors, and triggerfish.

Captain Morgan's offers a variety of diving and snorkeling trips and other excursions. If you have your own equipment (they'll supply a weight belt), a one-tank dive including boat transportation is $40; add $15 for a second tank. A one-tank dive from the shore costs $18. A night dive costs $55 with the boat and $30 from shore. They can supply you with all dive equipment for an additional $5 (one-tank dive) to $20 (two-tank dive).

For those who like to pretty much live underwater, the company offers a three-day package offering unlimited diving for $198. For novices, an open-water dive certification course costs $370 and lasts a week. A "resort course" costs $50.

Other offerings include a boat trip to nearby islands ($30 per person), a snorkeling trip (also $30 per person), and water-skiing ($35 per half-hour, $60 for a full hour). A ride on a banana boat is $6 per person. You can also just rent scuba equipment and one tank for $35 or snorkel equipment for $15.

Marina Las Perlas, 507/250-4109, is owned by Salvatore Morello, a very mellow Italian who has lived on Contadora for nearly 30 years. Morello runs the aquatic center at Hotel Contadora and will also run the one at Hotel Punta Galeón Resort if the hotel's ever completed. He offers a glass-bottomed boat ride followed by a hike around Pacheca Island for $35 per person. The boat ride alone is $20. You can get a four-hour tour of the islands on a catamaran, including a snorkel and beach stop, for $40 per person. Deep-sea fishing costs $50 per person for a half day. A banana-boat ride is $5 for 15 minutes. And if you're truly someone who loves to shatter the peace of fellow humans and innocent aquatic life, you can get a Jet Ski tour for $75 per couple.

If you want to explore the island with minimum exertion you can rent little golf cart–type vehicles for $15 an hour at the **Hotel Contadora**, 507/250-4033.

CAMPING/LODGING

Room options in the Perlas are severely limited, but new places are slowly appearing. At the time of writing, the only hotels were on Contadora. You can pitch a tent on any beach for free.

Hotel Contadora, 507/250-4033, fax 507/250-4038, islacont@sinfo .net, is a worn behemoth of a place that's not much loved by discriminating locals. It was feeling its age when I last stayed there in the late 1980s, and these days most of its clientele consists of large tour groups shipped in from overseas. The 354 rooms are scattered among two-story motel-like buildings out of keeping with the tropical ambiance. The rooms themselves aren't bad, but the place has been notorious for years for such unpleasant surprises as running out of water.

The hotel only offers all-inclusive packages, which means you're stuck eating its substandard food. There's a nine-hole golf course, a swimming pool, and tennis and volleyball courts. Those who loathe private zoos should know that monkeys and macaws are kept by the pool, though at least their cages are bigger than you normally find at such places. Rates are $80 per person double occupancy, $110 single. Prices include all meals, use of sports equipment, and all the local liquor you can drink. Special deals are often available; contact the Panama City office to check: 507/264-1498, fax 507/264-1178, hotcont@sinfo.net.

Hotel Punta Galeón, 507/250-4134, 507/263-4758 (Panama City), fax 507/250-4135, hpgaleon@sinfo.net, should be a pleasant place to stay when it finally opens. It was slated to be completely finished by December 2000 at the latest, but such projections are notoriously unreliable in Panama; be sure to check before packing your bags. The hotel has a lovely location on a low rocky bluff above Playa Galeón. Rooms are in a series of white-washed one-story buildings topped with thatch (purely for aesthetics—they're not real thatch roofs.) The rooms looked as though they were going to be simple but attractive. Every one I saw being built had a great view of the clear blue ocean and neighboring islands and opened out on a wide wooden deck that rings the point. There will be a swimming pool on the premises. Rates were unavailable at the time this book went to press.

Casa Charlito, 507/250-4067, on the south side of the island right above beautiful Playa Cacique, offers seven rooms on an Austrian family's land. The three new rooms in the main house are far nicer than the four run-down and dreary rooms in a second house farther inland that has a kitchen, dining room, and bar. Do not stay in these older rooms unless you don't mind stained carpets and aging mattresses. Two of the new rooms have waterbeds, and all three have tile floors, mirrored closets, and air-conditioning. The owners seem to be going for a romantic getaway vibe. That atmosphere is helped a lot by the large veranda and open-air restaurant, Restaurante Romántico (see Food, below), that look right out on the secluded beach. But it's diminished by the sense you're staying in someone's home; when I visited, baby toys were strewn everywhere. Rates are $70, $80, or $100 for the new rooms; $60 for the old. Guests can arrange breakfast for $8 and lunch for $15.

FOOD

Contadora is not known for good restaurants. What's worse, you'll usually have to pay quite a bit even for mediocre food, since everything has to be brought over from the mainland. All the places to eat on the island at the time of writing are listed below.

Restaurante Romántico, 507/250-4067, the restaurant attached to Casa Charlito (see Lodging, above), offers expensive food in a good location: It's an open-air place right above a pretty beach that's likely to be deserted when you visit. It's known for its "hot stove" shtick, in which you're given a piece of meat and a hot plate to grill it on. This is allegedly romantic, which may be why you're expected to pay $19 to $24 for a meal you cook yourself. Other offerings range from sandwiches (around $7) to fondue ($19).

The poor quality of the food at the **Hotel Contadora**, 507/250-4033, has long been a source of grumbling. The last time I visited, the main dining room didn't even have fans, never mind air-conditioning, making it almost unbearably stuffy. There's an open-sided dining room next door that at least has a breeze and a view of the nearby surf.

Restaurante-Bar Gerald's, on a hill just above the Hotel Contadora, offers grilled meats and chicken and a range of seafood, with most dishes going for $12 to $18. You can also order German food, but it's not on the menu. The restaurant is in a large, attractive rancho (thatch-roofed hut).

All the other restaurants on the island are within a five-minute walk of each other, clustered around the Aeroperlas office at the end of the airstrip. **Bar-Restaurante Angelina** is a deli-type place that serves eight-inch pizzas ($3.50 to $5.50), sandwiches ($4.50), gelato ($1.25), and a few other dishes. **Mi Kiosquito** is primarily a place to get a cup of coffee or an elaborate alcoholic potion. **Restaurante Sagitario** is a locals' hangout with zero atmosphere, though the tantalizing smell of grilling chicken may lure you in. **El Galeón Restaurante y Piano-Bar** was being renovated when I last visited, but chances are it'll be one of the better dining options when it reopens. It's perched on a hill with a view of the ocean.

man brothers who own Captain Morgan's Diving
un the island's only real nightspot, **Captain Morgan's**
It's an open-air, thatch-roofed place right on Playa
Gai..)py hour is 5 to 7 p.m. and it stays open "'til the last one
falls off the seat."

▣ *Pedasí and the Azuero Peninsula*

The Azuero Peninsula, Panama's heartland, is a paradoxical place.
It's a heavily settled, terribly deforested land where wilderness has
largely been supplanted by farms. In some places erosion has transformed forest into desert. Yet it still feels isolated from the rest of
Panama, and there's lots of natural beauty left.

The beauty is most apparent in the highlands, which are still
nearly inaccessible, and along the coast. The east coast beaches
resemble those within a couple of hours of Panama City, minus 30
years of development. They're easy to get to—in some cases, you
can drive right up to the beach—yet for dozens of kilometers at a
stretch there's little sign of human habitation. No condo towers
here—at least, not yet.

As with the beaches closer to Panama City, don't expect pure
white sand. In fact, the beaches here tend to be even darker. But if
you don't mind brown, gray, and in some cases black sand, you'll
have no trouble finding a seaside paradise you'll have all to yourself.
The beaches are wide and long, often backed by rugged cliffs and
ending at rolling surf.

Many of Panama's folkloric traditions and handicrafts originated on the Azuero, including the *pollera*, Panama's stunning national
dress, and handmade pottery that keeps alive pre-Columbian
designs. It's also home to some of Panama's most colorful festivals,
the biggest of which is Carnaval, held in the four days leading up to
Ash Wednesday. If you're in the country at the time and don't mind
a madhouse, you should consider checking out the celebrations,
particularly in Las Tablas and Chitré. Be warned, though, that every
place to stay in the area gets booked up a year in advance. *Note:* The
Carnaval celebrations in and around Las Tablas were canceled in
2000 because of an outbreak of hantavirus. This was being taken
seriously by the Panamanian government, and presumably the prob-

lem will be under control by the time you visit. But if you're considering a trip to Las Tablas, you may want to check with the U.S. Centers for Disease Control, 877/FYI-TRIP, www.cdc.gov/travel, or the U.S. State Department, 202/647-4000, www.travel.state.gov/travel.warnings.html, just in case.

It's beyond the scope of this book to detail all the cultural attractions of the area. But even if you're anxious to get to the beaches, I urge you to at least pull off the road for a quick visit to **Parita**, 10 kilometers (6.2 miles) north of Chitré. It's an amazingly well-preserved Spanish colonial town. The townspeople live adjacent to each other in narrow, block-long buildings with red-tile roofs. These are set around a plaza and quaint white church. The pride residents take in the place is evident in the spotless streets and the riot of flowering plants that cover the whole front of some buildings. It's a supremely mellow place, and so removed from the flow of modern life that many Panamanians don't even know it exists.

Chitré and **Las Tablas** are the biggest towns and the major transportation hubs on the Azuero. You can use them as bases for exploring the east coast of the peninsula, but you're probably best off heading all the way down to **Pedasí**, near the southeast tip of the Azuero. It's a quiet, peaceful, and colorful little town that makes a great base for exploring a number of nearby bathing and surfing beaches.

Like Parita, Pedasí is a Spanish-colonial town that time forgot, with the same kind of architecture and the same civic pride in keeping the place clean and quaint. There's little shaking in this friendly town, and that's part of its appeal: it's a haven of tranquillity surrounded by great natural beauty. I can't think of a more pleasant place to discover heartland Panama.

That kind of peace comes at a price. Pedasí offers only basic rooms, though ones with lots of character. The few restaurants are by and large el cheapo places whose backbone clientele is the local laborers. But now is the time to visit it, while there's still little traffic on its narrow, tree-lined streets. A tourism push is coming to Pedasí, helped along by a new airstrip, a French resort under construction nearby, and the fact that this is the hometown of Panama's president. That president, Mireya Moscoso, is renovating an abandoned U.S. military building on Punta Mala, on the southeast tip of the

Azuero a short drive south of town; it's intended as a kind of Camp David retreat. It's a controversial project, not least because Punta Mala is now off-limits to residents and visitors. But the presidential connection has raised the profile of this remote, sleepy town. Supposedly, IPAT is going to erect one of its monstrous CEFATI tourist centers in Pedasí. One hopes too much love won't wreck this special place.

Pedasí is only a couple of kilometers from the ocean, and you have your choice of good, easily accessible beaches. The ones listed below are just a sampling of the better options.

Playa Arenal is three kilometers (1.9 miles) east of town on a good road. It's absolutely massive. You have to take a short hike across the sand just to get to the water, and it stretches along the coast farther than the eye can see. Fishermen anchor their boats here, but there's more than enough beach and surf to go around. A basic, open-air place serves food and drink.

Playa El Toro is another big beach, 2.7 kilometers (1.7 miles) southeast of town on a well-marked dirt road. When the road forks, head left; the right fork takes you to **Playa La Garita**, which is okay but too rocky to recommend. El Toro is also a bit rocky, and there are huge boulders just offshore. But it gets nicer the farther north you walk. The sand here is brown. Warning: El Toro is the most popular beach with the townsfolk, which means it's the most crowded on dry-season weekends.

My favorite beach in the area is **Playa Los Destiladeros**, 10 kilometers (6.2 miles) south of town. Head down the main road through town until you get to Limón, three kilometers (1.9 miles) away. The turn will be on your left. When that road forks, take the right. The left leads to Punta Mala, which is no longer open to the public because the president of Panama is building a vacation home there. The road dead-ends at Los Destiladeros, seven kilometers (4.4 miles) away. It's a wide brown beach with a great view. Locals don't tend to come here since there are no facilities or shade, so you'll likely have it to yourself. However, a French resort is being built here, so it may be a more popular spot by the time you visit.

Playas El Toro and La Garita are a fairly easy hike from town, or you can take a taxi there for about $3. A trip to Los Destiladeros should run you $5. If you can't find a taxi in town, call 507/995-2275.

Playa Venado (aka Venao), 34 kilometers (21 miles) southwest of town on the main road, is a popular surfing beach, and it's easy to see why. The beach describes a huge, easy arc, and the surf offers an exceptionally long and gentle ride that breaks left and right. It's a good place for beginners. The beach itself is not very pretty, so it's not really worth the trip unless you're a surfer. You can drive right up to the beach on a good road. The turnoff is marked. There's a simple, open-air place that serves food and drinks. A taxi here costs about $12 to $15 one-way from Pedasí. On the way down from Pedasí, you'll notice the entrance to Laboratorio Achotines on your left. It's a tuna research center that's not generally open to the public.

Serious surfers, at least those with their own transportation, may want to check out two other popular spots farther west, along the bottom of the peninsula. These are **Playa Guanico** (about 75 kilometers, 47 miles, from Pedasí, 1.5 hours by car) and **Playa Cambutal** (a little under 100 kilometers, about 60 miles, two hours by car).

To get to them, continue west past Playa Venado until you get to the town of Tonosí. At the end of town the road forks; head left. You might want to make a quick stop one kilometer (0.6 miles) outside of town, when you come to an overpass. Look left across the road at the pond below. The place is absolutely crawling with caimans. The locals sometimes feed them bread as though they were ducks. (Don't worry: You're separated from the hungry critters by a fence.) If you have trouble finding the pond, ask in town where you can find the *lagartos*.

Keep heading west. The left turn into the town of Guanico is marked. There's a green iguana–breeding project in town, but there's no real facility to visit. If you're lucky, however, you'll see one of the big guys up in a tree. Head straight through town to find the beach, which is eight kilometers (five miles) away down a dirt road. There's a little open-air restaurant. The beach has black sand, and isn't worth the effort to get here unless you're coming to surf.

Back on the main road, take the left fork five kilometers (three miles) past the Guanico turnoff. (The right fork will take you to the nearly inaccessible Parque Nacional Cerro Hoya.) After about 10 kilometers (six miles) you'll come to the town of Cambutal. The paved road quickly turns into a very rough dirt one that follows the beach. It's impassable by regular car in the rainy season, but you may just manage it in the dry season. However, be prepared to ford two streams. This beach is more picturesque than Guanico, and it's certainly isolated if that's what you're looking for. There are no facilities.

There are two islands off the southeast tip of the Azuero you may be interested in visiting. The first, **Isla de Cañas,** has been called Panama's most important nesting site for sea turtles. Five species come here: the loggerhead *(Caretta caretta)*, Pacific green *(Chelonia mydas)*, leatherback *(Dermochelys cariacea)*, hawksbill *(Eretmochelys imbricata)*, and olive ridley *(Lepidochelys olivacea)*. They come by the thousands, which makes for a spectacular sight if you time your visit right. That's not necessarily an easy thing to do, since no one seems to agree on the best time to come. You should be able to see some action if you visit between August and November, though some claim nesting season begins as early as May and islanders told me there was a massive inundation of turtles on December 28, 1999. Your best bet is to contact a guide who knows the area before you plan to visit. Given the logistical hassles involved in getting here, you may want to arrange a guided trip in any case. See Guides and Outfitters, below, and Appendix B.

As hinted at above, it's kind of a pain to get to the island, but the trip is fun. From Pedasí, head south on the main road to the town of Cañas, 50 kilometers (31 miles) away. The turnoff is on the left, and it's easy to miss because the sign faces the northbound traffic. Head down the rocky but okay road until it dead-ends at the shore 2.5 kilometers (about 1.5 miles) away. You have to take a five-minute boat ride through mangroves to get to the island (50 cents each way). If you can't find a boat, you'll have to call the island's one phone; it's a pay phone and the number is 507/995-8002. Ask for Neyla or for a *"lancha"* or *"bote."* The closest pay phone to make the call is back in Cañas. The island is a colorful place with a small population that lives in cane houses. There are a few ultra-basic huts for rent near the beach for $10 to $15 per night, but if you want to hang out here you're better off pitching a tent on the beach for free. A local sugarcane farmer, Señor Fernando, will take you for a ride on his cane cart for $8 per group, but the beach where the turtles do their thing is just a five-minute walk across the island.

The other island is **Isla Iguana**, which is accessible from Playa El Arenal in Pedasí. The island is a popular spot for snorkeling as there is a large (14-hectare) coral reef. There's also a chance of spotting green and black iguanas on the island. You should be able to find a fisherman at El Arenal willing to take you over to Isla Iguana and back for about $40 for the day. I confess I skipped visiting the island during my last visit to Panama because I was running out of time and I'd heard too many negative reports about crowds dumping trash and damaging the reef, garbage that washes up from the mainland, and coral damage from El Niño. However, I have since learned that, while trash and crowds remain a problem, the coral has recovered pretty well from the last El Niño. If you're considering a visit here, you should contact Iguana Tours in Panama City (507/226-8738 or 507/226-4516, fax 507/226-4736, iguana@sinfo.net), which specializes in trips to the island and can tell you about current conditions.

One more point about the Azuero: The people are reason enough to visit. They're among the friendliest and warmest you'll find in Panama, and the percentages of smiles seems to go up the farther south you head. People seem not just content but genuinely happy. It'll probably rub off on you.

Details*: To drive to the east coast of the Azuero Peninsula from Panama City, head west on the Interamerican Highway until you get to Divisa, which is little more than a crossroads. Divisa is about 215 kilometers (133 miles) from Panama City, a drive that takes around three hours. Make a left turn at the fork, which will take you down to the peninsula (straight takes you to the city of Santiago and western Panama). The turnoff to the little town of Parita will be on your right after 26 kilometers (16 miles). Returning to the main road, Chitré is 10 kilometers (6.2 miles) south of Parita. To continue down the peninsula, make a right turn just past the church. Las Tablas is 30 kilometers*

Clea Efthimiadis

Squirrels in palm tree

141

(19 miles) farther on. To continue to Pedasí, make a left after the church. It's 40 kilometers (about 25 miles) farther south. The drive from Divisa to Pedasí takes a little under two hours.

You can get a bus to Las Tablas from Panama City between 6 a.m. and 6 p.m., 7 p.m. on Fridays. Buses used to leave from the Terminal de Autobuses al Interior in Curundu, but by the time you read this they will probably have been moved to the new Gran Terminal Nacional de Transportes, which was being built in nearby Albrook. Buses leave every 1.5 hours, except from 7:30 to 11:30 a.m., when they leave every hour. The ride takes 4.5 hours and costs $6.50. From Las Tablas you can take another bus for the 40-kilometer (25-mile) trip to Pedasí. Buses from Las Tablas to Pedasí ($2) run every half hour from about 6 a.m. to 5:30 p.m.

A bus from Pedasí to Cañas, the jumping-off point for a visit to Isla de Cañas, leaves at 8 a.m. There's also an 11 a.m. bus to Tonosí that stops at Cañas. Either bus can drop you off at Playa Venado. Buses to Cañas run more frequently from Las Tablas.

GUIDES AND OUTFITTERS

GUITUPESI, 507/995-2303, mirely@iname.com, is a local tour-guide outfit that's run kind of as a community project by folks eager to see Pedasí put on the tourism map. The president of the company is Mirna Batista, who is also the owner of Dim's Hostel, the unofficial headquarters of the company. Mirna is the only one of the guides who speaks English. She's very friendly and energetic and will cheerfully take you under her wing if you want her to. Though the guides are working on learning more about the natural attractions that surround them, please note that they are not nature guides and you won't learn much natural history on their tours. But as lifetime residents of the area they know everyone and can get you just about everywhere you might want to go, including Isla de Cañas and Isla Iguana. They're especially oriented toward cultural tours of this tradition-rich region. Day tours are $20 per group. There are also overnight packages available for quite reasonable rates, but bear in mind you'll be eating and sleeping very simply. Bike rentals are $3 an hour. Mopeds should be available by the time you visit. Mirna and her crew can arrange horseback rides for a reasonable fee, but there's not much demand for it.

CAMPING

As has been mentioned elsewhere, it's not a good idea to camp outside a tent because of the risk of being nibbled on by a rabies-carrying vampire bat. The area around Pedasí is very mellow, so you probably don't have to be as concerned about being molested by bad guys as you would closer to urban areas. Still, if you're camping alone you may want to think twice about pitching a tent in a very remote area, just as you would in your home country.

One spot to consider is **Playa Venado**. While there are five shacks on the beach you can bunk in, they're so far beyond basic you'd be ashamed to keep your tools in them back home. They go for an outrageous $16 to $24. If you must have a roof over your head, inquire at the basic restaurant/bar next door; the number is 507/995-8107. But you're probably far better off just pitching a tent on the beach for free.

You can also pitch a tent on the lovely beach at **Finca La Playita**, 507/996-6551 (in Chitré), car phone 507/994-0282, ext. 3418, for $10, which gives you access to bathroom facilities. See Lodging, below, for details.

LODGING

Residencial Moscoso, 507/995-2203, on the main road toward the end of town, is a simple but pleasant pension run by friendly folks. Both the people and the place possess lots of old Azuero character. Just to remind you how small Panamanian society really is, the place is owned by an uncle of Mireya Moscoso, the president of Panama. Rooms vary a lot; some are quite dark and small. None has hot water. Rates run $8 to $12 per room without air-conditioning, $17 to $22 with. Prices include tax. There is no restaurant on the premises, but there are places to eat nearby.

Hotel Residencial Pedasí, 507/995-2322, on the main road just before town, offers 16 clean, spartan rooms. The beds are a bit saggy and the rooms tend to be somewhat dark. But the spot is nice and quiet and the people are kind. Rates are $15, $20, or $25 for one, two, or three people. There's an open-air restaurant that's open on the weekend.

Dim's Hostel, 507/995-2303, mirely@iname.com, is on the right as you enter what passes for downtown in Pedasí. Accommodations consist of five rooms in the aging home of the owner, Mirna Batista, who is also the president of the GUITUPESI guide service (see Guides and Outfitters, above). Rooms are on the old side and are pretty basic, but they have character and Mirna should have finished renovating the house by the time you visit. In early 2000 she was midway through the construction of a small Azuero-style mud house in the backyard. It was being built the traditional way, in which everyone pitches in and the thing becomes a big party. It could be a pretty cool room option when it's done, especially since the rooms' one concession to modernity will be air-conditioning. Some of the other rooms also have air-conditioning, and all should be equipped when the renovation is complete. None has hot water. Simple but tasty meals are served to guests only, out on an attractive thatch-roofed patio area with a tree as the centerpiece. Breakfast is $2.50, lunch and dinner are $3.50. Mirna is an attentive and helpful host eager to see more tourists come to Pedasí. If you want to go to the beach, for instance, she'll pack you a lunch and provide drop-off and pickup service. Rates are $21, including tax, for up to three people; $5 more for a fourth person.

Finca La Playita, cell 507/680-5371, 507/996-6551 (Chitré; there's no permanent phone at the *finca*), cell 507/994-0282, ext. 3418, 30 kilometers (18.6 miles) south of Pedasí, halfway between the Laboratorio Achotines and Playa Venado, has by far the most attractive accommodations in the entire area. It's owned by Lester Knight, a horse-racing jockey with a Panamanian mother and an American father. If he's not there, ask to speak to the caretaker, Lover (seriously, that's his name), who speaks only Spanish. Knight's land is secluded and the *finca* is built right above a lovely beach that, given its location, is essentially private. A couple of islets offshore form a natural breakwater, so the surf is calm here. A short marble staircase leads down to the sand. The *finca* offers two large "cabañas" (actually, they're in a single building), and 15 more were planned at the time of writing. A restaurant was under construction as well. There is also a shared kitchen that guests can use. You can have food you bring cooked for you for $5 a day. The finished rooms were quite nice, done up in Spanish style with teak furniture. They're cold-water only. It's also possible to hire a boat and captain (expect to pay around $35) and rent snorkeling equipment ($5 for flippers, mask, and snorkel). It's a beautiful spot, isolated but very comfortable. Getting there: The left turn off the main road toward Finca La Playita is not marked. You turn onto a dirt country road that's okay in the summer but requires a four-wheel-drive in the rainy season. Taxis from Pedasí will take you there for about $12 one-way. The bus from Pedasí to Cañas or Tonosí will stop here, and in fact it may take you all the way in if you ask the driver to drop you at *"casa de Lester."* Each cabaña can sleep up to five people. Rates are $50 a couple, $5 extra per person, up to a maximum of $65 for five people.

FOOD

The nicest place to eat in Pedasí, **Restaurante JR**, 507/995-2116, is on the right as you enter town. It's run by an elderly French chef who's lived in Panama for 35 years and has cooked everywhere from Paris to Panama City. The place specializes in seafood and steaks, with prices ranging from $7 to $12.50. The fixed-priced menu, including salad, main dish, and dessert, costs $8. The restaurant is run out of his house, so let him know you're coming. To my everlasting regret, I've yet to eat there myself. The place is open for lunch and dinner.

Restaurante Angela, 507/995-2275, right next to Dim's Hostel, is patronized by local workmen. It's a bare-bones place that serves hearty local food. Nothing on the menu is more than $2. It opens at dawn and closes at sunset; let Angela know you're coming and she may stay open a little bit later.

Restaurante Marisco del Faro, 507/995-2317, by the Texaco station at the end of town, is an ultra-basic place where you can get a more-or-less edible breakfast for next to nothing.

Refresqueria y Dulceria Yely, on the right just south of Residencial Moscoso, is locally famous for its cakes. Try the rum or almond ones (25 cents a slice).

▣ *Playa Santa Catalina*

Santa Catalina is the best surfing spot in Panama, with one of the most consistent breaks in Central or South America. There's something to ride here every month of the year.

While Santa Catalina is of interest mainly to serious surfers, it's a lovely place even if you just want to watch the rollers from a distance. However, it's a remote and isolated spot and it's quite a haul to get here from Panama City. It's west of the Azuero Peninsula, closer to the Costa Rican border than the capital, and you'll be a long, rough road away from anything approaching civilization. It's definitely a get-away-from-it-all kind of place.

The best time for really big waves is February to August, when wave faces get as high as six to nine meters (20 to 30 feet). At other times the average is two to three meters (about six to ten feet). Waves break both right and left. The sea bottom is rocky, so you need booties.

The nearest sizable settlement you'll come across on the drive down to the beach is Soná, an unattractive crossroads town with nothing to offer travelers. You can get some provisions here, but you're better off planning ahead and stocking up on whatever you think you'll need back in Santiago, on the Interamerican Highway a two-hour drive from the beach.

The road ends right at the beach, where there are a couple of bars, a few simple homes, and little else. A left turn up a steep, bad road takes you to **Casa Blanca Surf Resort**, the only place I recommend staying. That's about all there is here other than the amazing surf.

Details: If you drive to Playa Santa Catalina from Panama City, you first have to get to the big town of Santiago. It's on the Interamerican Highway 250 kilometers (155 miles) from the capital, a drive that takes about 3.5 hours. (See the Visitor Information section at the beginning of this chapter if you need to spend the night in Santiago.) Head left off the highway into Santiago, then make a left toward the town of Soná when you reach the church. The streets here are confusing, and you may need to ask for directions. Soná is 50 kilometers (31 miles) southwest of Santiago on a mostly excellent road (beware, however, of the one-way bridges).

To continue on to Santa Catalina, make a left at the gas station just before you enter Soná; the turn is marked. The road is in great shape and very scenic for the first 48 kilometers (30 miles), at which point you make another left turn onto a rough road. After nine kilometers (5.5 miles) you'll come to the village of Hicaco. Make a right at the Hicaco police station onto a road so rough you won't be able to drive it in a regular car during the rainy season. The road ends at Playa Santa Catalina, eight kilometers (about five miles) away. The entire trip from Panama City takes about 5.5 hours if you drive straight through.

Buses from Panama City to Soná ($7) leave approximately every 1.5 hours from 8:30 a.m. to 6 p.m. At the time of writing, buses left from the Terminal de Autobuses al Interior in Curundu, but by the time you read this they will probably have been moved to the new Gran Terminal Nacional de Transportes being built in nearby Albrook. Buses from Soná to Santa Catalina ($3) leave at 5 a.m., noon, and 4 p.m., returning at 7 a.m. and 8 a.m. You can also get a taxi from Soná to Santa Catalina for $25–$30. If you have trouble finding a taxi, call 507/998-8322.

GUIDES AND OUTFITTERS

There are no real guides or outfitters here; surfers have to bring their own equipment. However, **Ricardo Icaza**, the owner of Casa Blanca Surfing Resort (see Lodging, below), will sometimes let guests rent his own boards if he's convinced you're experienced enough not to break them on the rocks.

Ricardo also makes trips to the nearby islands for fishing, snorkeling, or diving. Again, if you want to snorkel or dive, you must have your own equipment. I really don't advise diving these waters without a dive master. The most ambitious trip is to Coiba, which you can arrange for $300 for up to five people. Coiba is about 1.5 hours away on Ricardo's boat. For more information, see the Parque Nacional Isla de Coiba section in this chapter.

CAMPING

You can pitch a tent for free on the beach, but I'd suggest springing for a basic room at **Casa Blanca Surf Resort** instead; there's plenty of room to sleep under the stars there if you want to. (See Lodging, below.) Maybe it's just me, but it doesn't feel safe to camp out on this beach, at least near the village itself. I've gotten bad vibes from some of the characters that hang out around there.

Cabañas Rolo offers a few horrid cinder-block huts on the beach for $5 a night. They resemble jail cells, down to graffiti on the walls. The owner is reluctant to rent out to strangers in any case because surfer bums have cheated him in the past. If that doesn't discourage you, call 507/998-8600 and ask for Santiago.

LODGING/FOOD

Casa Blanca Surf Resort, tel/fax 507/226-3786 (Panama City; no local phone), is tucked away on an isolated bluff east of the village of Santa Catalina. It's a surprisingly pleasant and comfortable place to stay, given its location. To get there, make a left turn as you near the end of the road into Santa Catalina and head steeply uphill. Take the right fork at the sign.

Though not really a "resort," Casa Blanca offers eight rooms that vary in quality from basic but okay to simple but quite decent. Rooms are spread among several cabins on a spacious property with a spectacular view of the ocean. The cheapest rooms have fans and shared bathrooms. The nicest place to stay is a two-bedroom cabin with air-conditioning and private bath. But in any case the rooms don't matter nearly as much as the lovely surroundings. There's an open-air restaurant on the premises where you can get all your meals and watch satellite TV. The owner, Ricardo Icaza, is a surfer who's been riding waves in Panama for three decades. He's a nice guy. Rates run $15 to $40 per person.

Parque Nacional Isla de Coiba

The waters around Coiba Island offer world-class diving and deep-sea fishing. We're talking big fish. Very big fish. As in white-tip, hammerhead, and tiger sharks; orcas; dolphins; humpback whales; whale sharks; manta rays; barracudas; amberjack; big snappers; three kinds of marlin; moray eels; and on and on. Sharks and mantas are especially common, and you also have a good chance of coming face to face with a sea turtle. On the east side of the island is the second-largest coral reef in the central-eastern Pacific. Visibility can be unpredictable, but even on "bad" days you're likely to see some impressive creatures.

Coiba is actually just one part of the 270,000-hectare (1,042-square-mile) park, which also includes the 20-square-kilometer (about eight-square-mile) island of Jicarón, many smaller islands, and their surrounding waters, mangroves, and coral reefs. Coiba itself is, at 493 square kilometers (about 0.19 square miles), the largest island in Panama. It's still mainly covered in virgin forest, though there has been some deforestation and forest disruption. There isn't a huge diversity of animal species on the island, but there are least 36 species of mammals, including howler monkeys, and a range of amphibians and reptiles, including the deadly fer-de-lance snake. You're much more likely to come across beautiful birds, however; Coiba is just about the last stand of the gorgeous scarlet macaw. Other impressive birds common on Coiba include the bicolored hawk and the enormous king vulture.

Two things keep nature pristine and spectacular on and around Coiba: it's quite remote and hard to get to, and it's the home of a Devil's Island–style penal colony with convicted murderers, rapists, and other serious criminals. The Panamanian government has been making noises for years about moving the colony and developing the island for tourism, but for better or worse, definite plans have been slow to materialize.

Because of the penal colony, access to the island is tightly controlled. Visitors have to get a permit from the Panamanian government and are restricted to the area around an ANAM research station on the northeast tip of the island. It's well away from the prison camps, though some model prisoners work as servants at the station. The guest cabins are quite decent and air-conditioned, and the station is next to a sandy cove.

Because of the logistical hassles in getting to Coiba, you're almost forced to go with some kind of tour operator. This can get quite expensive, but you'll see a lot more and have a far more comfortable—and safe—trip than if you tried to get there on your own.

Details*: There is a landing strip on Coiba, but at the time of writing only charter flights made the trip. Otherwise, access to the island is a long* *haul by land and sea. As mentioned above, visits to the island are tightly controlled. See Guides and Outfitters, below, for suggestions on ways to get to this amazing place.*

GUIDES AND OUTFITTERS

The only operation that regularly makes diving and fishing trips to the Coiba area is the **Coiba** *Explorer II*, 800/733-4742, 504/871-7181, fax 504/871-7150, www.coibaexplorer.com, info@coibaexplorer.com. This is a high-end trip and a serious commitment of time: usually only week-long packages are offered, though a half-week fishing package may be available around Christmas. But if you can afford it, it's a very cushy way to see Coiba. The *Explorer II* is a modern 35-meter (115-foot) yacht with eight double staterooms and one deluxe stateroom. The mother ship is tended by a fleet of smaller boats from which the diving and fishing are done. The dive package gives you the chance to make about two dozen dives around Coiba and other islands in the region, including Jicarón, Contreras, and the Ladrones. The cost is $2,500 per person for the dive package and up to $4,000 per person for the fishing package. Packages include two nights in a luxury hotel in Panama City, the charter flight to Coiba, fishing or diving equipment, and meals. Snorkelers pay the same rate as divers. The diving season is June to mid-September, and the fishing season runs from approximately November to the beginning of May. Fishing trips are $750 cheaper in April, the last month of the season. Note that trips often book up a year ahead of time.

A far cheaper though more rugged trip is offered by **Nautilus**, cell 507/613-6557, 507/263-5742, fax 507/263-5892, kbmrossa @sinfo.net, a dive operator based out of Portobelo on Panama's Caribbean coast. Coiba trips are not regularly scheduled, but you should be able to arrange one as long as things aren't too busy around Portobelo. Minimum group size is five, and you have to give Nautilus at least 10 days notice to arrange permits. Five-dive weekend trips cost $350 per person, which includes transportation, food, lodging, and all equipment. It normally works like this: on Friday evening you're driven from Panama City to Santiago, about three hours away. You spend the night in a simple but okay hotel, then drive down to Puerto Mutis for the ride over to Coiba, which takes three hours on the Nautilus boats. You dive Saturday and Sunday, then return Monday afternoon after a final morning dive. Lodging is at the ANAM station. The owner of Nautilus refers to the Coiba trip as "diving from hell" because of the logistical hassles in getting there. But the rewards can be terrific. See Chapter 9, The Central Caribbean, for more information on Nautilus.

Scubapanama, 507/261-3841, 507/261-4064, fax 507/261-9586, offers a four-day trip with three days of diving for $467 per person. The price includes meals, tanks, weights, transportation from Panama City, and lodging above a live-aboard, the *Coral Star.*

If you're planning to visit Playa Santa Catalina, you may be able to arrange a trip to Coiba through Casa Blanca Surf Resort. See the Playa Santa Catalina section, above, for information.

LODGING/FOOD

The only lodging on the island itself is at the ANAM station, which also provides meals. See the Parque Nacional Isla de Coiba section, above.

▣ *Morro Negrito Surf Camp*

Started in June 1998, Morro Negrito is gaining a reputation as a haven for adventurous surfers. I was unable to visit it on my last trip to Panama, but I've heard enough good reports to recommend it to surfing buffs. It's located on two islands in the Gulf of Chiriquí, due north of Isla de Coiba. It's just off the opposite (northwest) side of the same little peninsula where you'll find Playa Santa Catalina, and it's even more remote. The actual surf camp, Morro Negrito, is on an island that the locals call **Ensenada.** The camp has rustic cabañas, running water, and a dining area. Electricity is generated in the evenings. The waves here are smaller than on the second island, with faces that range from 1.5 to 2.5 meters (5 to 8 feet) on average. The other island is **Isla Silva de Afuera,** a half-hour away by boat. This is the main surfing island, with wave faces that average 3.5 to 5.5 meters (12 to 18 feet). There are both left and right breaks on both islands.

Ten breaks have been discovered so far. The best time to find big waves is from April to October. For non-surfers there's a long beach, snorkeling possibilities (bring your own gear), horseback riding, and a 15-meter (50-foot) waterfall.

Details: Only week-long package deals are offered, and the place can accommodate a maximum of 20 people at a time. Packages cost $450 per person and include airport pickup, a night in a Panama City hotel, transportation to the camp (a five-hour drive from the city), all food, a surfing guide, and daily boat trips to surf spots. The package runs from Saturday to Saturday. Contact information: 800/846-2363, 760/632-8014, fax 760/632-8416, surferparadise@msn.com, www.surferparadise.com. The mailing address is Steve Thompson, P.O. Box 1266, Cardiff-by-the-Sea, CA 92007. Reservations must be made in the U.S. and require a $100 deposit check (made payable to "César Concepción").

GUIDES AND OUTFITTERS

The camp provides surfing guides as part of the package.

LODGING/FOOD

The camp is the only place that offers either. Vegetarian meals can be arranged with advance notice.

Parque Nacional Marino Golfo de Chiriquí and Environs

It's a bit of an adventure to get to the islands near the western Pacific coast of Panama; that's half the fun of visiting this area. You get the sense of being in the middle of nowhere without actually being that far from civilization or having to spend a lot of money to get there.

The easiest access to the islands is through the little town of Horconcitos, which is 40 kilometers (about 25 miles) east of David, the provincial capital of Chiriquí Province. (See Chapter 7, Western Highlands: West of Volcán Barú, for information on David.) Then you have to head south 13 kilometers (about eight miles) on a horrendous dirt road to the fishing village of Boca Chica. The road is supposed to be paved by the time you read this, but I have my doubts. When I visited in the middle of the rainy season, this short drive took 50 minutes and nearly ripped the bottom out of the pickup I was in. Once in Boca Chica, you have to get a fisherman to take you in his boat to Isla Boca Brava (a quick 1.5 kilometers away, about 0.9 miles), which will probably be your base during your stay.

If all this sounds more like fun than hassle, you have the right attitude to visit this place. The islands and ocean here are beautiful, and you can enjoy them with a certain degree of comfort while being quite intimate with nature. But be prepared for some rusticity.

Isla Boca Brava is the first island you'll come to, and it's probably where you'll be staying. Specifically, you'll probably be staying at **Restaurante y Cabañas Boca Brava** (see Camping/Lodging/Food, below). The island is 14 kilometers long, six kilometers wide (about 8.7 miles by 3.7 miles), and overflowing with wildlife. I hadn't been there an hour when a snake dropped from the rafters of the hotel's open-air bar. The owner instantly started slashing at it with a

Boca Brava, on the edge of Parque Nacional Marino Golfo de Chiriquí

William Friar

*Boca Brava offers an accessible "nowhere"
full of wildlife and unique flora and fauna.*

machete. Fortunately or not, it got away. An armadillo on the island
has been known to race across the dance floor in the evenings.

The forests on the island are also home to, among other things,
monkeys, anteaters, coatimundis, all kinds of birds, and a wealth of
trees and plants. The hotel's owner, Frank Köhler, proudly main-
tains that the island has "no poisonous spiders, but every kind of
poisonous snake." He says they're mellow, but don't go for a forest
hike without good boots. And watch your step.

Frank owns 50 hectares of Boca Brava, and through his land
he's built more than 10 kilometers (about six miles) of trails that
lead into the forest and down to the island's beaches. He also offer
tours to all the surrounding islands and other natural attractions
(see Camping /Lodging/Food, below).

Boca Brava is right on the edge of the 14,740-hectare (over
36,000 acres) **Parque Nacional Marino Golfo de Chiriquí**, a marine
park that encompasses two dozen islands and their surrounding
waters. The park is a refuge for all kinds of wildlife, including howler
monkeys, leatherback and hawksbill turtles, and tiger-herons.

From Boca Brava you can explore an endless maze of mangroves in the estuaries of several rivers that empty into the sea here. Or you can snorkel and swim in the clearer waters of the surrounding islands, including idyllic uninhabited ones. The closest are **Linarte, Saino,** and **Las Ventanas** (*ventana* means window; the name refers to the caverns that run straight through their rocky sides).

The best islands are farther away. The snorkeling is decent around **Isla San José**, a short boat trip away, but it's definitely worthwhile to head even farther out. **Isla Bolaños** is 13 kilometers (about eight miles) from Boca Brava, about 45 minutes by small boat equipped with a decent outboard motor. This is a lovely little deserted island with a couple of sandy beaches, lots of coconut palms, and snorkeling when the tide's low. It's easy to arrange a camping trip here. (See Camping/Lodging/Food, below.) Twenty minutes from Bolaños is **Isla Gámez** (sometimes spelled "Gámes"), also lovely and even smaller. This one, however, tends to attract yachts and the weekend Jet Ski crowd, while Bolaños is rarely visited. (Sadly, though, even Bolaños has its share of trash.) Both these islands are tended by the nonprofit environmental group ANCON.

The biggest island here is **Isla Parida,** just across from Gámez. It's an inhabited island with lots of trash, and you can easily skip it. There's an **ANAM station** on Parida next to a bunch of ramshackle huts and a dirty beach. You can spend the night at the station, but it's hard to see why you'd want to.

The scuba diving is said to be terrific around **Islas Las Ladrones** and **Islas Secas**, where the water is clearest and the sea life the richest. The diving visibility is up to 30 meters (almost 100 feet) at Las Ladrones. Two catches: (1) There's no place to rent diving equipment; and (2) the islands are very far away. Las Ladrones are 40 kilometers (about 25 miles) west and Islas Secas 30 kilometers (about 19 miles) east of Boca Brava. You should not attempt to go this far on the open sea without something more substantial than the little motorboats around here. If you do find a way to get there, the snorkeling's good, too.

If you haven't had your fill of beaches by the time you finish with all these islands, the most popular mainland beach in the region is at **Las Lajas**, the turnoff to which is about 30 kilometers (about 19 miles) east of Horconcitos on the Interamerican Highway. It's a wide, sandy beach with few facilities.

Details: The turnoff to Horconcitos is about 40 kilometers (25 miles) east of David on the Interamerican Highway. The turnoff is poorly marked; coming from David it'll be on your right, not far from a rustic restaurant on a little hill.

Unless the road has been paved or you have a four-wheel-drive vehicle, you can't drive from Horconcitos to Boca Chica, the jumping-off point for the islands. Only one pickup taxi made the trip at the time of writing, a black Toyota owned by Gregorio Tamayo. You can wait for him to make a run by the turnoff or hunt for him at his house, which is near the police station on the road to Horconcitos. (Horconcitos itself is five kilometers, a little over three miles, from the highway, on a good road.) Depending on the condition of the Boca Chica road and Gregorio's mood, the ride will cost you $15–$20. If you do drive yourself, you can park at the dock in Boca Chica.

The owner of Cabañas y Restaurante Boca Brava (see Lodging, below) can arrange a taxi from David to Boca Chica for $30 if you're staying with him. He'll also probably be able to give you a free ride back to the Interamerican Highway in his pickup truck, but be prepared for Mr. Toad's Wild Ride.

Any bus plying the Interamerican Highway, including the big ones that run between David and Panama City, can drop you at the Horconcitos turnoff; be sure to ask the driver when you get on. The fare from David is $1.50.

When you finally get to Boca Chica, the 1.5-kilometer (0.9-mile) boat ride to Boca Brava will cost $1. A fisherman willing to make the trip will probably find you as soon as you arrive.

GUIDES AND OUTFITTERS

This place is too far off the beaten track to support local guides and outfitters. Your best bet is Restaurante y Cabañas Boca Brava, which offers a range of interesting boat tours and snorkeling trips. See below.

CAMPING/LODGING/FOOD

Restaurante y Cabañas Boca Brava, cell 507/676-3244, is your only hotel and dining option in this entire region. (You may see listings for Isla Parida Island Resort, but it's been closed down.) It's situated on a cliff 20 meters (66 feet) above the ocean on the eastern edge of the island, giving it striking views of the Pacific and the surrounding islands.

The place has a wild and woolly vibe, but it's a good deal and surprisingly comfortable given its remote location, as long as you don't mind some rusticity and living close to nature. The German owner, Frank Köhler, is an architect who built the place himself (he was also a snow-ski instructor for 10 years; it's hard to imagine a more radical change than coming to this place). As noted above, he can arrange taxi pickup from David.

Frank offers boat tours to all the attractions in the area. A snorkeling trip to Isla San José, for instance, costs $25. A grand tour of all the major islands, including Bolaños and Gámez, costs $70. Prices are for up to four people; there's a slight additional charge for an extra person.

If you'd like to camp on an uninhabited island, Frank can set you up with tents and food and take you to Bolaños. (Keep the food away from the island's voracious crabs.) Price varies depending on the number of people and what you want to take with you.

The restaurant and bar is an open-air affair on the edge of the cliff, and the panoramic view is terrific. The food isn't fancy, but it's fine. Cambute, a kind of conch, is the house specialty. (If you're into that kind of thing, you can row out with Frank to the underwater net where the live critters are kept and help him extract them from their shells—definitely not for the squeamish.) Lobster costs $6.50; most other dishes are $4 or less. The piña coladas here are amazing, and the homemade papaya liquor is refreshingly sweet but potent.

Rooms at the hotel are clean but very simple: mattresses lie on raised platforms on the floor. Rates are $15 for one person or $20 for two in cabins with private bathrooms. You can also stay in simple bamboo huts with shared bathroom for $5 (one person) or $8 (two people), but you'll be living with the creepy-crawlies. Serious budget travelers with their own hammocks can hook them up on the grounds and use the showers for $2 per person.

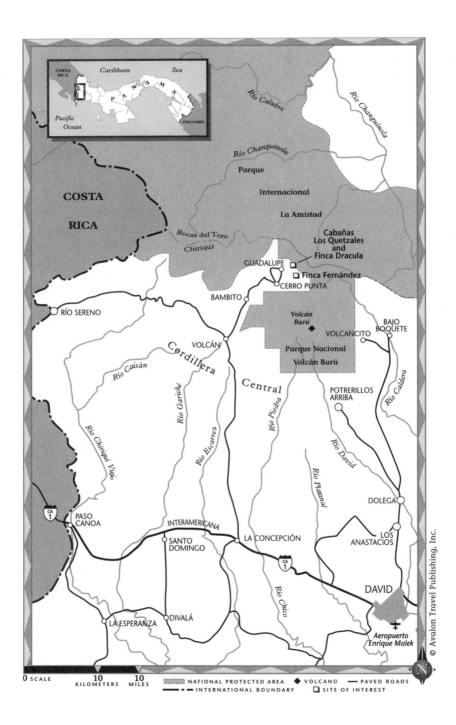

CHAPTER 7

Western Highlands: West of Volcán Barú

The western highlands of Panama have some of the most beautiful countryside in a beautiful country. If you come here after visiting the beaches or tropical rainforests of Panama, you'll feel you've entered a different world.

It's a world filled with white-water rivers, gigantic waterfalls, imposing mountains, secluded hot springs, and green forests bursting with life. At the time of writing, only two white-water rivers in Panama were being commercially run, and they're both in the western highlands. The highlands are also home to Volcán Barú, a dormant volcano that, at 3,475 meters (11,400 feet), is Panama's highest mountain.

Most of the sights of interest to visitors are clustered on the west and east sides of Volcán Barú. This chapter deals with the west side; Chapter 8 focuses on the east.

The phrase that comes to mind when you think of the west side of Volcán Barú is "pastoral paradise." As you wind your way up the foggy mountains, you pass one tranquil dairy farm after another. Soon you see neat quilts of green-and-brown farmland clinging at impossible angles to mountain slopes. Down in the valleys, racing horses romp in vast pastures. It's all so picturesque you have to remind yourself that the developed land borders two of Panama's most spectacular parks, and in some cases encroaches on them. The hikes through these parks are among the great attractions of the area. Here you'll find the most accessible entry into Parque Internacional la Amistad, a park so important it was declared a UNESCO World Heritage Site in 1990.

LAY OF THE LAND

The western highlands of Panama start at the Costa Rican border and head east for hundreds of kilometers along the Cordillera de Talamanca and the Cordillera Central. Much of Parque Internacional la Amistad and all of Parque Nacional Volcán Barú are in the highlands.

This chapter and the next deal mainly with the Pacific slopes of the Continental Divide, since the parks and other sights are more accessible from that side. But the highlands extend north into Bocas del Toro Province, where they descend toward the Caribbean.

It's refreshingly cool in the highlands, with temperatures that dip down to 7°C (45°F) and sometimes lower. And it's wet: rainfall can exceed 5,000 millimeters (197 inches). Even in the dry season, the mountains and valleys are often shrouded in what's affectionately known as *bajareque*, a foggy drizzle that can create lovely rainbows. No matter when you come, bring rain gear.

All the towns and tourist sights on this side of Barú are linked by a single road that starts in the lowland town of Concepción and ends at Guadalupe, elevation 2,130 meters (6,988 feet). The first town you'll come to is Volcán, officially known at Hato de Volcán, which has most of the visitor services but little else. The road forks here. Straight will take you to a Costa Rican border crossing at Río Sereno. A right turn will take you farther up the mountain toward Bambito, Cerro Punta, and Guadalupe. You'll find hotels in Bambito, but the "town" itself is really just a few roadside stands. The vistas open up at little Cerro Punta and tiny Guadalupe just beyond it. You're up in the clouds here, and you may feel you've found Shangri-la.

NATURE AND ADVENTURE ACTIVITIES

Just about any mountain activity you can think of is available here, including hiking, horseback riding, biking, white-water rafting, kayaking, even rock climbing and rappelling. The western highlands are popular with bird-watchers, since the forests attract hundreds of species, including many spectacularly beautiful ones. There are also inviting waterfalls and hot springs.

Evidence of little-known pre-Columbian civilizations, including some very ancient ones, has been found here. There are some petroglyphs and artifacts in the area (Barriles is popular with tour guides), but most of the good stuff has been taken to museums and the "archeological sites" are not very informative.

FLORA AND FAUNA

The western highlands harbor more virgin forest than any other region of Panama. The area's huge national parks are home to a bewildering array of plant and animal life, much of it endemic and some of it endangered. The mountain forests are threatened by encroaching farmland, which in turn is threatened by erosion. But there's a growing sense among highland dwellers that they're surrounded by something special that needs to be carefully preserved.

If you spend any time up here, you'll soon know how cloud forests got their name. At the highest elevations you are literally in the clouds, and it's quite a dramatic sight to see puffy white billows blowing through the moss-draped trees in the afternoons.

This is one of the best places in the Americas to see the resplendent quetzal, an absolutely stunning bird. In the dry season, visitors often see several on a single outing. You're likely to see several species of jewel-toned hummingbirds among the hundreds of other bird species that make their home here.

Though you'd be very lucky to spot one, the forests are home to all five species of endangered felines found in Panama, including the jaguar. It's also one of the last stands of the endangered Baird's tapir, the largest land mammal in Central America.

161

The highlands are well-known in Panama for several human-tended kinds of flora and fauna, especially oranges, orchids, coffee, and trout.

VISITOR INFORMATION

In David

There is an IPAT booth and an ATM at the David airport, Aeropuerto Enrique Malek. (David is the closest air hub to the western highlands.) There's also an IPAT office, 507/775-4120, in David proper. The office is on the second floor of the Edificio Galherna, the building on the left as you face the church from the plaza (Parque de Cervantes). You'll probably find the staff here friendly but not too enlightening. Hours are 8:30 a.m. to 4:30 p.m. weekdays. For visitor information in the highlands, see the specific area listed below.

The regional office for ANAM, 507/775-2055 or 507/775-3163, is on the road to the David airport. Heading into town from the airport it'll be on your right. You can get permits to visit Parque Internacional la Amistad and Parque Nacional Volcán Barú here. Hours are 8 a.m. to 4 p.m. weekdays. Park entrance is $3 and the camping fee is $5.

In the Highlands

The High Lands Adventure office in Volcán can give you information on sights and nature activities in the area; see Guides and Outfitters, below. You can get information about Parque International la Amistad at the ANAM ranger station at the Las Nubes entrance to the park; see the park sight entry for details.

The only banks on the west side of Barú are in the town of Volcán. Coming up from Concepción, the Banco del Istmo will be on your right shortly before the road forks. There's no ATM, but they cash traveler's checks. Hours are 8 a.m. to 3:30 p.m. weekdays, 9 a.m. to noon Saturday. A branch of the Banco Nacional de Panama is on the left straight past the fork, on the road to Río Sereno. Again, no ATM but you can cash traveler's checks. Hours are 8 a.m. to 3 p.m. weekdays, 9 a.m. to noon Saturday. There's a taxi stand at the fork. It'll be on your right as you turn toward Cerro Punta.

You can send and receive email and surf the Web for $1.50 an hour at Multi-Servicios Chips, near "downtown" Cerro Punta. As you head up the mountain, the office is a left turn off the main road toward the end of town. You'll see the office on your right. Hours are 8 a.m. to 7 p.m. daily. CyberCafé, attached to the Hotel y Restaurante Don Tavo just outside of Volcán, is another place to check your email (see Lodging, below). Guests at Hotel Los Quetzales can access the Internet for $5 an hour.

GETTING THERE

By car it takes six hours to get from Panama City to the lowland city of David, the hub for trips up to the highlands. From there it's about a two-hour drive to Cerro Punta.

Comfortable, air-conditioned buses from Panama City to the David bus terminal leave every hour or 1.5 hours from 5:30 a.m. to midnight. The schedule is slightly different on the return trip. The trip takes approximately seven hours and costs $11. The last two buses, at 10:45 p.m. and midnight, are expresses. The express ride is about an hour shorter and costs $15. See Transportation, Appendix A, for information on the Panama City bus terminal.

There are also many daily flights between Panama City's domestic airport and David. The flight takes about an hour and costs about $55 one-way, $110 round-trip. Aeroperlas (507/315-7500, 507/315-7580, iflyap@aeroperlas.com) flies from Panama City to David three times a day Monday through Thursday, four times on Friday, three times on Saturday and twice on Sunday. Mapiex Aero (507/315-0888) flies three times a day weekdays and twice a day on Saturday and Sunday.

David is about an hour by bus from the Costa Rican border crossing at Paso Canoa. See Appendix A for more information.

It's easy to rent a car in David. Four-wheel-drive vehicles are in shorter supply, so try to make a reservation as far ahead of time as possible. The cost is approximately $50 for a basic car and $100 a day for a four-wheel drive. Just about all the major and several minor rental car agencies have offices at the David airport and/or in town. Try Avis (507/774-7075), Budget (507/775-1667), Hilary (507/774-6440 in David or 507/721-2450 at the airport), Hertz (507/775-6828), or Interamerican Rent a Car (507/775-9280).

Regional buses to Volcán/Cerro Punta, Boquete, Chiriquí Grande, and many other destinations leave from the David terminal. Bus fare from David is $2.65 to all western highland destinations leading up to Cerro Punta. Look for the bus with "Cerro Punta" painted on the windshield; it stops at all the towns along the way. You can also catch the bus at Concepción, which will save you time if you're coming from Costa Rica. The Cerro Punta bus will usually take you all the way to Guadalupe, but ask to make sure. If not, taxi fare from Cerro Punta to Guadalupe is $1. Buses run every 15 minutes starting at 4:30 a.m. The last bus leaves at 8 p.m. from David and 6:45 p.m. from Cerro Punta. There's an air-conditioned lounge for passengers making the long haul to Panama City, and chances are good that if you're a gringo no one will ask questions if you're just waiting for a local bus and want to cool off.

Taxi fare from David to Volcán is $20, a bit more to go farther up the mountain. Some of the highland hotels will arrange pickup at the airport or bus terminal, for a fee. Check with your hotel.

If you're driving from David, take the Interamerican Highway west to Concepción, 26 kilometers (16.2 miles) away. Turn right and head uphill. After another 34 kilometers (21.1 miles) you'll come to Volcán. Turn right at the fork to get to Bambito, Cerro Punta, and Guadalupe. There may be no sign at the intersection except one pointing toward Hotel Bambito. Follow it. Cerro Punta is about 74 kilometers (46 miles) from David, a distance that takes a little over two hours to cover by bus and a bit less by car. The village of Guadalupe is three kilometers (1.9 miles) farther uphill.

A NOTE ON THE ROADS

Many of the highland roads are newly resurfaced and in great shape. Ironically, that can make them even more dangerous than usual. New roads are oily, and the lack of potholes encourages drivers to see how fast they can take those hairpin turns. If you drive, be extremely careful. Honk your horn at blind curves. Drive with low beams and hazard lights even in the daytime. (Don't forget to turn them off when you park.) If you're visiting in the rainy season, try to drive in the morning, when you're less likely to be hit by torrential rains. If at all possible, stay off the roads at night or when it's foggy.

If you take a taxi, don't be shy about asking your driver to slow the heck down. Remember, you're paying. A firm *"Despacio, por favor"* (des-PAW-see-o, por-fah-VOR) should get results. If you take a bus, just shut your eyes and hope for the best.

Gringo paranoia? Nope. One road in the highlands—fortunately, not one you're likely to take—is nicknamed *La Carretera de la Muerte* (Death Highway). Another one has a sign tallying the dozens of annual fatalities along a single stretch of road. I learned to drive on Panamanian roads, yet on my last trip to Cerro Punta my car was all but totaled by a speeding, hydroplaning truck coming down the mountain. The 3.5-hour wait for the cops on a dark, rainy night gave ample time to wonder what would have happened if someone had been hurt, which luckily no one was.

OVERNIGHTING IN DAVID

David, with 120,000, inhabitants, is the third-largest city in Panama and the capital of Chiriquí Province. It's the lowland hub for visits to the highlands and other parts of western Panama and has all the services you'd expect of a modern provincial capital. You can extend your stay in Panama or make arrangements to visit Costa Rica in David. (See Appendix A for information.) It's also a hot, humid, crowded, and unattractive city with little to offer visitors. If you spend much time on this side of the country, though, you'll probably have to spend at least one night here. Taxis anywhere within David cost $1.

If you do get stuck in David, the newish **Hotel Castilla**, 507/774-5236 or 507/774-5260/5261/5262, fax 507/774-5262, inmisa @cwp.net.pa, will give you a very comfortable night's stay away from the madding masses. It offers 78 pleasant, immaculate rooms with air-conditioning, phones, and cable TV. It's on Calle A Norte across the street from the west side of Parque de Cervantes. The restaurant here is fine though windowless. Bonus: The Aeroperlas office is in the same building. Double bonus for those driving: The hotel has an underground, gated car park. There's a bank nearby. Rates are a bargain at $25 for one or two people.

If the Castilla is full, the **Hotel Nacional**, 507/775-2221/-2222, fax 507/775-7729, is a decent alternative. It's the fanciest place in town, with a swimming pool and four theaters showing first-run movies. It has 75 modern, rather glitzy rooms. Rates are $40 for one, $48 for two people.

The no-frills **Restaurante Churrasco's Place**, around the corner from Hotel Castilla on Avenida 2 Este, is popular for its cheap, simple meals. You can stuff yourself silly with tasty but greasy food for around $2. The restaurant downstairs is open-air and sweltering. The *arroz con pollo* here is yummy. This is a good place to mingle with the locals, though you'll have to put up with desultory service. A fancier dining room upstairs is air-conditioned, but you're likely to be the only one up there.

NATURE AND ADVENTURE SIGHTS ON THE WEST SIDE OF VOLCÁN BARÚ

Finca Dracula—Don't worry, you don't need to bring garlic. Finca Dracula is named for the 100 varieties of the *Telipogon vampirus* that are among the more than 1,200 species of orchids found in this famous botanical garden. It has one of the most important collections in Latin America and is known for its experiments in propagating endangered species. The lovely landscaped grounds make for a pleasant walk. Tours are available in English and Spanish.

Details: Finca Dracula is located in Guadalupe, about a 20-minute walk or very short car ride past Hotel Los Quetzales. (If you get lost, you can ask for directions at the hotel.) You'll see a sign across the finca's gate on your left, at the turnoff to the entrance to the dirt road that leads to the Los Quetzales' cabañas. Call 507/771-2070 to arrange a tour. A $7 donation is requested.

Finca Fernández—This farm is famous as a prime place to see quetzals, often more than one. It's midway between Guadalupe and

A MOST BEAUTIFUL BIRD

The resplendent quetzal has been called the most beautiful bird in the world, and it's easy to see why. The male in particular is just incredible. It's luminous green above and scarlet and white below, with tail feathers that can grow to almost a meter (40 inches), twice the size of its body.

The resplendent quetzal's range extends from southern Mexico to the highlands of western Panama, where it's easier to spot than just about anywhere else. During the nesting season, which runs from February to May, you may see more than one during a hike. That doesn't mean they're always easy to find, though. They can spend a long time sitting quietly and inconspicuously. Quetzals often hang out at the edge of forests and in trees near clearings. Look for trees with holes in the side; they like to make their nests there.

Sadly, deforestation has forced quetzals higher and higher up into the mountains, and their numbers are dwindling. Conservation efforts and ecotourism dollars may help them survive.

Cerro Punta at the beginning of the Sendero Los Quetzales (see Parque Nacional Volcán Barú, below), which makes it a convenient excursion for visitors staying nearby or a quick side trip for hikers. You can go here on your own and ask a member of the Fernández family to give you a guided tour, which they're happy to do for a small fee. Settle on a price ahead of time; it shouldn't cost more than $10. You can also arrange the tour through a hotel or guide service, but you'll probably pay several times more, per person. The *finca* also offers guided hikes on the Sendero Los Quetzales and to the top of Volcán Barú; see Guides and Outfitters, below.

Details: *The turnoff to the* finca *is about 1.5 kilometers (0.9 miles) north of the Hotel Cerro Punta. Coming from that direction you'll see a huge sign for*

Sendero Los Quetzales on your right just after you cross a little bridge. Follow the road uphill to the right. After about three kilometers (1.9 miles) you'll come to the little town of Bajo Grande. Go past the town for about a kilometer (about a half-mile or more), until the asphalt ends. The farm is on the right.

Hotel y Cabañas Los Quetzales—This is *the* place to stay for nature lovers, so much so that it's really a destination in itself. Mostly this is because the cabañas are in a national park (Parque Nacional Volcán Barú) and at the edge of an international one (Parque Internacional la Amistad). The owners bought land here before the parks were founded.

As the name suggests, there are actually two Los Quetzales. The hotel is in the little town of Guadalupe, three kilometers (1.9 miles) past Cerro Punta. It's an attractive 10-room place with lots of handsome woodwork, on the edge of a fast-flowing river, and it resembles a ski lodge. It's a comfortable place, and the smells wafting up from the bakery/pizzeria on the first floor add to the cozy feel. The paintings you'll see everywhere, some of them rather spooky, are by Brooke Alfaro, your host's brother. At the time of writing, two new buildings were going up. The fancier one will house two large rooms and three suites, the latter with fireplaces and kitchenettes. The other will offer three single-sex dormitory-style rooms with bunk beds. Rates run $40 for a standard room up to $85 for suites. Prices are $10 less in the low season, between May and the beginning of November. Dorm beds will be $10.

There's a **health spa** right next to the river where you can recover from a grueling hike with a massage, sauna, or dip in an outdoor hot tub. An hour-long massage and sauna is $30, not including tip.

The four cabañas in the park are slightly rustic in the mountain-cabin sense, but three of them are very comfortable and nicely designed. Only Cabaña 4 has electricity, but all have wood-burning stoves or fireplaces, hot water, and a kitchen. You can hire a cook for $20 a day. Two daily guided hikes are included with your stay. Ten kinds of colorful hummingbirds are among the more than 100 species of birds identified near here. You'll see them buzzing around like mosquitoes.

Cabañas 2 and 3 are large, wooden, two-story structures built at more than 2,020 meters (over 6,600 feet) above sea level, right in the middle of a stunning cloud forest. The Chiriquí Viejo River runs through the property. Cabaña 2 costs $100 and can accommodate six people. It's slightly smaller than Cabaña 3, which sleeps up to eight and is $110.

Cabaña 4 is a short walk farther up into the park. It's huge and a bit fancier than the other wooden cabañas, with three bedrooms, two fireplaces, a modern living room, and electricity partly supplied by solar power. The drawback here is you're actually above most of the surrounding forest, so you're not in the thick of the bird action as you are at Los Quetzales. The rate is $120.

You can probably pass on Cabaña 1. It's a much more basic two-story cement structure just as you enter the property, shrouded by trees and therefore dark and rather gloomy. It's close enough to town that you'd do better to stay at the hotel and hike or drive to the trails in the park. Each floor has a separate entrance and can sleep two groups of five. Its rate is $60 per floor.

Prices for all these cabañas are $10 less in the low season. They offer enough privacy that friendly acquaintances who meet on the road can share them to save money.

Right next to Cabaña 4 is an unusual accommodation option: a semi-transparent geodesic dome on a wooden platform. However, you may find this to be niftier in concept than reality. You can't really see much through the dome, and it leaks in the rain so it's rented out only in the dry season. It has a bed, toilet, chair, and table, so it's a step up in comfort from camping. It costs $40.

The only real problem with Los Quetzales is the highly disorganized service. Ask for your bill at least an hour before you're ready to check out. On the other hand, the staff means well. When an acquaintance had her laundry done here, not only did the laundress refuse to charge her for a full load, she also returned $60 she found in a pair of jeans. And the owner, Carlos Alfaro, is a gentleman in every sense of the word.

Seven **trails** originate from the area around the cabañas. Foggy mountains, trees draped in moss, waterfalls, orchids, the lovely songs of countless birds—it's like a fairy kingdom up there. Two tours a day, led by Guaymi guides, are free to cabaña guests. Los Quetzales can supply boots, rain jackets, and horses. There's a very good chance of seeing quetzals here between January and May. See the Guides and Outfitters section for information on other tours available through Los Quetzales.

Details: The cabañas are only 2.5 kilometers (1.6 miles) from Los Quetzales Hotel in Guadalupe, but the road is so ferociously bad it takes about 25 minutes to get there by four-wheel-drive vehicle. (Transportation is included if you stay here.) Among other things, you have to ford a shallow river. That's something to bear in mind if you decide to hike in. Even if you go by four-wheel-drive, you have a short but steep walk up to Cabañas 2 and 3. You may have to carry your own bags. One strategy for staying at Los Quetzales is to spend a night or two at the hotel, seeing the nearby sights, then head up to the cabañas. The hotel can arrange taxi pickup in David for $30. Contact Information: 507/771-2182 or 507/771-2291, fax 507/771-2226, calfaro@chiriqui.com, www.losquetzales.com. For information in the United States, call 800/383-2107.

Lagunas de Volcán—These picturesque lakes are part of a protected area comprising Panama's highest wetlands (the elevation is 1,200 meters, or about 3,900 feet). They are famous for good bird-watching. On the lakes there's a chance of seeing masked ducks and northern jacanas. Look for pale-billed woodpeckers, flycatchers, antbirds, and the rare rose-throated becard in the woods.

Details: Unless you hike, you'll need to hire a taxi or use your own transportation to get to the lakes. It's a 15-minute drive, more if the road's in bad shape, and you need a four-wheel-drive in the rainy season. To get there, head through Volcán and make a left 0.5 kilometers (0.3 miles) past the fork to Cerro Punta. Ask directions from here, as the signs get confusing. Note: Vehicles have been broken into here. If you drive, keep an eye on your car.

Parque Internacional La Amistad (PILA)—The enormous and magnificent Parque Internacional la Amistad, which lies along the Talamanca mountain range, was established in Sept. of 1988 and declared a UNESCO World Heritage Site in 1990. It's "international" in that a little less than half of it is in Costa Rica. That leaves 207,000 hectares (80 square miles) on the Panama side. Nearly all of this land is in the province of Bocas del Toro, but the 3 percent that poke into Chiriquí province is far more accessible.

The park's plant and animal life are among the most diverse in Panama. The forests range from lowland tropical to subalpine, and

much of the vegetation is virgin.
Five of the six species of Central
American felines—the jaguar,
puma, ocelot, jaguarundi, and
margay—are still hanging on
here, as is the also-endangered
Baird's tapir. Among the nearly
600 types of birds identified in
the area are such spectacular
species as the resplendent quetzal, the three-wattled bellbird,
and the rarely seen bare-necked
umbrellabird.

All that said, you may not see
much wildlife other than birds
on a day hike near Cerro Punta.
But the park is well worth a visit
even if you're not a birding
fanatic. The forests are lovely
and there are several miles of
well-maintained trails near town.

*Waterfall in Parque
Internacional La Amistad*

The main entrance to the park is at **Las Nubes**, about seven
kilometers (4.3 miles) west of Cerro Punta. There's an ANAM
ranger station on your right at the end of the road, where the trails
start. Here's where you pay your entrance fee and get trail maps
from the friendly staff. There's also a small display on the park and
a few of its denizens.

There are two main trails that start from here. **Sendero La
Cascada** is a 3.4-kilometer (about two-mile), two-hour round-trip
hike that leads to a picture-perfect 55-meter (180-foot) waterfall.
The trail is wide and well-maintained. It's a 1.7-kilometer (about
one-mile) uphill hike to the falls, with the elevation climbing from
2,180 to about 2,500 meters (7,100 to 8,200 feet). There are three
miradors (observation platforms) along the trail with sweeping views
of the mountains and valleys. However, if it's a foggy day you won't
see a thing from them.

The first *mirador* is unmarked, but it will be on your right as the
trail levels off and you come out of the woods. **Mirador La Nevera** is

171

on the left a little farther on. The trail forks at **Mirador El Barranco**. To get to the falls, head down the steep wooden staircase to your right. (*Note:* Some of the stairs are loose and slippery. Watch your step.) If you're in the mood for more exercise you can take the left fork. If it's a clear day, a two-hour hike from here will give you a view of the Caribbean.

Sendero El Retoño, a two-kilometer (1.2-mile) loop trail, is much less strenuous but even more beautiful. The trail is mostly level and remarkably varied. It takes you through lush green forest, over bridges spanning rushing streams, and into a tunnel formed from leaning stands of bamboo. The hike will take you about an hour at a very leisurely pace.

You may be confused by a few forks along the trail: to stay on the main trail, just take every left fork. If you want a longer hike, though, about halfway down the trail a marked fork to your right will take you to a loop within the loop. It ends near the exit to the main trail. There's also a short mini-trail near the station for those not up to a hike.

Serious hikers may be interested to know that you can also take an eight-hour hike through the forest to some hot springs. That's one way; you'd have to camp out by the springs. For the truly hardcore, there's also the possibility of multiday treks over the cordillera toward the Caribbean coast. Hotel y Cabañas Los Quetzales offers an eight-day trek for those feeling brave. See Guides and Outfitters, below.

Do not attempt any of these longer hikes without a good guide. The forest here is rugged wilderness, and it's very easy to get lost. If you speak Spanish, you can ask the forest ranger at Las Nubes, Mail (mah-EEL) Villarreal, for guidance. He's been working in Panama's parks for 20 years and is a very good guy; he'll remind you of a favorite uncle. Mail also leads hikes on the two shorter trails. He won't expect a tip, but given how little Panama's rangers earn you might want to give him one.

You can camp in the park or stay in a dormitory at the ANAM station. See Camping, below.

Details: The Las Nubes entrance to PILA is about a 10-minute drive from Cerro Punta. As you head up the mountain, look for the sign indicating a left turn off the main road that runs through town. Round-trip taxi *fare from Cerro Punta is $5–$7. The road gets a bit rough, but a four-wheel-drive is not essential to get to the first gate. The short uphill drive past the gate to the ANAM ranger station and trailheads does require a four-wheel-drive. The station is open from about 8 or 8:30 a.m. to 4 p.m. every day. Entrance is $3.*

Parque Nacional Volcán Barú—Though only a fraction of the size of its imposing neighbor, La Amistad, this park is still plenty impressive. Its centerpiece is the dormant volcano that gives the park its name and whose summit, at 3,475 meters (11,400 feet), is the highest point in Panama. The park was founded in 1976.

This is a good place for long hikes, camping (see below), and bird-watching. Because of the change in elevation, the park has quite a range of life zones for its size (14,000 hectares). You'll pass through several different kinds of forests before reaching its barren and rocky summit. In the bushes near the top you can spot the rather plain-looking volcano junco. This is its only Panamanian habitat. Other birds you might encounter at the higher elevations before the forest ends include the timberline wren, black-and-yellow silky-flycatcher, and large-footed finch.

There are three major trails in the park. Two of these lead to the top of Barú from either side of the mountain. On a clear day (hah!) you can see both oceans from the summit. From either entrance it takes about five or six hours up and four or five hours down. It's a very strenuous climb but not technically difficult.

The **summit trail** on the west side of the mountain is at Paso Ancho, about three kilometers (1.9 miles) north of Volcán. See Chapter 8, Western Highlands: East of Volcán Barú, for information on the summit trail (actually a very rough road) on the east side of the mountain.

You can probably hike either summit trail without a guide, but it's essential that you plan ahead. Visitors accustomed to Panama's hot and steamy side forget just how cold it can get up in the mountains. The *average* temperature at the higher elevations is 7.2°C (45°F) and it can get down to freezing. And, like every place else in the highlands, it's often incredibly wet. Do not treat this climb casually: People have died of exposure attempting it. Plan either to start very early or else camp out on the mountain. As an incentive, your best chance of a clear view is to be at the top close to dawn. Be sure to dress warmly, and if you camp bring a good tent and a change of clothes.

One bummer about this hike is that many thoughtless people have scrawled graffiti all over the rocks near the summit. Try to ignore it; concentrate on the view and your sense of smugness for making it to the top.

The third trail is **Sendero Los Quetzales**. As its name suggests, this is an excellent hike for spotting quetzals, among many other birds. Rather than leading you up the mountain the trail curves around its northern face, linking Cerro Punta and Boquete. It's far less grueling than a summit attempt but is still a serious undertaking. It takes five to six hours one way and you stand a good chance of getting lost if you don't go with a guide. You can also hire horses and ride the trail. Ask about this at Hotel y Cabañas Los Quetzales.

The hike requires advance planning since you end up far away on the other side of the mountain. The bus ride back takes at least three hours, not including waiting time in David, where you have to switch buses. The best strategy is to leave early in the morning and either have someone meet you with a car at the end of the trail or plan to spend the night in Boquete. See Guides and Outfitters in the Boquete section of Chapter 8, Western Highlands: East of Volcán Barú, for suggestions.

It's much easier to hike the trail from Cerro Punta to Boquete than vice versa since you're heading downhill most of the way, descending nearly a kilometer in altitude. See the Boquete section in Chapter 8, Western Highlands: East of Volcán Barú, for information on taking the trail in the other direction.

Details: For the hike to the summit of Barú you should drive to the trailhead, unless you're up for an even longer trek than you anticipated. To get to the Paso Ancho entrance from Volcán, head north toward Bambito for three kilometers (1.9 miles), at which point you'll see a park sign on your right (it doesn't say Paso Ancho, by the way). Turn right onto the gravel road and head across the plain toward the mountains. You need a four-wheel-drive for this road. It's about a 40-minute drive, depending on the condition of the road, before you reach the trailhead. Admission to the park is $3, $5 more to camp.

The entrance to Sendero Los Quetzales is much farther up the main road. It's located halfway between Cerro Punta and Guadalupe, or about 1.5 kilometers (0.9 miles) past the Hotel Cerro Punta. Heading uphill, you'll see a huge trail sign on your right just after you cross a little bridge. Follow the road leading up and to the right. If you're driving, keep going until you run out of road. Don't leave anything of value in the car. If you're staying in Cerro Punta or Guadalupe you can just walk here instead.

Río Chiriquí Viejo—You'll come across this powerful river again and again during your stay, as it snakes by many of the places listed above. The only white-water rafting company that runs the river is based in Boquete, on the east side of Barú. See the Guides and Outfitters section in Chapter 8, Western Highlands: East of Volcán Barú, for information.

Truchas de Bambito—If shooting fish in a barrel sounds too challenging, Truchas de Bambito might be to your liking. This is the Hotel Bambito's trout farm (*"trucha"* is Spanish for trout). Tons of the big guys swim about in a series of concrete tanks, and you're welcome to fish one out or ask the workers to catch one for you. *Note:* Catch and release is not allowed here.

Details: *The trout farm is on the left 0.4 kilometers (0.25 miles) past Hotel Bambito as you head uphill. You can rent a fishing pole for $5 an hour, or use our own for $2.50 an hour. Then you have to pay for what you catch, at $2.60 a pound. The place is open 7 a.m.–4 p.m. every day.*

TOWARD RÍO SERENO

So what happens if you stay straight on the road through Volcán rather than turning right toward Cerro Punta? Eventually you end up in Río Sereno, a tiny town with nothing to offer visitors but a border crossing with Costa Rica.

The road to Río Sereno is one of the prettiest in Panama. Bright, tiny flowers dot the shoulders. The road crosses over rivers and winds past lovely waterfalls, rolling forested hills, coffee plantations, tall stands of evergreens, and plump cows grazing in fields.

But this is no place for a pleasure drive. The road also features blind curves and trucks that barrel down the hills without a thought for what might lie around the bend. You can count on landslides and washouts in the rainy season and savage potholes year-round. Given the limited services at Río Sereno, I suggest entering or exiting Panama through the far less attractive but much more convenient crossing at Paso Canoa. See Appendix A for information on both routes.

The 42 kilometers (26 miles) from Volcán to Río Sereno take about an hour and 45 minutes by car. That's how bad the road is at times. Taxi fare from Volcán is $20. *Note:* Only take a pickup-truck taxi, though it's unlikely a regular cab would be willing to make the trip anyway.

The one thing that might entice you out this way is **Finca Hartmann**, 507/771-5144, fincahartmann@hotmail.com, www .angelfire.com/pa2/hartmann/, in Santa Clara, about an hour along the road. The entrance to the *finca* is near a small gas station; there'll be a sign right before you come to it. It's a shade-grown coffee farm that's a great favorite with birders—more than 230 species of birds have been identified here. The *finca* offers simple rooms with hot water and kitchen facilities. Bus drivers plying the road know the place; ask them to stop at Finca Hartmann. Rates run from $10 for a bunk bed to $30 for a cabaña for two. Optional food service is $20 a day. You can also just get a guided tour of the grounds for $10.

GUIDES AND OUTFITTERS

Several of the hotels in the area can arrange nature tours and outdoor adventures whether or not you're staying with them. At the time of writing these included **Hotel y Cabañas Los Quetzales**, **Bambito Camping Resort**, and **Hotel Bambito**. See Lodging for contact information. Daily guided hikes are included with your stay at Los Quetzales.

Hotel y Cabañas Los Quetzales offers a couple of unique tours. If you're up for a true adventure, they can arrange a rugged eight-day trek over the cordillera to the town of Changuinola, near the Caribbean coast. If you're a good hiker, you can shave a couple of days off that estimate. Be warned that this is a hard-core trip through mountainous wilderness and deep mud. You'll spend the last two days traveling in *cayucos* (dugout canoes) through Teribe Indian territory. For food and shelter you'll mostly rely on lonely, friendly folk living in huts in the woods. (You should offer to pay, but your hosts will probably be happy with gifts of lighters, fishhooks, and other items about which the hotel management will advise you.) The guide will cost $20 a day per group. You must have your own tent, sleeping bags, and all other equipment. The hotel also offers day and overnight trips to southeast-

William Friar

On the porch at Cabañas Los Quetzales

ern Costa Rica, including a visit to the Wilson Botanical Gardens. If you want to hike Sendero Los Quetzales, the hotel can arrange a taxi back from Boquete or, for about $5, it can send your luggage ahead to meet you in Boquete if you're planning to stay in that area.

High Lands Adventures, 507/771-4413 or 507/771-4341, cell 507/685-1682, jcaceres@Chiriqui.com, offers a variety of tours. The operation is run by brothers Nariño and Gonzálo Aizpurúa, who are trying to learn a bit of English and German. Their prices average around $40 per person, going up to $70 per person for an overnight hike to the top of Barú. Their office is in Volcán, next to the Shell station at the fork in the road. Look for the building with "High Lands Adventures, Oficina de Ecotourismo" painted on the front. If they're not guiding you should be able to find them in the office between 7 a.m. and noon. Otherwise call their cell phone. They also work with some of the area hotels.

At **Finca Fernández**, the Fernández brothers, Juan and José, and their sister, María, offer tours not only to see the quetzals on their property but also to the top of Volcán Barú ($50 per group) and to

177

Boquete on the Sendero Los Quetzales ($30 to $45, depending on the size of the group). If you don't want to walk all the way back down from Barú, one of them will meet you at the top of the mountain in a four-wheel-drive vehicle and drive you back via Boquete for another $90.

Tony Cadogan, the activities director at Bambito Camping Resort, offers trips ranging from inner-tubing on a river to kayaking on the Lagunas de Volcán to a hike up Barú. Prices range from $10 to $90 per person. (By the way, the "canopy adventure" the resort offers is much tamer than it sounds. You can easily skip it, especially if you're planning to do the real thing in El Valle. See Chapter 5, The Central Highlands, for information.)

Tony can also take you rock climbing and rappelling in Cañon de Macho Monte, a rocky canyon noted for its waterfalls. Personally, I wouldn't go rock climbing or rappelling with anyone until he showed me home movies of his one-handed ascent of El Capitan, but you may be more trusting and adventurous.

Note that for nearby, less rugged destinations, you're probably

White-water rafting in the Chiriquí Highlands

Courtesy Chiriqui River Rafting

better off making arrangements on your own than going through a guide service. This is especially true of visits to Finca Fernández and Finca Dracula, which supply their own tour guides for a fraction of what third-party outfits charge. (The exception is Hotel y Cabañas Los Quetzales, which charges little or nothing extra to arrange visits to these and other sights near the hotel.) You should, however, use a guide for more ambitious outings or for those requiring a four-wheel drive (if you don't have your own).

A number of hotels and guides offer white-water rafting trips. You should note that all of them contract out to **Chiriquí River Rafting** (see the Boquete section in Chapter 8, Western Highlands: East of Volcán Barú), so find out if your tour planner is getting you a discount over what the rafting company normally charges. You may do better to contact the company directly, especially since they provide pickup service for $15 (groups of four or more) to $25 (groups of three or less) per person.

Hotel y Cabañas Los Quetzales rents bikes and horses for $6 an hour and rubber boots for $1.50 a day. Hotel Bambito rents mountain bikes for $5 an hour and horses for $8 an hour. Bambito Camping Resort rents mountain bikes and fishing equipment for $5 an hour and horses for $10 an hour. They'll also rent you a bow and arrow for target practice on their land for $5 an hour.

CAMPING

Be sure to bring plenty of warm clothing and a good tent if you camp out. It can get quite cold and drizzly even in the dry season.

You can camp in **Parque Internacional la Amistad** for $5, but as usual with Panamanian parks don't expect developed campsites. You can also stay in a surprisingly pleasant dormitory at the ANAM station at the main entrance to the park for the same price. It offers bunk beds in shared rooms, a large fireplace, and a kitchen. Bring your own bedding. You can sometimes arrange to have food cooked here. Ask at the station, or call the ANAM regional office in David, 507/775-2055 or 507/775-3163. This place is a great deal.

As mentioned earlier, you can camp in **Parque Nacional Volcán Barú**, which you may want to do if you hike to the summit. The fee is $5, but good luck finding someone to pay it to. If you want to do things by the book you can buy a permit ahead of time at the ANAM office in David or Panama City.

If you want to camp in cushier surroundings, you can pitch a tent on the 170-hectare grounds of **Bambito Camping Resort**. The resort has a developed campsite a few minutes farther up the mountain by four-wheel drive. It offers hot-water showers and a bathroom. For $40 the resort will supply a couple with a two-person tent, sleeping bags, pads, lanterns, and a meager continental breakfast back at the hotel. If you have your own gear, you can camp at the site for $10, but you have to hike in and you're on your own for breakfast.

LODGING

There are several other lodging options besides Hotel y Cabañas Los Quetzales (described above) on this side of the mountain.

In Cerro Punta

Hotel Cerro Punta, 507/771-2020, is on the left just as you come into downtown Cerro Punta. It offers 10 decent rooms. Six of the rooms are in an annex facing a gorgeous view of the mountains. Perversely, the windows are in the back, looking out on nothing. The rooms in the main building are nicer, and two have a good view for no extra charge. The service here is friendly. *Note:* That mangy-looking stuffed creature in the lobby is a puma the owner's uncle supposedly shot in the 1980s, before environmental consciousness began to take hold in Panama. Still, its presence may be off-putting to some. Rates are $25 per couple, $5 more for a third person.

You can choose from 19 quaint cottages at **Cabañas Kucikas**, tel/fax 507/771-4245 or 507/269-0623 (Panama City), just 0.7 kilometer (0.4 miles) up from Hotel Bambito, just past the trout farm. It's on the left, but there's no sign so it's easy to miss the turn. The cottages are on forested grounds snug up against the mountains. It's a pleasant place. All the cottages are different, with some more cheerful and well-appointed than others. There's no restaurant on the premises, but all the cottages have full kitchens. This place is a

Cabañas Kucikas in Cerro Punta

good deal for larger groups. Rates run $60 to $150 for cottages that hold from two to 10 people. There's a fancy "honeymoon" cottage for $60.

In Bambito

The **Bambito Camping Resort**, 507/771-5126, fax 507/771-5127, 507/265-5103 (Panama City), eproject@chiriqui.com, www.bambito-forest-resort.com, is sometimes known by the more accurate name Bambito Forest Resort. This is a place for wealthy Panamanian families to get close to the woods without giving up any comfort. The location is pretty, with the Chiriquí Viejo River racing by the front of the hotel. It's about nine kilometers (5.6 miles) past the Hotel Bambito; look for the large sign by the side of the road. Turn left and continue along the one-lane dirt road for 0.6 kilometers (0.4 miles). You don't need a four-wheel drive.

Most of the rooms here are elegantly wood-paneled, high-ceilinged suites, ranging in size from big to gigantic. They have all the amenities you'd expect in an upscale hotel. So in a place this fancy you wouldn't find thin walls, hard beds, toilets that don't flush right, five minutes' worth of hot water, and light switches that electrocute you, right? Wrong. If you stay here, inspect your room carefully.

A major step down in quality are the basic and musty rooms in the resort's *"explorador"* cabins. You can do much better for less money elsewhere.

This place also offers nature tours and other outdoor activities (see Guides and Outfitters, above) and has a cushy campsite nearby (see Camping, above). Rooms in the explorador cabins are $50. Suites start at $100.

Hotel Bambito, 507/771-4265, fax 507/771-4207, bambito @chiriqui.com, is an aging luxury hotel that's pretty imposing but which some find out of keeping with the natural beauty of the surroundings. It's not related to the Bambito Camping Resort. It offers surprisingly plain standard rooms and several varieties of large suites. Common denominator in all types of rooms? Saggy beds. The place has seen much better days. There are tennis courts, an indoor/outdoor swimming pool, sauna, hot tub, and a few pieces of gym equipment. To show just far eco-chic can go, the hotel also boasts an "ecological miniature golf" course, which consists mainly of a ramp on a sloping lawn. Rates are $39 to $45 per person; suites are $155.

West of Volcán

If you need to stay farther down the mountains, there are several hotels just west of Volcán on the road to Río Sereno. Stay straight on the main road through Volcán rather than taking the right fork up to Bambito and Cerro Punta. The hotels listed below are two of the best options.

Hotel y Restaurante Don Tavo, tel/fax 507/771-5144, volcan @chiriqui.com, www.chiriqui.com/hotel/dontavo, is on the right just past downtown. It's set around a pretty courtyard and offers 16 simple but clean rooms with TV. Singles are $25, doubles are $33, and triples are $45. Attached to the hotel is **CyberCafé**, 507/771-4461 or 507/771-4055, an Internet café that charges $1 an hour, $1.50 in the evenings. The hours are 8 am. to 11 p.m.

Hotel Dos Ríos, 507/771-4271 or 507/771-5708, is 2.5 kilometers (1.6 miles) from Volcán. As this was written, the hotel was closed for a major renovation so prices weren't available. It will almost certainly be open by the time you read this, with a restaurant and bar and tour service to the surrounding sites. It was an attractive hotel before and should be even better when the renovation is completed.

FOOD

The hotels are your best dining bet on this side of Volcán Barú.

The fare at **Hotel y Cabañas Los Quetzales,** 507/771-2182 or 507/771-2291, is decent, featuring trout from its own pond, produce from its own garden and tasty pizza from its own pizzeria. Other dishes include pasta and the usual array of meats. Entree prices are in the $4-to-$8 range. It's open from 7:30 a.m. to 8 p.m.

The decor is plain in the dining room of the **Hotel Cerro Punta**, 507/771-2020, but the food is surprisingly tasty. The veggie rice dish *(arroz jardinero)* will be a godsend for those tired of meat and deep-fried starches. Be sure to try one of the delicious fresh-fruit shakes *(batidos);* the strawberry one is to die for. Most dishes here are under $6.

Restaurante Las Truchas, in the Hotel Bambito, 507/771-4265, features plate-glass windows that look out on the artificial terraced pond in front of the hotel and the side of a mountain right across the street. The house specialty, as the name of the restaurant implies, is trout from its own trout farm up the street, prepared any way you can think of for $11. Pasta here is around $6, and most other dishes are in the range of $10 to $12. If you're feeling terribly hungry, you can tuck into the ample Sunday brunch for $14 a head.

The restaurant at **Bambito Camping Resort**, 507/771-5126, includes most of the usual suspects (beef, pork, chicken, etc.) at inflated prices. Most dishes are $10 to $12. The trout is fine as long as you don't mind staring a big ol' fish in the face. The restaurant is housed in an attractive building that also has a fireplace, bar, and small lounge. If nothing else, this is a good place to stop for a drink.

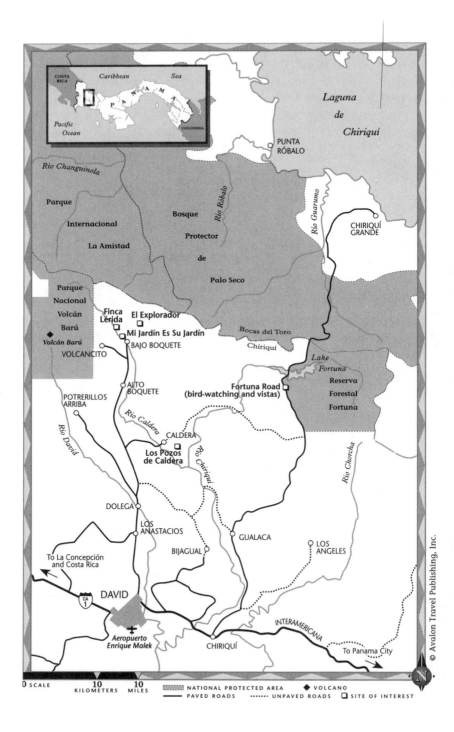

COSTA
RICA
Caribbean   Sea
PANAMA
Pacific
Ocean   COLOMBIA

*Laguna
de
Chiriquí*

PUNTA
RÓBALO

Río Changuinola

Parque

Bosque
Internacional
Protector
La Amistad

CHIRIQUÍ
GRANDE

Río Róbalo

Río Guarumo

de

Palo Seco

Parque
Nacional
Volcán   **Finca   El Explorador**
Barú   **Lérida**
◆   □ **Mi Jardín Es Su Jardín**
Volcán Barú   □ BAJO BOQUETE
VOLCANCITO

Bocas del Toro

Chiriquí

*Lake
Fortuna*

ALTO
BOQUETE   **Fortuna Road**
POTRERILLOS   **(bird-watching and vistas)**
ARRIBA

**Reserva
Forestal
Fortuna**

Río Caldera

CALDERA

Río David

**Los Pozos
de Caldera**

Río Chiriquí

Río Chorcha

DOLEGA

LOS
ANASTACIOS   GUALACA

LOS
ANGELES

To La Concepción   BIJAGUAL
and Costa Rica

CA
1

DAVID

*Aeropuerto
Enrique Malek*

INTERAMERICANA

CHIRIQUÍ   To Panama City

0 SCALE   10   10
         KILOMETERS   MILES

▨▨▨ NATIONAL PROTECTED AREA   ◆ VOLCANO
── PAVED ROADS   ······ UNPAVED ROADS   □ SITE OF INTEREST

N

CHAPTER 8

Western Highlands: East of Volcán Barú

You could start a lively argument by asking Panamanians whether the west side or the east side of Volcán Barú is more lovely. While the west side is a bit wilder, cooler, and more dramatic, the east side has both great beauty and something its western neighbor lacks: a charming little town.

That town is Boquete, and most of this chapter is devoted to the attractions in and around it. The end of the chapter heads quite a bit farther east to describe a couple of other worthwhile spots along the Fortuna Road, which links the Pacific and Atlantic slopes of the western highlands.

BOQUETE

Boquete, a pretty town that may remind you of a village in the Alps, is the center of action on the east side of Volcán Barú. At a little over a kilometer above sea level (about 3,300 feet), it doesn't get quite as chilly here as it does in the higher mountain towns on the west side of Barú, but it's still pleasantly cool compared to most of Panama, and it can sometimes get surprisingly cold. You can expect foggy drizzle, known as *bajareque*, even in the dry season. Bring warm,

185

The valley of Boquete

William Friar

waterproof clothes. The town is tiny and laid-back, a very relaxing place to hang out and plan day trips to the many attractions nearby.

LAY OF THE LAND

What most people think of as Boquete is officially Bajo Boquete (Lower Boquete), so called because it's in the middle of a picturesque valley surrounded by mountains. On a clear day, the Barú volcano dominates the landscape to the northwest. The town is bordered on the east by the churning waters of the Río Caldera.

Boquete's main drag is Avenida Central, which descends from Alto Boquete (Upper Boquete), runs north through town, and continues past a small church to the hills beyond. The plaza midway through town, on the east side of Avenida Central, is the town hub.

NATURE AND ADVENTURE ACTIVITIES

As with the west side of Barú, popular activities here include hiking, bird-watching, white-water rafting, and horseback riding. While there are plenty of rugged trails on this side of the mountain, you'll find many more options for less strenuous walks than in the Cerro Punta/Guadalupe area. Depending on the route you take, you can warm up in hot springs or cool off under waterfalls. There are also great opportunities for heart-pumping bike rides on well-paved mountain roads.

Boquete is headquarters for Chiriquí River Rafting, the only white-water outfit in Panama. At the time of my last visit, a group of top-notch kayakers from North Carolina's highly regarded Nantahala Outdoor Center were down for the winter. These guys were spending just about every day making first descents, including some very hairy ones. They raved about the world-class runs they were discovering and were planning to spread the word. By the time you read this, Panama may have taken off as a trendy white-water destination.

FLORA AND FAUNA

The flora and fauna here are similar to what you'd find on the west side of Barú. Boquete is also famous for its coffee and oranges. The Fair of Flowers and Coffee is a major event that takes over the fairgrounds on the east side of the Río Caldera the third week of January.

VISITOR INFORMATION

IPAT's new Centro de Facilidades Turisticas e Interpretación Volcán Barú-Boquete (CEFATI) is in Alto Boquete, on the main road just before it heads downhill into the town of Boquete. The place, almost as imposing as its name, was a costly undertaking (a reported $450,000) for a glorified information booth. It hadn't opened when I last visited, but a friend who's a Boquete native tells me the staff knows little about the area and just hands out brochures. It's worth stopping for the decent map of Boquete that IPAT puts out. Supposedly the place will eventually have a café and an exhibit on the area's attractions. There's a great view behind the building of the Boquete valley and Río Caldera.

Also in Alto Boquete, before you get to CEFATI, is an ANAM office, 507/720-3057, where you'll have to go to get permits to enter or camp in Parque Nacional Volcán Barú. As you head toward Boquete, the office will be on your right near the Seminario Franciscano. It's open 8 a.m. to 4 p.m. weekdays.

In Bajo Boquete, the town proper, you'll find the post office on the east side of the plaza; hours are 7 a.m. to 6 p.m. weekdays, 7 a.m. to 5 p.m. Saturday. Banco Nacional de Panama and Colabanco are right across the street from each other as you come into town on

MADE IN THE SHADE

Boquete is coffee country, but as you look around you may wonder where they're hiding the coffee plants. Scanning the hillside farms, all you see are shady trees, particularly orange trees. Look closer: If it's a coffee farm, you'll see tall shrubs below the trees. In the picking season, these will have ripe, cherry-red berries. The seeds are coffee beans.

Coffee here is shade-grown, a traditional method in which coffee bushes grow in the shade of a forest or among trees planted by farmers. Coffee grown in cleared fields produces a greater yield, but conservationists say it's a poor trade-off. They argue that trees protect the crop from pests, produce natural mulch, and prevent erosion. Shade-grown coffee therefore requires less pesticide and fertilizer and is less disruptive to the environment. Also, the trees provide a habitat to hundreds of bird species, particularly migratory birds. This habitat becomes ever more important as forests disappear in other parts of the coffee-producing countries. In other words, don't feel too guilty about drinking that third cup of coffee.

Avenida Central, open 8 a.m. to 3 p.m. weekdays, 9 a.m. to noon Saturday. You can access the Internet at Cafe Net 2000, on the west side of Avenida Central just as you come into Boquete. It's on the second floor, next to Chiriquí River Rafting. You can use the two computers here for $1.75 an hour or 3 cents a minute.

You probably won't need transportation in town since you can walk from one end of Boquete to another in just a few minutes. If you do take a taxi within town, it shouldn't cost more than 50 cents. "Urbana" buses that roam around the nearby hills leave from Avenida Central just north of the plaza, but taxis here are generally so cheap you should try them first. Taxis to places just outside of Boquete, such as El Explorador and Mi Jardín Es Su Jardín, shouldn't cost more than $2.

GETTING THERE

Boquete is 45 minutes by car from David, seven hours from Panama City. For information on David, see Chapter 7, Western Highlands: West of Volcán Barú. If you're driving west from Panama City, turn right at the first major intersection just as you come into David. The turn is not well marked, but it's located at the first major crossroads you'll have seen for many miles. Follow the road all the way into Boquete, which is less than 40 kilometers (24.8 miles) north of David.

Buses run between the David bus terminal and Boquete every 25 minutes. The trip costs $1.20 and takes about 45 minutes. The last bus leaves David at 9 p.m. The return bus leaves in front of Hotel Palacio on the northwest side of the plaza. Buses are hard to miss: they're yellow or white school buses. The last bus leaves Boquete at 6:30 p.m. Taxis between Boquete and David cost $12 during the day and $15 at night.

NATURE AND ADVENTURE SIGHTS AROUND BOQUETE

El Explorador—This peculiar private garden in the hills above town is worth a visit if you approach it with a sense of humor. A winding path leads you through two hectares of terraced land with orange and lemon trees, a rose garden, stands of papyrus, a bonsai nursery, and much more. But what's likely to strike you about this place are the human touches. All kinds of junk—shoes, bottles, shopping carts, TVs—have been turned into planters. Cartoon eyes peer at you from trees and topiary shrubs. Classical music is pumped throughout the place. And dotted around the garden are wise sayings and encouraging words in Spanish. One tells you that "If before you die you plant a tree, you haven't lived in vain." Another sign leads the way to the "greatest miracle in the world." When you get there, of course, you find a mirror. What starts off seeming kitschy ends up making you feel rather, well, loved. This is a good place to recharge your batteries. If you see a gardener, thank him: they take great pride in the place. There's a great view of the valley from the rose garden.

Details: El Explorador is about three kilometers (1.9 miles) northeast of town, near La Montaña y el Valle. Head north through Boquete on Avenida Central, pass the church, and then take the right fork toward Hotel Panamonte. You'll soon see signs for La Montaña y el Valle and El Explorador. The road gets rocky toward the end but you don't need a four-wheel drive. You can also walk from town, but it's uphill most of the way, steep at times. The garden is open 9 a.m.–6 p.m. weekends and holidays. On other days it's open by appointment. Call 507/720-1989 (Boquete) or 507/775-2643 (David). There's a small food stand. Admission is $1.

Finca Lérida—This is the most famous birding spot on the whole east side of Barú. Though a working coffee plantation, the *finca* contains primary and secondary forest that is home to hundreds of species of birds, as well as howler monkeys, peccaries, deer, and other mammals. You have a good chance of seeing resplendent quetzals here between January and August. The *finca* is up in the hills northwest of town, in a setting so picturesque you may find yourself humming the theme from *The Sound of Music.*

Details: Finca Lérida is owned by the Collins family, the same folks who own the Panamonte Hotel and the Pozos de Caldera. That means you can visit the finca only if you take the quite expensive tour offered by the Panamonte. For information see Guides and Outfitters, below.

William Friar

Hiking up a waterfall near Caldera

Los Pozos de Caldera—These hot springs are located a fair haul southeast of Boquete near the town of Caldera, famous in Panama as a home of cowboys and witches. If you're really into hot springs, you'll enjoy the Pozos de Caldera. If you can take them or leave them, you'll find the trip here a bit of a hassle for the payoff. That said, the springs are attractive, situated in a secluded stretch of forest near the bank of the roaring Río Chiriquí.

Those put off by the sulfurous stench of many hot springs will be pleased to find that these barely smell at all. There are four pools. The first one you'll see is the warmest, supposedly 42°C (108°F). There's one closer to the river that's hard to spot but quite nice. It's not as warm as the first one, but it's surrounded by trees and is less developed (the others are lined with large, flat rocks).

Not far from the springs is a tributary to the Río Chiriquí, which, if you don't mind quite a bit of scrambling over slippery rocks and muddy banks, you can follow upriver to **five waterfalls**, each more picturesque than the one before. This hike is best done with a guide. At the very least, don't go alone. A dip in the hot springs is especially pleasant after splashing about in these brisk waters.

Details: To get to the pozos from Boquete, head south out of town on Avenida Central. After about 12 kilometers (7.5 miles) you'll see a blue sign that says Caldera. Turn left here and continue past the town of Caldera. You should see another blue sign indicating a right onto a gravel road. If you have a four-wheel drive, you can follow this road to within a 15-minute walk from the springs. If not, you'll soon have to park and hike the rest of the way, about a 40-minute walk. After you cross the cable-and-plank bridge, make a left turn uphill (there should be a sign). Make your first left at the barbed-wire gate, which is easy to miss because there's no sign. From here the springs are about 15 minutes straight down the trail. Admission is 50 cents, which goes to keeping the area clean. A man will appear from a house to collect the fee just before you reach the springs, which are on private land owned by the same family that owns the Panamonte and Finca Lérida.

Mi Jardín Es Su Jardín—There must be something about the Boquete air that makes folks' dream gardens come out a little wacky. Mi Jardín Es Su Jardín ("my garden is your garden") is a formal garden as it might have been conceived by a miniature

Cerro Punta, obscured by fog

192

golf–course designer. We're talking a topiary dinosaur, brightly painted cow statues, a toy windmill, etc., set on a sloping lawn crisscrossed by fountains and artificial streams. There's an impressive view of the valley and surrounding mountains from the observation tower. It's a toss-up whether this garden or El Explorador is quirkier.

Details: The garden is on private land, but it's open to the public and entrance is free, no reservations necessary. From the plaza, head north on Avenida Central past the church, keeping left at the fork. You'll soon see the entrance on your right.

Ríos Chiriquí and Chiriquí Viejo—At the time of writing, the powerful Chiriquí (east of Barú) and Chiriquí Viejo (west of Barú) were the only white-water rivers in Panama any company was running, and the only company running them was Chiriquí River Rafting.

Even if you're an experienced rafter you'll likely find the runs here pretty darn thrilling. I've been on Class V rapids in California that were not as intense as some of the Class IIIs and IVs on these rivers, which feature very long wave trains, relentless runs, hair-raising moments, and lots of variety. And if you're a timid beginner, there are much more peaceful sections of the river where you can get your feet wet.

One of the great things about rafting on these rivers is the sense of solitude. Yours might be the only raft on the river, and you may not see a soul along the banks. Other than the occasional cow, all you're likely to encounter are forest, gorges, tributaries, and huge, beautiful birds. And, of course, big water.

Chiriquí River Rafting offers four different day trips, on rapids ranging from Class IIs and IIIs to solid Class IVs. The most hardcore of these is the Palon section of the Chiriquí Viejo, a four-hour blast through deep canyons. The gentlest is the Barrigona section of the Chiriquí, a 2.5-hour ride through Class II and III rapids that are suitable for families.

Word is finally beginning to spread about the exciting runs in the highlands, so by the time you read this you may have a little more company on the rivers. But chances are good you'll still have the sense of being a trailblazer.

Details: See Guides and Outfitters, below.

Sendero Los Quetzales—This trail arches across the north side of Volcán Barú, connecting Boquete with Cerro Punta to the west. You have a good chance of seeing a quetzal along the trail during the dry season. Bear in mind that Cerro Punta is nearly a kilometer higher in elevation than Boquete, so you'll be walking uphill most of the way. In this direction, the hike takes about six to seven hours one way. You should arrange transportation back from Cerro Punta or plan to spend the night there. See Parque Nacional Volcán Barú, in Chapter 7, Western Highlands: West of Volcán Barú, for more information on the trail.

Details: The trail starts about halfway along the very scenic Bajo Mono loop road. Do not attempt this hike without a guide, as you will likely get lost.

Volcán Barú—Those wanting to climb to the top of Volcán Barú, Panama's highest mountain, will find the Boquete **summit trail** easier to get to than the one on the west side of Barú. When the road is in slightly less horrendous shape than normal, which means the dry season, you can even drive to the summit from this side. Even then, however, you'll need a good four-wheel-drive with a winch.

If you hike instead, it'll take you about four to five hours up and three to four hours back down. The hike is strenuous but not technically difficult. Remember, people stranded on the mountain overnight have died of hypothermia, so be sure to dress warmly. See the entry on Parque Nacional Volcán Barú, in Chapter 7, Western Highlands: West of Volcán Barú, for hiking and camping tips and more information on Barú.

Details: Unless you're looking for a marathon hike, you should drive or hire a taxi ($5) to the trailhead. You'll need a four-wheel-drive vehicle. From Boquete, head north through town and take the second left past the church (you'll see a blue "Volcán Barú" sign). Continue straight past the first intersection then take the right fork uphill. You'll come to a fork after 6.7 kilometers (4.2 miles). Take the right fork. The road forks again in about 800 meters (0.5 miles). Take the left fork. After another 600 meters (0.4 miles), take the right fork up the very steep gravel road. Entrance is $3, payable at the ANAM office in Alto Boquete (see Visitor Information, above). There's a little ranger station at the entrance that may or may not be staffed when you visit.

William Friar

Farmland in Cerro Punta

Volcancito—If you're at all into orchids, you should take time to visit John Hackett's house in Volcancito, a short drive west of Boquete. Hackett is a very friendly retired U.S. Navy officer who has lived in Panama more than 30 years. He has turned his land into a haven for orchids, with 7,000 plants on the property. Be sure to check out the tree in the driveway—it's absolutely covered with orchids. When I last visited Boquete, Danny Poirier at Pensión Marilós was building a greenhouse behind the pension to sell some of Hackett's orchids, so you may be able to see a sample of his collection without driving to Volcancito.

Details: This is a private home, so call ahead at 507/720-3284 to make an appointment and get directions. The Hacketts are happy to let you poke around their property for free, but please be considerate. Try to come in the morning, as they take naps in the afternoon. Besides, you're more likely to encounter sunshine in the morning.

Palo Alto Cloud Forest—There are many great trails in the Boquete area. The Palo Alto Cloud Forest trails are popular and easily acces-

195

sible. If you're able to rent mountain bikes by the time you read this, beautiful bike routes offering a good workout include the 20-kilometer (12.4-mile) **Bajo Mono Loop**. If you're feeling lazy, the loop also makes a great car excursion. However you go, be extremely careful—many of the truckers plying these roads seem to have a death wish.

Details: The Bajo Mono Loop starts north of Boquete. Follow Avenida Central and keep left at the fork past the church. The loop is well marked. For details on other trails and bike routes, ask any of the guides mentioned in the Guides and Outfitters section, below.

GUIDES AND OUTFITTERS

Chiriquí River Rafting, 507/720-1505 or 507/720-1506 (tel/fax), www.panama-rafting.com, rafting@panama-rafting.com, enjoys a great reputation as a safe, highly professional operation, and at the time of writing it was the only company in Panama offering true white-water rafting. It's run by Hector Sanchez and his daughter, Kara, though these days Kara spends more time managing the business to allow Dad more time to guide. Both are bilingual. Not all the guides are, though, which can create some exciting moments when you're trying to figure out if your guy just yelled "Back!" or "Stop!" in his broken English.

The company offers four options for day trips, two on the Río Chiriquí and two on the Río Chiriquí Viejo, ranging in price from $75 to $100 per person including a picnic lunch by the river. (See Ríos Chiriquí and Chiriquí Viejo, above.) Trips last from 2.5 to four hours and run the gamut from serious white-water to more easygoing sections for beginners and families. Kayaking trips are also offered for around the same price. Experienced kayakers can rent the kayak and gear alone for about $25 per day. Multi-day rafting trips are offered for $280 per person. The usual trip lasts two days and includes rafting both sections of the Río Chiriquí Viejo, with a night on the river in between runs. The price includes camping equipment and all meals. At the time of writing, mountain-bike rentals, hiking tours, and sea-kayaking trips in Bocas del Toro were in the works.

The company also offers all-inclusive multi-day kayaking clinics every October and November.

Danny Poirier, a Canadian who fell in love with the highlands a few years ago and decided to move here, is an easygoing hiking guide. He knows most of the trails in the area, though he's still learning about the wildlife. He lives at the Pensión Marilós, 507/720-1380, and you can also arrange hikes with him through La Montaña y el Valle. *Note:* Danny is a born hiker who has trekked all over the world. What is for him a kick-back stroll you might consider a hard-core hike. Be honest with him—and yourself—about the shape you're in and how rugged you want your outing to be. He charges $40 for a group of up to four people. An average hike is six to seven hours. Danny speaks French, English, and Spanish and is available seven days a week.

Several reliable sources recommended **Gonzalo (Chalo) Miranda,** cell 507/637-6023, as a hiking guide. You can also contact him through La Montaña y el Valle (507/720-2211). He speaks only Spanish, but those who've hiked with him say his enthusiasm makes up for any language barrier. He charges $35 to $50 per group, depending on the destination. He can also drive you to the top of Volcán Barú for $50 per person when the road is passable by four-wheel-drive. He's available only on weekends.

The owners of the **Hotel Panamonte,** 507/720-1327 or 507/720-1324, also own Finca Lérida, which means you have to go through the hotel to visit the *finca.* They make you pay for the pleasure: Tours are a whopping $150 for one or two people and $65 per person for a group of three or more. Prices include a box lunch. Given the unique attractions of the *finca,* you may

La Montaña y el Valle, in Boquete

197

want to grit your teeth and fork over the cash. All their other tours are the same price, including an early-morning drive to the top of Volcán Barú. That tour includes a continental breakfast in addition to the box lunch. The Panamonte can also hire horses for you for $5 an hour, plus an additional $5 an hour if you want a guide.

Pensión Topas, tel/fax 507/720-1005, also offers tours and rents bikes and horses. Contact them for details.

CAMPING

Though it's not as cold around Boquete as it is in the higher elevations on the west side of Barú, it can still get plenty chilly. As always in the highlands, be sure to bring plenty of warm clothing and a waterproof tent if you camp out. Even in the dry season you should expect drizzles.

You can camp in **Parque Nacional Volcán Barú**, but if you pitch your tent in the higher altitudes be prepared for weather that can approach freezing. You have to get a permit from the ANAM office in Alto Boquete (see Visitor Information, above). Camping permits are $5, in addition to the $3 park entry fee.

La Montaña y el Valle, tel/fax 507/720-2211, offers three wonderful campsites tucked away among citrus trees (you can pick the fruit) and coffee bushes, with a great view of Barú and the valley when the weather's clear. The sites, each of which accommodates three people, consist of concrete platforms with picnic tables. There are hot showers and a changing room a few steps away. You must call ahead to reserve. See Lodging, below, for more information on La Montaña y el Valle. Rates are $10 for up to two people, $3 more for a third person.

LODGING

Well above the other places to stay in Boquete, literally and otherwise, is **La Montaña y el Valle**, tel/fax 507/720-2211, montana@chiriqui.com, www.ncal.verio.com/~ptpub/montana. It consists of three large, modern cottages set on forested grounds in the hills just northeast of Boquete. Each has a balcony, sitting room, full kitchen, and, on a clear day, a terrific view of Barú and the valley. Guests can dine in their cottage by candlelight on reasonably priced, near-gourmet meals you wouldn't expect to find outside Panama City (moussaka, pesto, Indonesian curried rice, etc.). The Canadian owners, Jane Walker and Barry Robbins, are attentive hosts who run a very tight ship. They're a great source of information on the area's attractions. Guests are invited to walk the kilometer (0.6 miles) of trails on the property and use the library in the house, which has a few volumes on the natural history of Panama and lots of good, trashy mysteries. There's also a great campsite here; see Camping, above. To get to La Montaña y el Valle, take Avenida Central north past the church and follow the signs. The entrance gate is near El Explorador. Rates are $70 for one or two people, $10 for an extra person.

Pensión Marilós, 507/720-1380, is one of the better deals in all of Panama. It offers seven simple but clean and tidy rooms at bargain prices. It's two blocks south of the plaza, on Avenida E Este, which is parallel to and two blocks east of Avenida Central. Guests can use the kitchen and dining room. Rates run $6 for one person with shared bath to $14 for two people with private bath.

Just across the street from Pensión Marilós is **Hotel Rebiquet**, 507/720-1365. It's a modern place with nine large, pleasant rooms set around an interior courtyard. All have small TVs and refrigerators. Rates are $20 for singles; $30 for doubles. Prices include tax.

Hotel Panamonte, 507/720-1327 or 507/720-1324, fax 507/720-2055, panamont@chiriqui.com, is a Boquete institution—it was built in the 1920s—that's feeling its age but still has lots of Old World charm. Rooms are quaint and clean but on the small side and rather dark. Its charming, semiformal restaurant makes it worth a visit even if you don't stay here. The hotel also offers a couple of special tours that are difficult or impossible to get elsewhere; see the Finca Lérida sight and the Guides and Outfitters section, above, for details. The Panamonte is about 0.7 kilometers (0.4 miles) north of the town center. Follow Avenida Central past the church and head right when you come to a fork. It's the blue wooden building on your left. The rate is $54 including tax.

The German-run **Pensión Topas,** tel/fax 507/720-1005,

schoeb@chiriqui.com, is three blocks south of the plaza on Avenida Belisario Porras, which is parallel to and one block east of Avenida Central. This is a cheerful place with six rooms set in a garden. Two more rooms were planned at the time of writing. You can have a full breakfast on the terrace for about $6. The owners speak English. Ask them about their new beer garden, El Tuki, up in the hills of Volcancito. Rates are $25 for singles, $35 for doubles. Very simple and small rooms with shared bath cost $10 to $12.

A new, rather odd place is **Residencial Campestre Los Pinos**, 507/720-1668 (Boquete), or 507/775-1521 (David), just outside of town. It's a left turn shortly past the church as you head north on Avenida Central. Follow the signs. This place seems to have been built for people who like narrow, vertical spaces. It offers split-level "cabañas" (actually tiny apartments in a single building), each with a bedroom and sliver of a balcony upstairs and a kitchen and couch downstairs. The place is terribly dark, but it has cute, lovingly tended gardens, and a friendly caretaker. Rates are $44 for two people, $10 more in the high season. Prices include tax.

The 40-room **Hotel Fundadores**, 507/720-1298, is another Boquete stalwart. It's on the left side of Avenida Central just before you come into town; its faux Arthurian–castle facade is hard to miss. Rooms here are small, drab, and past their prime, but a babbling creek runs right through the middle of the place, which makes up for a lot. Rates run $22 to $30.

FOOD

La Casona Mexicana, cell 507/685-4120, on the left side of Avenida Central as you enter town, is a funky little Mexican restaurant with decent food. It consists of a honeycomb of brightly painted rooms in a slightly ramshackle wooden building. Only two dishes on the menu are over $5. It serves good, if relatively pricey, margaritas.

The restaurant at **Hotel Panamonte**, 507/720-1327 or 507/720-1324, is the fanciest place in town, with tablecloths, fresh flowers, candles, etc. The food here is good but not cheap. Entrees start at $12 and top out around $15. But you can stuff yourself silly, as meals include soup, salad, vegetables, dessert, and coffee or tea. If you're a guilty meat-eater, this is a good place to indulge in a filet mignon. The rum cake is excellent.

Restaurante Merendero el Oasis, 507/720-2224, is on the east bank of the fast-flowing Río Caldera, just below the Calle 4 Sur bridge. You can get pasta or sandwiches here for around $3. Oddly, the most expensive seafood dish on the menu is the locally super-abundant trout, at around $10. If it's not raining, you can sit outside in the flower garden and commune with the river.

The restaurant at the **Hotel Fundadores**, 507/720-1298, has a good reputation for its way with the usual assortment of meats and seafood, priced from about $6 to $9. And again, it's got that cool creek running right through it.

If you have an irresistible craving for pizza, **Pizzeria La Volcánica** serves mediocre individual-size pies for around $5. You can also get a whole chicken here for $6. It's one block before the park on the main road.

If you don't mind a short road trip, you can choose from an array of unusual (for the Panama countryside) pastas at the reasonably priced, middle-of-nowhere **Trattoria Villa Florencia**, cell 507/614-8172. The restaurant is an open-air terrace behind a home up in the hills around Volcancito. The view is supposedly great on a clear day; the elevation is more than 1,500 meters (4,900 feet). At night, when I went, you can see the lights of Boquete twinkling below. It's open noon to 9 p.m. Saturday and Sunday. Call ahead if you want to come during the week. To get there from Boquete, head back up to the CEFATI building above town and turn right toward Volcancito. Just when you think you've gone too far you'll see a marked driveway on your left.

One of the many things that makes Boquete such a cozy place are the bakeries, with their seductive aromas wafting into the streets. **Panaderia y Dulceria King's House** carries that rarest of commodities in Panama: something resembling real brown bread. It's one block north and east of the plaza, near the northeast corner of the little park with the train in it. **Panaderia Victoria** is on Avenida Central, a short walk up from the plaza. It's on the west side of the street.

Coffee junkies should stop by the processing plant of **Café Ruiz**, 507/720-1000, a gourmet coffee company that grows its crop in the hills around Boquete. There's an espresso machine on the premises, and you can have a free sample of the strong, non-bitter brew it makes. The company also offers free half-hour tours of the plant or two-hour tours of a coffee plantation. November to March is the best time for the latter, since that's when they're harvesting the crop. There's also a small store where you can buy bags of coffee, some of it gift-packed. Cafe Ruiz is located just north of town on Avenida Central. Keep left at the fork past the church. There's no sign so it's easy to miss; it's the white complex on your right, near Mi Jardín Es Su Jardín. It's open 7 a.m. to noon and 1 to 4 p.m. Monday through Saturday.

ALONG THE FORTUNA ROAD

The area around the Fortuna reservoir, farther east along the cordillera, is known for its sweeping vistas and great bird-watching, but so far it doesn't see that many visitors or even have that many residents.

Because the Fortuna Dam generates more than 30 percent of Panama's electricity, there's an economic incentive to keep its watershed well protected. That's good news for nature lovers, as the forests here are overflowing with life. It can get cool at the higher elevations, down to about 14°C (57°F), but it's significantly warmer than the area around Volcán Barú.

LAY OF THE LAND

The reservoir, located just south of the Continental Divide, is surrounded by the Fortuna forest reserve (19,500 hectares), which in turn is bordered by the enormous Palo Seco buffer forest (244,000 hectares) to the northwest. The Continental Divide marks the border between the provinces of Chiriquí and Bocas del Toro.

A good, though dangerous, road—often referred to as the Fortuna Road—cuts north across the mountains from the town of Chiriquí on the Interamerican Highway to Chiriquí Grande on the Caribbean coast, 100 kilometers (62 miles) away. Chiriquí Grande is the jumping-off point for water taxis and ferries to the archipelago of Bocas del Toro. Along the way there are rugged access roads into the forest, making it relatively easy to explore the area.

NATURE AND ADVENTURE ACTIVITIES

It's all about hiking and bird-watching here.

FLORA AND FAUNA

More than a thousand plant species have been identified just in the Fortuna Forest Reserve, which is also home to 40 mammal and 70 amphibian and reptile species. Endangered mammals here include the white-lipped peccary and Baird's tapir.

The area between the Fortuna reservoir and the Continental Divide has some of the best bird-watching in Panama. Besides the ever-popular resplendent quetzal, there's a chance of seeing such spectacular specimens as the bare-necked umbrellabird, azure-hooded jay, black-bellied hummingbird, lattice-tailed trogon, and yellow-eared toucanet, to name just a few. Some of these are rare and nearly impossible to spot, so you'll get a lot more out of your hike if you go with a good guide. Fortunately, one of the best bird guides in Panama owns a campsite in this area. For details, see the Rancho Ecológico Willie Mazu sight, below.

VISITOR INFORMATION

This is a remote area with few services of any kind and certainly no tourist information booths. Your best bets for information and guides are Finca La Suiza and Rancho Ecológico Willie Mazu; see below. Don't attempt a hike into the forest without a guide.

GETTING THERE

You can do this area as a day trip from one of the more touristed areas, but you're in for a long day. You're better off spending at least one night.

Access to hikes and the only accommodations you're likely to be interested in are from the main road linking Chiriquí and Chiriquí Grande. From the Interamerican Highway turn north at the town of Chiriquí, about 15 kilometers (9 miles) east of David, and head toward the hills. Keep left when you come to the fork at Gualaca.

To get to the area by public transportation, take any bus running between David and Chiriquí Grande. Just tell your driver ahead of time where you want to get off. Buses leave David bus terminal and Chiriquí Grande every hour from 5 a.m. to 6 p.m. (If you're coming down from Chiriquí Grande, you can take any bus that goes at least as far as Gualaca. Ask the driver.) The trip the whole way takes about three hours and costs $6, so you'll pay some fraction of that. To return to David or Chiriquí Grande you'll have to flag down a bus by the side of the road.

NATURE AND ADVENTURE SIGHTS
AND LODGING IN THE FORTUNA AREA

Two appealing places to stay are aimed at ecotourists and are nature sights in themselves. They are also good bases for exploring the area.

Finca La Suiza—Sort of a cross between a mountain B&B and a nature reserve, Finca La Suiza, 507/615-3774, afinis@chiriqui.com is well worth a visit. It consists of 205 hectares (0.8 square miles) of mountainous primary and secondary forest through part of which the friendly Swiss owners have built a terrific trail. Those owners, Herbert Brullmann and Monika Kohler, rent out two large and cheerful bedrooms with private bath in their small house, which is set on a ridge 1,220 meters (about 4,000 feet) above sea level. The views are spectacular. On a clear day, you can see lovely valleys,

William Friar

Waterfall on Finca La Suiza trail

Pacific islands, Volcán Barú, and even a slice of Costa Rica.

The food here is gourmet and includes such unexpected treats as pesto, gnocchi, watercress and endive salad, and blackberry parfait. The produce is from the *finca's* garden. The full four-course dinner, which I recommend you go for, is $10. A big breakfast featuring home-made jams is around $4. You're on your own for lunch.

You do not have to stay here to hike the **trail**. It's one of my favorites in all of Panama, both because of its beauty and because it's so well marked and maintained. (Red flags mark the trail going up, silver ones the trail back down.) For much of the trail you're in the thick of the forest, then suddenly you come upon spectacular waterfalls or sweeping valley views. The forest is alive with sights and sounds. On my first visit I had hiked in only a few hundred meters when a group of white-nosed coatis scampered through the trees right above my head. There are big cats in the forests here, but it's very unlikely you'll have the good fortune to see them. However, a puma attacked a neighbor's cattle in 1997.

Be advised that this is a somewhat strenuous hike that goes from an elevation of 1,150 to 1,700 meters (3,770 to 5,580 feet). It's relentlessly uphill for the first half, and the trail "down" has lots of uphill parts. You have to cross several streams, which can be tricky in the rainy season when the water is high and the trail is slippery. As with any forest trail in Panama, do not hike alone. If you get lost, the rescue fee is $100. Officially it takes 5.5 hours to hike the trail, but that's being very conservative. Going at a reasonable clip you can shave at least an hour off that estimate. By the way, don't eat the things that look like blueberries growing along the side of the trail. They're poisonous.

Rates to stay at the *finca* are $25 for one person, $32 for two. Trail fee is $6. *Finca* guests pay only once no matter how many times they hike. Rooms are not rented out in June, September, and October, but the trail is open year-round.

Details: Finca La Suiza is 55 kilometers (about 34 miles) from David on the road to Chiriquí Grande, just past Los Planes and the one gas station on the road. A sign for the finca *is on the right. Park just inside the fence, watching out for muddy stretches. If you're just planning to hike the trail, pay the fee to one of the Guaymi women in the house just up the hill and get a map of the trail from her. You must start the trail between 7 and 10 a.m. This is for your own protection, as you don't want to be stuck out there at night. The trailhead is a steep, seven-minute walk up the dirt road. The trailhead is to the left. Finca guests can continue straight to get to the house. If you don't have a four-wheel drive, leave your luggage in the car. The owners will help you retrieve it.*

Rancho Ecológico Willie Mazu—Owned by Wilberto (Willie) Martínez, one of the best birding guides in Panama, Rancho Ecológico, 507/225-7325, tel/fax 507/225-7314, panabird@sinfo .net, www.nattur.com, is a unique camping retreat. (See Appendix B for more information on Martínez and his tour company.) This lovely campground is 31 kilometers (19.3 miles) north of Finca La Suiza, just on the other side of the Continental Divide, and borders protected forest. There are two main **trails** into the surrounding forest that originate from the campground. One leads to a 90-meter (295-foot) waterfall, Chorro El Mazu, an hour's hike away. The second leads to a cloud forest about 1.5 hours away.

The main campsite is a rancho (open-air thatched hut) with a number of large and small tents. It's set in a garden next to a river and has electricity and a hot-water bathroom. There's a kitchen and dining area, and food service is included.

Note: This is not the sort of campsite where you can just show up and pitch a tent. It's designed as an ecological retreat offering an all-inclusive package, and you have to call ahead of time to make reservations.

Martínez is also building a botanical garden to protect indigenous local plants, some of which are endangered. So far he estimates he's gathered 250 species of orchids and is adding bromeliads, heliconias, ferns, and other plants. It's also a sanctuary for the poison-arrow frog, with 13 varieties of the species identified on the property.

The most basic package is $42 per person per day, including three meals, all camping equipment, and daily guided hikes. Minimum group size is four people. Another $50 buys your group round-trip transportation to and from Panama City. Martínez's tour company, Nattur Panama, offers other tours that include stays at the rancho. (See Appendix B.)

Details: The campground is 86 kilometers (53.4 miles) from David, or 29 kilometers (18 miles) south of Chiriquí Grande. It's not easy to see from the road, but it's on a river just before the road makes a steep, sweeping turn. If you're heading north, you'll see an orchid booth on the right side of the road a few dozen meters before the campground. The booth is run by the Martínez family (no relation to Willie), which also acts as caretaker for Rancho Ecológico. They will not be able to accommodate you if you show up without a reservation.

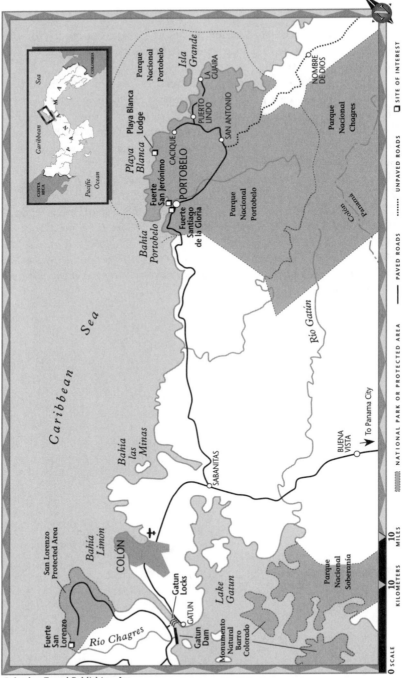

© Avalon Travel Publishing, Inc.

CHAPTER 9

Central Caribbean: Panama's Gold Coast

The strip of Caribbean coastline that stretches from the mouth of the Chagres River east toward the border of the Comarca de Kuna Yala is rich in history and even richer in natural beauty. Evidence of the former include the well-preserved ruins of Spanish forts, built to protect looted Inca treasure, as well as some of the most awe-inspiring structures in the Panama Canal. The area's natural beauty can be found among the mangroves, coral reefs, beaches, and forests that still abound with wildlife. And all this is about a two-hour drive from Panama City. No wonder this area is sometimes known as the "Gold Coast."

A new era for some of these riches began in 2000, when the United States turned over complete control of the canal to Panama. The Panamanian government has declared promotion of tourism in this newly acquired territory a national priority. Resort hotels and facilities catering to the cruise-ship crowd are going up, as are more modest ecotourist ventures. Which approach to tourism proves more attractive to visitors will help shape the future of this beautiful and important region.

LAY OF THE LAND

All the attractions described in this chapter are in Colón Province, which lies along the central Caribbean coast of Panama. Its capital is Colón, Panama's second-largest city.

The San Lorenzo Protected Area, Gatun Locks, Gatun Dam, and what were once Canal Zone townsites are all clustered around the Atlantic (or Caribbean) entrance to the Panama Canal and the mouth of the Chagres River, very close to the city of Colón.

The stretch of coast east of that city is known as Costa Arriba, which is where you'll find Portobelo, Playa Blanca, and Isla Grande. For most of the way this is a lovely drive: it's quite striking to zip along the lush, quiet coastline and suddenly come upon the ruins of ancient Spanish forts. A large swath of this area is part of Parque Nacional Portobelo, whose boundaries extend into the surrounding waters. It's under a lot of pressure from the human populations.

Please note: Though the city of Colón has a long, colorful history, I strongly advise you to avoid the place. For one thing, it has nothing to offer nature tourists, and you can get to all the region's sights without ever stopping here. But more important, it's just too dangerous. Extreme unemployment and poverty give this crumbling city a terrible reputation as a place where it's a surprise if you *don't* get mugged. Colón loyalists argue that these fears are exaggerated, but they'll sometimes follow that up by saying you should have no problem—as long as you take taxis everywhere and never set foot on the streets. There's always a lot of talk about revitalizing Colón. These days that includes a fancy cruise-ship port at the heart of a controversial tourism project called Colón 2000. But your best bet for the foreseeable future, sadly, is to stay well away from the city.

NATURE AND ADVENTURE ACTIVITIES

This stretch of the Caribbean has long been a favorite place for Panamanian and American locals to enjoy water sports, particularly scuba diving. While the diving is better in the San Blas Islands, it's much more convenient here, and finding outfitters is easy. There's also some surfing on Isla Grande.

It's also prime bird-watching country. The Audubon Society has identified 350 species on a single day during its annual Christmas Bird Count. Especially popular spots include what is now the San Lorenzo Protected Area and the Achiote and Escobal Roads. The latter are located just a few kilometers from Gatun Dam. You should go with an experienced guide.

Other activities include organized walks through the forest and a short boat ride to the mouth of the historic Chagres River.

FLORA AND FAUNA

As noted above, the bird life is impressive in this region. There is a lot of nominally protected forest in the area, but deforestation, hunting, and other human pressures limit the amount of other wildlife you may see. Still, you can have good luck spotting critters remarkably close to population centers. These include mammals such as coatimundis, agoutis, and the occasional crab-eating raccoon.

Mangroves near Isla Grande

The waters near the coast harbor extensive mangroves and coral reefs. Even a brief snorkeling trip will give you a chance to swim with lots of small- to medium-sized tropical fish.

VISITOR INFORMATION

Until and unless tourism really gets off the ground here, your best bet for information is a tour or dive operator. See Guides and Outfitters, below.

GETTING THERE

At the time of writing, a toll highway, the Corredor Norte, had been completed across 25 kilometers (15.5 miles) of the isthmus, a little under one-third of the way from ocean to ocean. Even that little bit of good road makes the drive from Panama City much quicker, easier, and scenic than it's ever been. The toll from Panama City to the end of the line is $3, after which you have to continue along the old Boyd-Roosevelt Highway (commonly known as the "Transístmica"). If the toll road is ever extended all the way to the Caribbean, the drive will be a snap.

Portobelo is less than 100 kilometers (62 miles) from Panama City, and the village of La Guaira—the jumping-off point to Isla Grande—is just 20 kilometers (12.4 miles) farther along the same road. You can reach these places by bus, but you'll have to change buses at the little town of Sabanitas, located on the Boyd-Roosevelt Highway 60 kilometers (37 miles) from Panama City. Buses heading east from Sabanitas to Portobelo and La Guaira run only during daylight hours. It's a bit of a hassle to go the whole way by public transit.

The drive from Panama City is fairly easy, so if you don't go with a tour guide or group you should consider renting a car. At the time of writing, the Corredor Norte came to an end near Chilibre. From there you have to make a left turn onto the Boyd-Roosevelt Highway (or Transístmica), and head north 40 kilometers (25 miles) to Sabanitas. The turnoff to Portobelo is on the right side of the road just past the El Rey supermarket as you head north.

There's no direct public transportation from Panama City to the San Lorenzo Protected Area and the other sights west of Colón. Again, you'd probably do best to go with a guide or drive yourself. If you drive, continue north on the Boyd-Roosevelt Highway instead of turning at Sabanitas. Just before you reach Colón you'll come to a four-way stop with a traffic light. Turn left, then make another left, and drive past the townsite of Margarita. The roads aren't well marked, so you'll probably have to ask for directions. If you miss the turn and end up in Colón, *do not* stop to ask for directions. Turn around and head back to the traffic light. It takes about 1.5 hours to get to this area from Panama City. For sights west of the canal you have to cross over a swing bridge that spans the locks. If a ship is transiting, the wait can be up to half an hour.

NATURE AND ADVENTURE SIGHTS

Isla Grande—This is the most accessible of the Caribbean islands from Panama City. If you're planning to go to Bocas del Toro or the San Blas Islands, you can easily give Isla Grande a miss; those archipelagos have much more to offer. If not, though, this is a good place to get a quick dose of natural Caribbean beauty and tranquility. This is quite a humid place; be prepared for some serious afternoon napping.

The island is only a few hundred meters from the mainland. Isla Grande is not really all that grande—it's about five kilometers long and 1.5 kilometers wide (3 miles by 0.9 miles), and has around 300 inhabitants. Though there are a couple of okay beaches, in front of Hotel Isla Grande and Bananas Village Resort, this is not the place for vast expanses of sand. What the island offers mostly is the chance to laze about and enjoy some beautiful views of the forested mainland, clear blue ocean, and palm-covered islands nearby. There's a decent surf break along the rocky shore just down from Sister Moon (see Lodging, below), but you'll have to bring your own board. There are also a couple of short, hilly forest hikes on the island.

The beauty of this place is marred somewhat by the trash inhabitants and visitors think nothing of tossing into the crystal waters. Little wonder the coral nearby is in sad shape. You'll encounter most of the trash around the small town that runs along a single waterfront path facing the mainland. It consists mainly of a handful of simple hotels, some run-down houses, and a few tiny stores and open-air restaurants.

Fortunately, there are less-disturbed spots a short boat ride away. A popular boat excursion is to **Isla Morray**. This is a tiny, uninhabited private island with a nice beach and relatively calm, shallow waters. You can snorkel or scuba dive here. Boat tours to Morray often take you through some beautiful mangroves near the mainland. Farther out to sea are the dramatic **Farallones**, which offer challenging scuba diving (see Guides and Outfitters, below).

Forest trail on Isla Grande

William Friar

Details: Access to Isla Grande is from the down-at-the-heels village of La Guaira, 20 kilometers (12.4 miles) past Portobelo on a good new road. It's 120 kilometers (75 miles) from Panama City, a drive that takes around two hours. As you enter La Guaira you'll see a sign that reads Isla Grande. Take the left turn indicated. You can park by the dock. You can also park in the partially fenced-in area on your left, behind Doña Eme's kiosk. The $1 a day to park there probably buys you nothing but a specious sense of security, but I always go for it anyway. Obviously, don't leave anything valuable in the car. When you come back, one or more kids may hit you up for change for "watching" the car. It's up to you whether you want to pay one of them or not, but they can be unpleasant if you don't.

If you're coming by bus from Panama City, take a Colón-bound bus and make sure ahead of time that it stops in Sabanitas. Get off in Sabanitas and take the bus to La Guaira ($2.25). Any of the boatmen hanging around the dock at La Guaira will take you to the island (don't expect life jackets). The ride takes about five minutes. The fee is $1, but if you look like a dumb *gringo they may ask for more. Settle on a price ahead of time, and name the hotel near which you want to be dropped.*

Playa Blanca Lodge—This is a cool little place. Playa Blanca is a cove on a forested peninsula a 20-minute boat ride from Portobelo. There's little on it besides the lodge, which is set on 4.5 attractive hectares. You can get to Playa Blanca only by boat: no roads have yet been cut through the forest. That isolation gives the place the feel of an island. (*Note:* Don't confuse the lodge with the Playa Blanca residential resort going up on the Pacific side of the isthmus.)

The lodge is just a few feet away from blue-green ocean and a rocky beach; a sandier swimming beach is just behind it. There are coral gardens literally a one-minute swim away that are alive with colorful small- and medium-sized fish and the occasional bigger guy (I came across a rather large and curious barracuda when I visited).

Snorkeling equipment and boat transportation from a dock near Portobelo are included with your stay. Several Sunfish sailboats ($10) and sailboards ($5) are available for rent. You can also get a boat tour of the Portobelo ruins ($15) or go deep-sea fishing ($40 an hour). A trail through the forest leads to José Pobre, about an hour away, where there's a little Swiss-run restaurant. Horseback riding can be arranged with 48 hours notice. The lodge can supply you with filled diving tanks, but there's no dive master on the premises and you have to bring your own diving gear. (Equipment and dive masters are available near Portobelo; see Guides and Outfitters, below. The lodge can arrange this for you.) Everything but deep-sea fishing is included if you go for the full package.

The place is owned by four Americans who are taking pains to get everything right. It's simple but comfortable. Little lights and bedside fans run on 12 volts of electricity, mostly supplied by solar panels. The bathrooms have solar-heated warm water.

The main lodge is an attractive, open-sided wooden building with a corrugated roof. It's sunny and airy, but don't expect much privacy. (The walls don't reach all the way to the ceiling.) There are four rooms and three bathrooms in the lodge; the room upstairs is a bit like a tree house. There's also a full kitchen you're free to use.

The best rooms are in a separate building on a nearby point. Two spacious upstairs rooms with balconies were nearing completion in early 2000. The view is absolutely beautiful. A kitchen and third room downstairs were in the works.

All the (quite comfortable) beds have mosquito nets, which you need here. As with many beach areas the *chitras* (sand flies) can be a nuisance; the owners were working on the problem.

Details: The dock for boats to Playa Blanca is located just before Portobelo, about 90 kilometers (56 miles) from Panama City. Make a left turn at the police station immediately past Restaurante La Torre as you head toward Portobelo. Your car should be safe here. The lodge will schedule a boat to pick you up when you make your reservation. Rates are $150 per room, which includes boat transport to and from the dock, snorkeling equipment, and kitchen privileges. For $150 per person (not per room), add three meals a day and access to all the equipment and activities described above except for deep-sea fishing. The prices are the same for the borderline rustic rooms in the main lodge and the significantly nicer ones in the new building. The lodge was just getting fully underway in 2000, so rates may be adjusted somewhat by the time you read this. Contact information: 507/441-0672, ext. 7801 (radio phone at Playa Blanca), cell 507/613-1558, 507/232-4985, fax 507/276-7181, rgoedjen@panama.c-com.net, www.pblodge.com.

San Lorenzo Protected Area—This is one of Panama's newest protected areas. Its 12,000 hectares (nearly 30,000 acres) include a former U.S. military base (Fort Sherman), the impressive ruins of the Spanish fort of San Lorenzo, and four types of forest, including mangroves and freshwater wetlands. The United States left most of this forest standing, and with the departure of the military all kinds of wildlife have returned even to formerly populated areas. The big question is what happens next.

Conflicting demands are being made on the area. On the one side are those who want to preserve this vital ecosystem, restricting its use as much as possible to ecotourism and scientific research. Conservationists consider this area a crucial link in the biological corridor that runs the length of Panama, especially since so much of the land to the east and west of it has already been deforested. On the other side are those who see this entire region as prime real estate. At the time of writing, for instance, it looked like a very real possibility that a petroleum storage facility was going to be built on nearby Galeta Island. Also, slash-and-burn farmers, hunters, and loggers were beginning to invade the area following the departure of the U.S. military.

Still, it seems likely that those pushing for conservation will be at least partly successful. In the short term, only organized tour groups are being allowed into the protected area. That's probably just as well for now, because you really wouldn't want to wander around here by yourself. Besides the usual hazards found in a tropical forest, there is unexploded ordnance in the area. The U.S. military conducted jungle-warfare training and had a firing range here.

The ruins of **Fort San Lorenzo** (official name: Castillo de San Lorenzo el Real de Chagres) are impressive and surprisingly intact. They sit on the edge of a cliff with a commanding view of the Caribbean coast and the mouth of the Chagres River, which the Spaniards built the fort to protect. As imposing as they must have been, the fortifications weren't impregnable: the Welsh buccaneer Henry Morgan won a bloody battle here in 1671, which opened the way for him to cross the isthmus and sack Panama City. The ruins, along with those at Portobelo, were declared a UNESCO World Heritage Site in 1980. *Note:* Be careful as you wander around the fort. There are few guard rails and it'd be very easy to walk right off a roof or a cliff. Supposedly at least one tourist has.

Details: The entrance to the area is 12 kilometers (7.5 miles) past Gatun Locks in the former U.S. military base of Fort Sherman; stay straight after you cross over the locks. Fort San Lorenzo is another 11 kilometers (6.8 miles) up a rough but passable road. It's a left turn past the entrance to Fort Sherman. Again, at the time of writing only organized tour groups were allowed into this area. See the Guides and Outfitters section, below.

Scuba Diving Around Portobelo—There are 16 dive spots around the Portobelo area, with attractions that range from coral reefs and 40-meter-deep walls (about 130 feet) to a small airplane and a cargo ship. But any honest dive operator will be the first to tell you the diving here is just average: you should expect no more than 10 meters (33 feet) of visibility on a typical day. Portobelo does, however, have two major things going for it: the diving is inexpensive and it is easily accessible. See the Guides and Outfitters section for more information.

Sierra Llorona Lodge—If you need a place to break your travel on the way to or from the sights on the central Caribbean coast, this is a good bet. Sierra Llorona means "crying mountain," an apt name for a place that sees rain 286 days a year. Even in the "dry" season you can expect predawn rains.

The plus side of all that precipitation is evident in the lushness of the 140 hectares (346 acres) of private primary and secondary rainforest surrounding the lodge. The owner of all this, Ida Herrera, is a dentist who has lived here for 30 years and is determined to leave the forest as untouched as possible. She limits the number of visitors, which means you're likely to have the forest pretty much to yourself. There are two kilometers (1.2 miles) of well-maintained **trails** that start about a 10-minute walk from the lodge. One leads down to a pretty little waterfall; you can go for a dip in the pool. This is a prime birding spot; the lodge can supply you with a list of nearly 150 species you may encounter here. Also keep your eye open for small mammals and other critters. You should go with a local guide, which the lodge will arrange for you. There's no fee for the guide, but you should give him a tip.

The lodge sits on a ridge 300 meters (984 feet) above sea level. Even this modest elevation is enough to give the place cool, pleasant breezes in the morning and evening as well as views of the Caribbean, Limón Bay, and, at night, the lights of Colón. The "lodge" is really a sprawling house with an attractive indoor fish pond, a swimming pool and deck, and a separate building a short walk down the hill. The three rooms in the house each have twin beds. Only one of them has a private bathroom. The rooms are nothing fancy but they're clean and comfortable. The rooms near the pool have a view and are larger and nicer, with private baths and two double beds in each. There's also a deteriorating tennis court on the property.

One of the best things about this place is Ida and her extensive family. They couldn't be kinder and more welcoming. You'll immediately feel yourself at home, which is good because meals are served family style. Dinners consist of tasty local food, and plenty of it.

Details: Rates are $65 per person, including breakfast, dinner and a guided hike. Sierra Llorona Lodge is located near the small community of Santa Rita Arriba (not to be confused with nearby Santa Rita). If you're coming from Panama City, it's reached by a right turn off the Boyd-Roosevelt

Highway (Transístmica) a couple of kilometers before you reach Sabanitas. The turnoff isn't marked and is easy to miss. Turn when you see a sign that says Ciudadela de Jesús y María. If you end up in Sabanitas, turn around and head back up the hill. This time you'll see a Santa Rita Arriba sign on your right; make a left turn there.

After the turn, head uphill about 2.5 kilometers (1.5 miles), then make a left turn onto a rutted dirt road. The lodge will be on your left after another 1.5 kilometers or so (about a mile). It's next to several radio antennas.

You'll need a four-wheel-drive vehicle to get up this rough road in the rainy season. Call the lodge for current conditions. Ida can also arrange transportation from Sabanitas ($8), Cristobal or Colón ($15), or Panama City ($80) for up to four people; larger groups pay more. You can also get a pickup-truck taxi in front of the El Rey supermarket in Sabanitas for $6–$8. If they don't recognize Sierra Llorona Lodge, ask them to take you to Santa Rita Arriba near the radio antenna towers ("cerca de las torres").

Contact information: 507/226-3128, fax 507/441-5414), sierrallorona @panamacom.com or ghorna@sinfo.net, www.panamacom .com/sierrallorona.

OTHER SIGHTS

Gatun Dam—This huge (nearly 2.5 kilometers long, about 1.5 miles) earthen dam was built to create Gatun Lake, a vital part of the Panama Canal. It was the largest such structure in the world when the canal opened in 1914. The dam controls the flow of the mighty Chagres River, a major obstacle to canal builders, and supplies electricity used at the locks and the surrounding communities. It's an impressive sight when the spillway is opened to control the level of the lake. A small bridge runs right by the spillway, and you can get a good view of the canal from the road that runs along the shore.

Details*: To get to Gatun Dam, you have to cross over the swing bridge that spans Gatun Locks. Take the first left after the bridge and head up the road for about two kilometers (1.2 miles).*

Gatun Locks—On the Pacific side of the Panama Canal it takes two sets of locks, Miraflores and Pedro Miguel, to raise or lower ships 26 meters (85 feet). Gatun Locks, on the Caribbean side, do the job by themselves. Each lock chamber is the same size as those on the Pacific—1,000 by 110 feet (almost 305 by 34 meters)—but there are three pairs of them on this side, versus two (Miraflores) and one (Pedro Miguel) on the Pacific. That makes Gatun Locks absolutely massive, more than 1.5 kilometers (a little less than a mile) from end to end. All this is by way of saying that the Gatun Locks are an especially impressive sight. There's an observation platform up a long flight of stairs that gives an excellent view of the locks, the Atlantic entrance, and Gatun Lake.

Details: The locks are open to visitors 8 a.m.–4 p.m. seven days a week. The number of tourists visiting the locks was increasing at the time of writing, but the free bilingual talks on the Canal offered regularly by the Panama Canal Authority at Miraflores were still sporadic here. Your best bets are Thursday, the occasional Friday, and whenever a cruise ship disgorges it passengers for a tour of the locks. Call the Panama Canal Authority Guide Service at Miraflores, 507/276-8325 or 507/276-3187, for information on the current guide schedule at Gatun Locks. Call at least a week ahead of time to arrange a tour.

Portobelo—Though the Spanish ruins scattered all over this seaside town hint at its long history, it still may come as a surprise to learn that Portobelo was once one of the most important ports in the Spanish empire. Today it's sleepy and impoverished, its decaying houses built near or in some cases into the crumbling stone ruins.

Inca treasure brought from South America was carried across the isthmus and stored here, drawing European merchants to renowned trade fairs for nearly 150 years. Columbus discovered Portobelo Bay in 1502, reportedly giving it its name when he exclaimed *"¡Puerto bello!"* (beautiful port). The city, originally called San Felipe de Portobelo, was founded in 1597 after the Spanish abandoned Nombre de Dios farther east. (There's little to see in Nombre de Dios today.)

Portobelo endured constant assault from those seeking its riches. It was first attacked, five years after its founding, by the English pirate William Parker. Sir Henry Morgan, for years the scourge of the isthmus, sacked the city in 1668. The assaults continued into the 18th century. Sir Francis Drake, the most famous thorn in Spain's side, was supposedly buried at sea in Portobelo Bay, though mod-

Spanish ruins around Portobelo, first attacked by the English pirate William Parker

ern-day searches have failed to discover his leaded casket. Given the attacks, it's a wonder so much survives. But large sections of the forts, their cannons still guarding the entrance to the bay, still stand.

The first one you'll come to as you enter Portobelo from the west is **Fort Santiago de la Gloria**. It's the third incarnation of a fort by that name here; these ruins date from 1753. In the town itself you can explore **Fort San Geronimo**, from the same period. The nearby Custom House was restored in February 1998 by the Spanish government. If you hadn't seen its state before the restoration, you might have a hard time figuring out what was done to it. Still, the place has been through a lot: originally built in 1630, it was seriously damaged in a 1744 attack, then rebuilt, then damaged again in an 1882 earthquake. The future of a small museum here was in doubt the last time I visited.

The large white church is the **Church of San Felipe**, which is still in use. It dates from 1814, but its tower wasn't completed until 1945. It's famous as the home of the effigy of the Nazarene of

THE BLACK CHRIST FESTIVAL

Every October 21 Portobelo comes back to life at the Festival of the Black Christ. It's quite a spectacle. Thousands throng the Church of San Felipe, home to the effigy of the Nazarene of Portobelo, otherwise known as the Black Christ. Some come crawling on their hands and knees, and many wear purple robes in emulation of Christ. Devotees circle the church carrying the Black Christ on a litter. It's a very slow process, as they bear the statue around the church with a peculiar rocking, back-and-forth gait.

What's this all about? There are several legends of the origin of the statue and its festival. One has it that the statue arrived in Portobelo on a ship bound for Cartagena, Colombia. A storm arose that kept it from sailing on, and the crew members decided the effigy wanted to stay in Portobelo. Variations on the story have the ship either sinking in the storm and the statue washing up on shore or the crew members throwing the statue overboard in fright.

Then, the story goes, on October 21, 1821, Portobelo residents prayed to the Black Christ to be spared from a cholera epidemic sweeping the isthmus; they were.

Every October 21 since, people from all over Panama who have prayed to the Black Christ for help with an illness or other problem during the year give thanks by making a pilgrimage to Portobelo, often performing some sort of act of devotion or penance along the way. Many find just walking here from Colón in the heat and humidity to be sacrifice enough.

If you decide to attend the festival, be forewarned that it's a major mob scene. Be prepared for epic traffic jams and keep on the lookout for pickpockets.

Portobelo, better known as the Black Christ (see sidebar).

If exploring these ruins and buildings doesn't satisfy your historical urges, you can try to persuade a fisherman to take you across the bay and visit a few more. At the time of writing, the one local entrepreneur offering this as a regular tour had a busted outboard motor. You can also take a short hike above town to some fortifications with a good view of the bay; if you're heading east, it'll be on to the hill to your right just before you enter town. You can park by the side of the road.

Ruins of a Spanish fort at Portobelo

Details: *Portobelo is about 100 kilometers (62 miles) from Panama City. The road from Sabanitas to La Guaira runs right through it. The town's poverty can be a bit intimidating, but you shouldn't have any problems if you come here during the day. If you come by Colón-bound bus from Panama City, you'll have to change in Sabanitas to a Portobelo bus ($1.25).*

GUIDES AND OUTFITTERS

San Lorenzo Protected Area
At the time of writing, the tour operator with the biggest presence in this area was **Nattur Panama**, 507/225-7325, fax 507/225-7314, panabird@sinfo.net. An all-day tour including transportation to and from Panama City, a stop at Gatun Locks, a forest hike, lunch, and a boat trip down the Chagres to Fort San Lorenzo costs $75 per person, four-person minimum.

On Isla Grande

Isla Grande Dive Center, 507/448-2298, cell 507/688-4073, dive_islagrande@hotmail.com, is in a small concrete building near Cabañas Super Jackson. The place is run by Andres Hernandez, an enthusiastic Chilean-Colombian who has lived in the region since the late 1980s and knows all the good spots. He's a very nice guy, and he has his own certified compressor. Andres doesn't speak much English, but he's made himself understood to legions of American military guys over the years. He may also have an English-speaking assistant when you visit. He's the only dive operator on the island.

One dive, including all equipment but not the boat ride, will cost you $22. The boat will cost around $5 to $7, or $10 if you want to go all the way out to the Farallones. If you're not certified, Andres also offers a "resort" course that consists of two dives and two to three hours of training for $40. A full, five-day course costs $150 and includes a bunk in a very basic concrete cottage that Andres was talking about upgrading.

Andres also rents snorkel equipment for $6 for the whole day, by far the best deal on the island. A snorkeling trip to Morray Island costs $12. He's quite open to other trip proposals.

Club Turqueza, 507/448-2990, cell 507/687-8702, rents sea kayaks for $10 (one person) and $15 (two people) per hour. Aluminum canoes cost $15 per hour. The hotel also offers a variety of boat tours, including a snorkeling trip to a nearby reef ($45 per person, two person minimum), a 1.5-hour trip around the islands ($25), snorkeling at Manzanillo Bay ($25), and an Isla Morray snorkeling trip that includes a tour of the mangroves and monkey-watching on Isla Linton ($45). A sportfishing trip costs $18 for three hours. *Note:* All prices are per-person, and the snorkeling trips don't include equipment.

If you stay at **Bananas Village Resort**, snorkeling, sea kayaking, and daily boat trips are included.

Around Portobelo

As this was written, four dive outfits had operations running within five kilometers (three miles) of each other on the road to

Portobelo. The closing of the American bases was hitting them hard, as military personnel and their families constituted much of their business. By the time you read this, a couple of the operators listed below may have folded. The ones who looked like they had the best chance of making it were Scubaportobelo and Nautilus: The last time I visited the area, Scubaportobelo was hopping, and Nautilus was in the middle of a major expansion.

These outfits offer similar packages for more or less the same price. Unless you're a real nickel-and-dimer, your best approach in deciding which to go with is to visit some or all of them and see which place you feel most comfortable with. Expect to pay around $25 for equipment rental, one tank, and a dive at a nearby location. A second dive at a second location will cost you around $10 extra, more if you want to go farther. If you have your own equipment you'll pay less. As always when you dive, bring evidence of certification and ask to see the dive master's credentials.

All these places also offer utterly basic rooms, though Nautilus was in the middle of a serious upgrade when I last visited. Rooms start at around $10. Expect to pay $30 for a three-bunk room. The best of the lot are probably the simple but clean and air-conditioned rooms at Nautilus and Scubaportobelo.

Nautilus, cell 507/613-6557, 507/263-5742, fax 507/263-5892, kbmrossa@sinfo.net, is the first place you'll come to as you head toward Portobelo; it's about 10 kilometers (6.2 miles) west of town. Look for the sign that says Happy Lobster Steak-House (presumably the lobster's happy because you're eating steak). The restaurant and bar, which were being renovated in 2000 and may have a different name when you visit, share quarters with the dive operation. This outfit is run by Javier Freiburghaus, a long-established dive operator.

Besides working all the Portobelo spots, Javier was the only dive operator offering trips to the San Blas Islands at the time of writing. (See Chapter 11, San Blas Islands, for details.) He also runs weekend trips to hard-to-get-to Isla Coiba on the Pacific side of the isthmus (see Chapter 6, Pacific Islands and Beaches). A significant expansion of the facility should be completed by the time you read this and could be quite decent. It was slated to include five two-unit cabins with air-conditioning and hot water. Each unit will have double beds and private bath. Rates run $25 to $35.

Next up is **Buzo**, 507/448-2175, 507/447-2900, cell 507/676-3655. The place is fine, but the trash and stagnant water around the shore suggest this may not be the best place to spend the night. You can also take a snorkeling trip to nearby spots from here for $5 for the gear and $5 for the boat, minimum four people.

Scubaportobelo, 507/448-2147, is five kilometers (three miles) west of Portobelo. There's a huge yellow sign on the way that you can't possibly miss. The spot is quite nice, with a wooden *mirador* built on rocks over the ocean.

Just past La Torre restaurant is **Diver's Haven**, 507/448-2003 and 507/448-2111. As you head toward Portobelo, make a left at the police station. It's just beyond the station, next to the dock. When I last visited, the place had closed down but was looking to reopen under new management.

CAMPING

Campers have traditionally pitched their tents on pretty stretches of beach along the coast. But everything was so much in flux in this area at the time of writing it was impossible to know where this would be either tolerated or safe in the future. Try contacting ANAM or a tour operator before you visit. Unless a developed camp site has been established, I really don't recommend camping on the mainland. If you just can't resist, bear in mind it's often too muggy for tent camping, and if you don't use a tent you'll likely be eaten alive by mosquitoes and *chitras* (sand flies). In the rainy season, you'll be camping in a mud hole. There's even a chance of being bitten by vampire bats, which carry rabies. Given the poverty in this area, you should also consider the possibility of human predators.

On Isla Grande you can pitch a tent on the grounds of **Villa Ensueño**, cell 507/685-2026 or 507/269-5819 (Panama City). The price is $10 for up to three people and includes use of a bathroom and shower.

LODGING

A Spanish-owned 300-room resort hotel, the **Hotel Meliá Panama Canal**, 507/470-1100, fax 507/470-1200, was nearing completion at the time of writing. It's located near the San Lorenzo Protected Area in what was once Fort Gulick, close to Colón and Gatun Locks. The hotel was built on the site of the U.S. military's notorious School of the Americas, which had a reputation for training Latin American dictators. Friends who visited the hotel as it was preparing to open were impressed with the food and the service. Facilities will include a swimming pool, gourmet restaurant, piano bar, casino, business center, and so on. The hotel was also planning to offer excursions to Gatun Lake, ranging from kayak trips to night "safaris" to observe crocodiles. Rates are $99 for a single or double room. Special weekend packages will also be available.

A 140-room **Radisson Hotel**—complete with a pool, casino, health spa, business center, and other resort amenities—was sched-

William Friar

View from Sister Moon, on Isla Grande

uled to open in May 2001 as part of the ambitious Colón 2000 cruise-ship complex. At the time this was written that seemed like an optimistic opening date. It will be located in the complex itself, near the Colón waterfront. For the project's status visit www.colon2000 .com or send an email to info@colon2000.com.

Other than Playa Blanca Lodge and Sierra Llorona Lodge, described above, the rest of the hotels described in this chapter are on Isla Grande. There are quite a few options, of wildly varying quality and price.

Sister Moon, 507/448-2182 or 507/226-2257 (aka Moon Cabins), was still a work in progress when I last visited, but it was expected to be finished by the time you visit. If so, it should be a great place to stay. It sits by itself on the hills of a palm-covered point overlooking a picture-postcard bay, rolling surf, and the emerald green mainland. The main accommodations consist of a series of thatched-roof cabins on stilts dotted along the hillside. Each has a double bed. The cabins are simple but extremely pleasant and tastefully designed. You'll feel you're in a fancy treehouse, and the breeze here is a welcome respite from the island's humidity. There are also eight cabins with bunk beds for backpacker-types. There's a pool and restaurant jutting out right above the surf, a pub with a billiard table and dartboard, and a sun deck. A small, rocky beach with a good surf break is close by. Rates are $50–$60 for the private cabins and $15 for the bunk-bed cabins.

Bananas Village Resort, 507/263-9510 or 507/263-9766 (Panama City reservations), fax 507/264-7556, 507/448-2252 or 507/448-2959 (Isla Grande), gram@sinfo.net, is the fanciest place on Isla Grande. Heck, it's one of the fanciest places outside of Panama City. It's on the north side of the island, tucked away in a lovely isolated spot facing the ocean. You can get to it only by boat or forest trails. (*Note:* The $1 boat trip to the island from La Guaira is included with your stay; don't pay the boatman, even if he makes you think you should. Take him to the reception desk, where he'll be reimbursed.)

The place, which opened in 1998, is nicely designed, cheerful, and small. Most of the rooms are in a handful of A-frame cottages on stilts. Each cottage has three units: two large rooms below and one very large room above. They're the same price, but the upstairs ones are nicer. All have balconies, hammocks, and air-conditioners, and all look out on the ocean (but palm trees block the view in some cases—shop around). There's a swimming pool and guests have free access to sea kayaks, snorkeling equipment, beach chairs, etc. Boat excursions to the surrounding area are included. Afro-Caribbean dancers entertain guests on Saturday.

So what's not to love? For one thing, the hefty price. And though you get a fair amount for the money, you don't get as much as you're promised. For instance, you may find that "kayak lessons" consist of a staff member giving you a paddle and kayak and pointing you toward the ocean. The service is poor and slow, and no one seems to be in charge. You can't even count on hot water. You may have better service if you come on the weekend, when the place is in full swing, but you'll also have a lot more neighbors. One plus: For $15 each way, the hotel will shuttle you between their office in Panama City and the dock at La Guaira. The Panama City office is located at the corner of Avenida Federico Boyd and Avenida Balboa; it's the Parque Urraca building. Rates run $75 to $110 per person, which includes a $16 credit toward breakfast and either lunch or dinner. There are sometimes promotional discounts during the week. A couple of less attractive rooms are available for $60 per person. You can also rent an even more exclusive complex with private pool if you have six people or a fat wallet.

Club Turqueza, 507/448-2990, cell 507/687-8702, fax 507/448-2271, jym97@hotmail.com, is at the edge of town before the beach path to Sister Moon. It's a simple but pleasant place with 10 rooms and more on the way. Each room has double beds, mosquito nets, screened windows, and ceiling fans (they're working on air-conditioning). The major drawback here is the very loud backup generator right next to the rooms. If the electricity goes out, which can happen two or three times a week, the noise from this thing would be pretty annoying. The French owners speak English, Spanish, and, of course, French. Rates are $45 for one or two people, $15 more on the weekend. There are also weekend package deals.

Heading into town you'll come to **Villa Ensueño**, cell 507/685-2026 or 507/269-5819 (Panama City), which offers a wide variety of simple, spacious rooms set around a garden. This place isn't fancy, but it's comfortable. All the rooms have air-conditioning. There's a little store here where you can buy snacks and such. This is a very popular place with the party crowd on the weekend, so bear that in mind if you're looking for a quiet spot. You can also camp here (see Camping, above). Rates are $35 for one or two people, $5 more between mid-December and the end of April.

Right next door to Villa Ensueño is **Cabañas La Cholita**, 507/448-2962, 507/232-4561 (Panama City), which offers 12 very simple and rustic rooms. There's no hot water, but there is air-conditioning. Again, this place is often packed on the weekend. Rates run $35 to $40 for up to two people.

About a five-minute walk farther into town is **Cabañas Super Jackson** (no phone), which offers four rustic rooms of varying quality. The place has little atmosphere but will do in a pinch. The rates are $20 for one or two people.

Hotel Isla Grande, 507/225-6722 (Panama City—no local phone), fax 507/225-6721, is the biggest hotel on the island, with 52 rooms. It has the largest beach on the island, which curves in a half-circle in front of the hotel. The rooms here are dreary and the service is torpid. When I last visited, rooms in unfinished buildings, with ducts sticking out everywhere, were being offered without hesitation. Eventually these are supposed to have air-conditioning. There are also 10 units in five air-conditioned cabañas right on the beach, but these aren't very nice either. The place is popular with Panamanians, but I don't recommend it. It's a cheap deal for groups, though. Rates are $40 for rooms, $50 for cabañas. Both can hold up to four people.

FOOD

On the way to Portobelo, Playa Blanca, and Isla Grande **Los Cañones**, about six kilometers (3.7 miles) before you reach Portobelo, is a charming little open-air place on a small bay. Looking out at the Caribbean, you'll find it easy to imagine Sir Francis Drake's ships gliding past on the way to a sneak attack. Seafood is the specialty at this popular place, with most entrees going for $6 to $8. The food here is good. The elderly owners were trying to sell the place at the time of writing, so cross your fingers it's still there when you visit. It's open until 10 p.m. every night.

If Los Cañones is closed or too crowded, **La Torre** is a cute little open-air restaurant 1.3 kilometers (0.8 miles) farther up the road toward Portobelo. It's easy to spot because of the stone tower that gives the place its name. It also specializes in seafood, with most dishes at $6 to $9. I wasn't too impressed with the jumbo shrimp ($9). The service is friendly and courteous. There's an illustrated history of Portobelo, in Spanish and English, along one of the wooden walls.

On Isla Grande, the hotels are your best bet. **Club Turqueza**, 507/448-2990, cell 507/687-8702, has a breezy open-air restaurant right over the water. It's a pleasant place to eat or have a drink (the bar "stools" are actually swings suspended from the rafters). The menu tells you right away that this is a French-owned place. Offerings include such exotic fare, for the location, as escargot, homemade paté, salad nicoise, and seafood crepes alongside more expected seafood and meat dishes. Breakfast dishes cost $4 to $6, lunch and dinner entrees about $4 to $12. They also serve a veggie plate ($7). The food here is good.

I didn't get a chance to eat at **Villa Ensueño** (no local phone), but friends who are Isla Grande regulars, and whose taste can be trusted, recommended the food as simple but good. It's not rock-bottom cheap, but most dishes are reasonable: breakfast tops out at $4, and most seafood dishes hover around $7.50.

Bananas Village Resort, 507/448-2252, 507/448-2959, has a very limited menu. Seafood appetizers will run you around $5. Entrees include the usual Panama trinity of meat, chicken, and fish ($8 to $12). The food is reasonably tasty but the chef has a fondness for fried stuff and strong sauces. The setting is nice. You can sit on a veranda near the ocean or dine upstairs in a circular open-air building with pleasant sea breezes. The staff sometimes blares dance music at high volume here, seemingly more interested in entertaining themselves than you.

The restaurant at **Hotel Isla Grande** (no local phone) is large and drab. It serves all the usual Panamanian specialties, especially the fried ones. You can get a burger with coconut rice and fried plantains for $3.

Near Gatun Locks the **Restaurante Tarpon Club,** 507/443-5316, 507/443-5216, right next to Gatun Dam and two kilometers (1.2 miles) from the west side of Gatun locks, is a good place to stop for lunch while visiting the area's attractions. This old standby is well-known for its seafood. The décor is plain—the best thing about it are the nifty old photos of the canal construction—but the plate-glass windows look out on a great view of the dam and the fast-flowing waters it spills into the Chagres River. You'll probably also get an impressive glimpse of some of the bird life for which the area is famous. The restaurant isn't cheap, but the food is tasty. It offers corvina 14 ways ($9 to $15). You won't go wrong by sticking just with corvina à la plancha (grilled corvina). Other offerings include jumbo shrimp, octopus, crab, and lobster. The service is friendly, bilingual, and slow. The place is open 10 a.m. to 11 p.m.

▲ Isla Grande (William Friar)

▲ John Hackett's orchids near Boquete (William Friar)

▼ Colorful houses in Casco Viejo, Panama City (William Friar)

▲ El Explorador garden in Boquete (William Friar)

▼ Kuna women (Clea Efthimiadis)

▲ Canopy Tower in
Parque Nacional Soberanía
(Courtesy of Canopy Tower)

▲ Scarlet macaw and blue-and-
yellow macaw (Clea Efthimiadis)

▼ Kwadule, San Blas Islands (William Friar)

▲ Touring Piñas Bay (Bachmann/Photo Network)

▼ Bridge of the Americas (Clea Efthimiadis)

▲ Girl in *pollera* (Clea Efthimiadis)

▲ Portaging in the Chiriquí Highlands (Courtesy of Chiriquí River Rafting)

▼ Sailboat in San Blas Islands (William Friar)

▲ Exploring Panama's rivers via Zodiac (Dave G. Houser)

▲ Boquete is a charming town nestled in the highlands on the east side of Volcán Barú. (William Friar)

▼ Panama is well-known for its brilliant, jewel-toned frogs. (Len Kaufman)

▲ Abandoned locomotive, Cana (William Friar)

▼ Bright colors, animal imagery, and geometric patterns are common features of *molas*, cloth works of art made by the Kuna. (Bachmann/Photo Network)

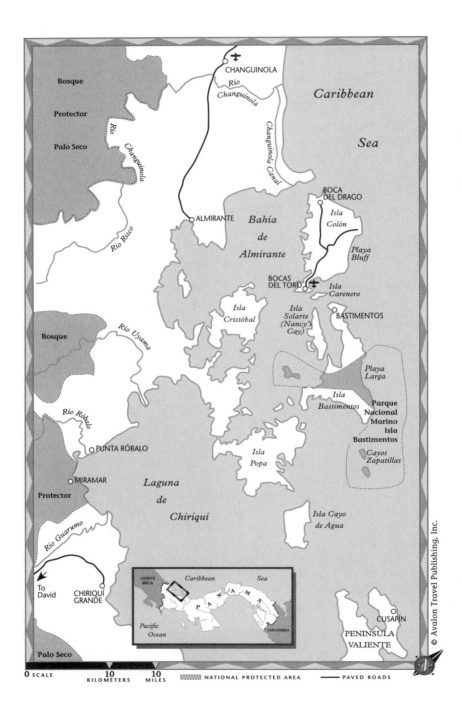

© Avalon Travel Publishing, Inc.

CHAPTER 10

Bocas del Toro Archipelago

You may find it hard to leave Bocas del Toro. It's a terribly relaxing place, and at the same time it exudes a funky, romantic charm that has something untamed about it. The place is filled with colorful characters you'll find nursing drinks in wooden bars by the waterfront or running rustic hotels on deserted beaches. It's the kind of Caribbean hideaway one expects to find only in old Bogart films.

And it's just gorgeous. It has pristine beaches, blue-green waters, dense jungle, exotic wildlife, and more. If no other place in Panama takes off as a major tourist destination, Bocas probably will. People are betting on it—literally. Much of the good land is being snatched up by foreigners.

Most of the hotels and restaurants are already owned by Europeans, Canadians, and Americans. There's an especially strong Italian presence; it's easy to find pizza and pasta here. The local population includes Guaymi Indians as well as Jamaicans, who have worked on the region's enormous banana plantations for generations. You'll likely find a greater variety of people here, and more English-speakers, than anywhere in the country outside of Panama City.

Bocas's biggest shortcoming is the rain. It never completely stops here, though your best chance of a dry visit are in the semidry seasons of September/October and February/March.

Bocas seems to be evolving from a great backpackers' secret to a slightly more upscale destination. It's a good place for people who've seen the rest of the Caribbean and are looking for something a little different. A word of advice for those contemplating a visit: Hurry.

LAY OF THE LAND

The archipelago is only part of the province of Bocas del Toro, but it's the part that most visitors come to explore.

By far the most developed island in the archipelago is Isla Colón, and by far the most developed part of Isla Colón is the town of Bocas del Toro, at the southeast tip of this large (61 square kilometers, about 24 square miles) island.

Bocas town is nearly an island in its own right; it's connected to the rest of Isla Colón by a causeway. (*Note:* Here's where the names start getting confusing. The town, the archipelago, and the province share the same name, often shortened simply to "Bocas." And just to really mess you up, the whole of Isla Colón is sometimes referred to as Isla Bocas.) Almost all the archipelago's hotels, restaurants, tour outfits, and visitor services are in Bocas town. Most of the action is on either side of Calle 3, the broad main street that runs past the town plaza, Parque Bolívar, and peters out at water's edge.

The other commonly visited islands in the archipelago are east of Isla Colón, which is the point of departure to all of them. The services diminish the father east you go.

Throughout the archipelago, the great beaches and pounding surf tend to be on the north side of the islands, where there's nothing but ocean until you get to Jamaica. Generally the sea is too rough for safe swimming. The water tends to be glassy on the southern side of the islands and in sheltered bays on the eastern sides. Here's where you can find good snorkeling.

NATURE AND ADVENTURE ACTIVITIES

Scuba diving, snorkeling, bird-watching, surfing, and water-skiing are big here, but you may find it tempting just to lounge in a hammock and stare at the ocean. When it comes to nature activities, a dive operator here put it best: Bocas doesn't have the best of anything, but it has a little bit of everything. For instance, the diving can be good, but not as good as it is in the San Blas. Several rivers empty into the sea here, so visibility tends to be 15 meters (49 feet) on a good day, 22 meters (72 feet) on an excellent day, and less than three meters (10 feet) when I visit. But there are many other attractions to make up for a so-so day of gawking at fish.

There is some decent surfing in Bocas, particularly off the northern beaches of Islas Bastimentos and Colón. You have to bring your own surfboard, as no one rents them on the island. (You might be able to buy a used one though. See Guides and Outfitters, below.) The surfing is best from mid-December to April..

FLORA AND FAUNA

Four species of endangered sea turtles lay their eggs on the north side of the islands. Little Swan Cay, really just a rock in the ocean, is the only Panamanian nesting site of the beautiful red-billed tropicbird. The forests on the islands are home to several endangered species of amphibians and reptiles. Among these are some tiny neon-colored frogs that are easily spotted on one of the beaches. There are impressive mangroves here, especially red and white mangroves, and several kinds of coral. The fish tend to be small but colorful.

VISITOR INFORMATION

IPAT recently built, at a reported cost of nearly half a million bucks, a Centro de Facilidades Turísticas e Interpretación (CEFATI), 507/757-9246, about halfway down Calle 1, the street that borders the waterfront. The huge, two-story, Caribbean-style complex—located, oddly enough, next to the town jail—is one of the biggest buildings in the archipelago. At the time of writing, though, it offered tourists little more than a map of Bocas town and the islands and a few brochures. However, an exhibit about the natural and social history of the archipelago should be open on the second floor by the time you visit. The center is open 8:30 a.m. to 4:30 p.m. weekdays.

You can get park permits and marginally useful maps and brochures from the tiny ANAM office, 507/757-9244, near the corner of Calle 1 and Avenida E, one block east of the park. It's open 8 a.m. to noon and 1 to 4 p.m. weekdays.

The Banco Nacional de Panama, northeast of the park on Avenida E between Calles 1 and 2, has an ATM and cashes traveler's checks. It's open 8 a.m. to 2 p.m. weekdays and 9 a.m. to noon Saturday. There's another ATM in the same building that houses Expresso Taxi 25, the water-taxi service near the jail.

Note: These are the only two ATMs in the archipelago, and they've been known to go on the blink simultaneously. Theoretically, many places on Isla Colón take credit cards. In reality many of them don't, or they charge an extra fee for their trouble (be sure to ask ahead of time). This is a good place to come well stocked with traveler's checks and/or cash.

You can buy telephone calling cards from the Cable and Wireless office, located along the waterfront on Calle 1 near Expresso Taxi 25, a water-taxi service. The office is open 8 a.m. to noon and 1 to 4:30 p.m. weekdays, but the vending machine outside is available 24 hours a day.

The biggest annual party in Bocas is the Feria del Mar (Festival of the Sea), held at the end of September.

WATER QUALITY

This is one of the few places in Panama where you shouldn't drink water out of the tap, although by the time you read this the new water purification plant may be finished. If not, you can buy 1.5-liter bottles of water from many of the local shops for $1.50, and some restaurants and hotels serve filtered water.

GETTING THERE

There are daily flights from Panama City and David to the town of Bocas del Toro, on Isla Colón. Direct flights from Panama City take about an hour and cost $45 one-way, $90 round-trip.

Aeroperlas, 507/315-7500, 507/315-7580, iflyap@aeroperlas .com, makes the trip twice a day weekdays, and once a day on weekends. Mapiex Aero, 507/315-0888, has one flight a day to Bocas. Sometimes planes make unannounced stops in Changuinola. Make sure you know where you are before you get off the plane.

You can get a *transporte cooperativa* van from the airport to Bocas town for 50 cents each, or a taxi for $1. But you can easily walk to any of the town's hotels if you're not weighted down with luggage.

If you're coming by car or bus, you can get as close as Almirante (if you're coming from Costa Rica) or Chiriquí Grande (if you're coming from mainland Panama). The drive from Panama City to Chiriquí Grande will take you a full day. When you get to the coast you have to take a water taxi or ferry. The water-taxi fare is $2 to $3 from Almirante and $10 from Chiriquí Grande. The direct trip takes 25 minutes and 50 minutes, respectively.

Two companies offer this service: Expresso Taxi 25 (in Almirante: 507/758-3498; in Bocas: 507/757-9028; in Chiriquí Grande: 507/756-9712) and Galapagos Tours (in Almirante: 507/758-3058; in Bocas: 507/757-9073; no Chiriquí Grande number).

The Almirante–Bocas del Toro route is far more traveled. The companies make the trip every 45 minutes to an hour during daylight hours.

Trips between Chiriquí Grande and Bocas del Toro are less frequent and dependable. Count on about three taxis a day, depending on the number of passengers waiting. Call ahead of time to confirm, and try to make the trip early in the day. If you arrive after mid-afternoon, you may have to wait until the next day.

In Bocas town, Expresso Taxi 25 is located near the town jail and the CEFATI tourist office. Galapagos Tours is midway down Calle 3, near Restaurante Le Pirate and other water-tour operators.

A terribly slow ferry also runs between Bocas, Almirante, and Chiriquí Grande on Wednesday, Saturday, and Sunday. The fare is

$1.50 from Chiriquí Grande and $3 from Almirante. The only reason you'd take it is if you were bringing a car from the mainland, which would cost you $30 to $40 more. For more information you can try calling 507/757-9691 (Chiriquí Grande) or 507/757-9260 (Bocas del Toro) but be warned that both phones are frequently out of order.

You'll have to take tour boats or local water taxis to get to all the other islands. See Guides and Outfitters, below.

NATURE AND ADVENTURE SIGHTS

Around Isla Colón—There are no real beaches in Bocas town, and the waterfront is too busy to make wading in the water here much fun. The **beaches** are past the causeway on the main part of Isla Colón. The best beaches start about a 15-minute drive from town up the east coast. The surf is too rough to land boats anywhere along this part of the island. You can bike there, but the rocky dirt road gets a bit rough in places. The land along the coast has been gobbled up recently, mostly by gringos building dream homes, so you may also have to contend with construction equipment along the road. A taxi may be your best bet. If you take one, arrange a time to be picked up and don't pay until the driver returns and takes you back. Taxis don't cruise this strip looking for passengers.

Go at least as far as **Playa Bluff**, about a 25-minute drive from town. It's an absolutely gorgeous beach you're likely to have to yourself during the week. This is also an important nesting site for endangered sea turtles. The surf can get rough here, so it's probably not a good idea to do any real swimming. The same is true of the equally lovely beaches that continue up the east and north coast. At the time of writing, the road ended at a stream just past Playa Bluff, so you'll have to hoof it if you want to keep heading up the coast. About an hour hike away is **La Piscina** (the swimming pool), a protected lagoon on the north side of the island. Ask for directions at Finca Verde, a little hotel just past Playa Bluff.

If you want to break your trip on the way back, **La Coralina** (no phone) is a good place to stop for a cold drink. It's a small, Spanish-style house on a hill that offers three large, dreary, and run-down rooms for $25, $29 with breakfast. It's a pretty grim place to stay, but it has a great view of the ocean from the patio. It's south of Playa Bluff.

Another popular beach area, mainly because it's easily accessible by boat, is **Boca del Drago**, on the northwest side of the island. Boca del Drago is also the name of the canal separating this part of Isla Colón from the mainland. The water is tranquil on this side of the island, so landing a boat is not a problem; many of the island tours include a stop here. You can also take a scenic drive across the island from Bocas town. *Note:* A resort being built in this area may make Boca del Drago a bit too popular for those who like secluded beaches.

There's a little thatch-roofed, sand-floored restaurant on the beach called **Restaurante Yarisnori** (closed Tuesday). The grilled lobster ($9) is pretty good, as is the mixed ceviche. Through the restaurant you can rent a small boat for $5, a pedal boat for $3.50, or snorkel gear for $6 all day. There are coral gardens all along the west side of the island. The snorkeling can be decent, but the coral is not in great shape and the visibility isn't always the best.

William Friar

Playa Bluff, Isla Colón

Halfway across the island on the road to Boca del Drago you'll find **La Gruta** ("the cavern"), home to zillions of bats. If your idea of fun is to wade through guano in a claustrophobic cave and inhale disease-carrying particulates, then by all means walk through the thing. The rest of us will be happy with a snapshot of the highly photogenic entrance to the cave, a green grotto with a little statue of the Virgin standing guard.

A standard boat tour around Isla Colón includes a stop at lovely **Swan Cay**, a craggy rock that juts out of the ocean north of the island, about a half-hour by motorized boat from Bocas. It's so impossibly picturesque that a friend of mine decided it looked like it was designed by Disney. Swan Cay is also called Isla de los Pájaros (Bird Island) for reasons that become obvious when you visit it. Most notably, it's the only known nesting grounds in Panama for the red-billed tropicbird, an elegant white bird with tail feathers about a meter (39 inches) long. Do not disturb the birds by walking on the island; you can, however, snorkel around it. The current isn't too strong, but the water can get pretty churned up at times, creating a washing- machine effect that drastically reduces visibility.

Your boatman may ask if you'd like him to motor through the narrow cleft in the western crag. It may not look it, but it's possible if the boatman times the waves right. It's a fun thing to do—you can see crabs scuttling along the rocky walls inches from the boat. Go for it if you trust your boatman's navigational skills.

Details: Taxis can take you as far as Playa Bluff on the east coast (25 minutes) and to Boca del Drago (45 minutes) across Isla Colón. Playa Bluff is a nicer beach, but the surf is much rougher. La

William Friar

A skilled boatman can navigate the cleft through Swan Cay.

William Friar

Swan Cay—the only known nesting grounds in Panama for the red-billed tropicbird

Gruta is about halfway across the island on the road to Boca del Drago. Expect round-trip fare to be $10 for Playa Bluff and La Gruta and $25 for Boca del Drago. You have to take a boat to Swan Cay. It and Boca del Drago are typically included in an Isla Colón boat tour. See Guides and Outfitters, below.

Changuinola Canal—If you're looking for a break from beaches and splashing about, a boat trip up the Changuinola Canal, on the mainland east of the town of Changuinola, is an interesting off-the-beaten-track jaunt. The eight-mile canal was built in 1903 by Michael T. Snyder, a pioneering plantation owner, to shelter his banana barges from the open sea on their way between the mainland and the islands. The canal parallels the coastline from the mouth of the Río Changuinola to Almirante Bay.

When the canal was bordered by forest on either side it was a prime birding spot. Unfortunately, slash-and-burn farmers and cattle ranchers have cut away much of the forest in recent years. But you can still see quite an array of birds. Manatees are occasionally spotted

William Friar

Birding at the Changuinola Canal

here as well. It makes for a tranquil jungle cruise.

Details: *It takes about a half-hour to reach the entrance to the canal by boat from Bocas town. Reaching the Río Changuinola takes about 45 minutes at a leisurely pace, but you don't have to go that far to get a good look at the wildlife that's left; there are tons of birds at the very entrance of the canal. Early morning or late afternoon is the best time to go. You may want to include this as part of an Isla Colón tour, since the entrance to the canal is just opposite Boca del Drago. Expect to pay an extra charge, but agree on a price ahead of time.*

Isla Bastimentos—This big, beautiful island (52 square kilometers, about 20 square miles) has a lot to offer nature lovers. The north shore has pounding surf and miles of gorgeous sandy beaches, some of which attract sea turtles in nesting season. The protected waters to the southeast are shallow and glassy, making it easy to explore a vast underwater playground of coral reefs. To the southwest are mangrove islands. And the island itself is home to dense forest that harbors many exotic and endangered species. In fact, the midsection of the island and some of its surrounding waters are part of a national marine park (see Parque Nacional Marino Isla Bastimentos, below).

Boats from Isla Colón that approach Bastimentos from the south will pass a series of idyllic mangrove islands, protected as part of the marine park, before coming to **Coral Cay**, a shallow channel between Isla Bastimentos and Isla Popa. In keeping with the Bocas name game, Coral Cay is sometimes called **Crawl Cay**. It's about a half-hour by boat from Bocas town.

The water here is a luminous light green, smooth as glass, and only a couple of feet deep before you hit the sandy bottom. The channel harbors two rustic thatched-hut restaurants, built on stilts over the water, that are tourist destinations in their own right. Tours to Cayos Zapatillas (see Parque Nacional Marino Isla Bastimentos, below) and around Bastimentos usually include a stop at one of these photogenic spots.

The one to your left is **Restaurante Adonis**. In the water next to the dining area is a wooden corral that at the time of my visit was home to a jewfish, rockfish, sea turtle, and other largish sea creatures. Given that, for starters, sea turtles are endangered, this menagerie might put off environmentally conscious customers. For what it's worth, the owner's cousin assured me the turtle was going to be released once it got bigger. Critters to be consumed, namely conch and lobster, are kept in another corral. There's a meager general store here where Guaymi Indians pull up in their canoes to do their shopping.

Across the channel on your right is **Restaurante El Paso de Marisco**, which is even more charming. Here each table is housed under its own thatched hut, connected to the rest of the place by a series of boardwalks. Since you're only a few feet from the crystalline water, you can watch slender needlefish and brilliant parrotfish, angelfish, snapper, and other aquatic life cavort at your feet. If you don't want to eat, you can just snorkel around here for $3. The fish in the area are so spoiled by free feedings that the restaurant even boasts a "tame" barracuda. It's too well fed to bother with you, but don't push your luck by swimming too close.

William Friar

Restaurante Adonis in Coral Cay

If you want to eat at either of these places, a good strategy is to place your order an hour ahead of time and then go snorkeling. The catch of the day can include lobster, conch, crab, shrimp, or calamari, at least in theory. A full meal averages about $5 and cold beer is a buck. Note that both these places are bare-bones establishments, but at least you know the food is fresh.

Warning: Some tour operators, wanting to save on gas, take you only as far as Coral Cay and call that your snorkeling trip. Given that coral reefs don't start until you round the point and head up the coast of Bastimentos—at which point there are miles of them— you're cheating yourself if you agree to this. Find out ahead of time exactly where your boat is heading.

The sheltered waters from Coral Cay to Punta Vieja, about eight kilometers (about five miles) up the southeast coast of Bastimentos, offer some colorful snorkeling. The sea here is so shallow and calm you'll feel like you're swimming in a tropical aquarium. There's a variety of coral and lots of small but dazzling fish. However, as elsewhere in the archipelago, the visibility can be disappointing.

As soon as you round Punta Vieja you meet open sea. The beaches along the north side of Bastimentos are generally much too rough to swim out past wading depth. But there are several spectacularly beautiful beaches here. The one most popular with sea turtles is **Playa Larga**. For details, see Parque Nacional Marino Isla Bastimentos, below, and the sidebar on sea turtles.

The sea is often too choppy to land boats on the beaches. An exception is **Playa Polo**, which is partly protected because waves break on rocks about 100 meters (320 feet) offshore. This means it's easier to go for a swim here, but it also means it's more likely to have visitors than some of the other beaches, and it's far too small to accommodate many people comfortably. There's a little house that sells cold beer here, but there are nicer beaches farther west.

If the sea is rough, the best way to get to the beaches is to walk across the western neck of the island from Bastimentos's only town, known alternately as **Old Bank** or (here we go again) Bastimentos. The town is poor but mellow, with tons of local color. Its inhabitants are primarily of West Indian descent. They'll likely be supremely indifferent to your presence. The town has little to offer visitors, and the trash strewn along the shore—not to mention the outhouses over the water—are a turnoff.

The trail to the beach starts toward the eastern edge of town, just past the soccer field. You'll have to walk through townspeople's yards to get to the trail; ask for directions to the "playa" (PLY-yah) if you can't find your way. It's a very pretty 20-minute walk over a hill to the beach. If the guy who built the trail is around he'll ask you to pay a $1 toll.

The first beach you come to is called, logically enough, **First Beach**, aka **Playa Wizard**. It's a wide, stunning stretch of sand and big rollers and, if you're lucky, very few people. Again, beware of the strong surf here. You can walk east to other beaches, but it's hard to see why you'd have to.

Actually, there's one other beach worth checking out, at least if you're into amphibians. **Red Frog Beach**'s namesake is a tiny creature *(Dendrobates pumilio)* that's easier to spot here than anywhere else in Panama. In reality it comes in a variety of vibrant colors besides red.

You can land on this beach only when the water is dead calm. Otherwise, your boatman will take you to nearby Playa Wizard and tell you to walk over, or drop you at a trail east of Old Bank which will take you over a narrow isthmus to Red Frog Beach. The last is the best option, as the trail is good and it's an easy 10-minute walk to the beach. There are lots of other frogs in the forest here. The noise they make is amazing; it's like a huge frog convention. You'll have to pay $1 a head at the end of the trail to get to the beach, as the access is across private land. (You can also rent rooms here.)

It can be hard to spot red frogs when the weather's dry. Look among the fallen leaves at the end of the trail near the beach. If a local is around, ask him or her for help in finding the *rana roja* (RAH-nah ROH-ha).

Details: Old Bank is about 10 minutes from Bocas town by water taxi. The fare is $2. Other Bastimentos destinations are usually included as part of a boat tour. See Guides and Outfitters, below.

Isla Carenero—This little island is just a banana's throw across the water from Bocas town. Because it's so close to the busy waterfront, and is pretty built up itself, it's not a popular tourist destination. But it's home to the archipelago's most upscale hotel, the Buccaneer

Resort, and one of its best restaurants, El Pargo Rojo. See the Food and Lodging sections below.

Details: The island is less than five minutes by water taxi from Bocas town. Water taxis stopping at Carenero leave frequently from the pier next to Restaurante Le Pirate, on Calle 3. Look for the sign that says Taxi Marítimo Galapagos Tours. The fare is 50 cents.

Isla Solarte (Nancy's Cay)—Solarte is a seven-kilometer-long (4.3-mile-long) island located two kilometers (1.2 miles) east of Isla Colón. Its western tip, **Hospital Point**, is one of the most popular diving and snorkeling spots in the archipelago. There are coral reefs just a few feet from the surface, but the sea floor also drops down surprisingly deep in places.

The point is named for the hospital the United Fruit Company built here in 1900 for its labor force, which was being decimated by malaria, yellow fever and other tropical diseases. The hospital closed in 1920 after a fungus known as Panama disease wiped out the banana plantations on the islands and surrounding shore, forcing the company to move its operations farther west.

The house on the point is the home of Clyde Stephens, who for 32 years was a banana researcher for United Fruit. He gives lectures on the history of the banana industry, and his books include a history of Hospital Point. You may be able to find copies at the Buena Vista Bar and Grill or Cocomo-on-the-Sea.

Details: Solarte is about 10 minutes by boat from Bocas town. A diving or snorkeling trip to Hospital Point is usually included as part of a tour of the islands. See Guides and Outfitters, below.

Parque Nacional Marino Isla Bastimentos—This 13,226-hectare (about 32,700 acres) park is shaped like a bridge and, as its name suggests, most of it is underwater. It starts among the mangrove islands on the southwest side of Bastimentos, arcs across its midsection, and curves down to two lovely little islands.

These islands, the **Cayos Zapatillas**, are the most visited parts of the park thanks to the good snorkeling and diving among the nearby coral reefs and underwater caves. Nurse sharks live in this area, as well as two different species of lobsters and the usual assortment of vibrant tropical fishes.

There is an interpretive trail called **El Bosque Detrás del Arrecife** ("the forest behind the reef") on the more easterly of the Zapatillas (farther away from Bastimentos). It starts behind the ranger station. ANAM has put out a glossy booklet, in Spanish only, that describes the trail. The ranger at Zapatillas may have copies, but don't count on it. Before you leave Bocas town ask for the booklet at the ANAM office or CEFATI. You can camp on either island. See Camping, below, for details.

Most visitors to Isla Bastimentos come only for the beach, but the inland forest is a natural treasure trove, which is why a big swath of it is included in the marine park. For one thing, it is home to 28 species of reptiles and amphibians, more than half of which are threatened or endangered. You have a good chance of spotting sloths, monkeys, and many species of birds in a trip through the forest, especially in the early morning. The **Laguna de Bastimentos**, near the north coast midway across the island, is home to freshwater turtles, caimans, and crocodiles. Do not attempt a hike through the forest without a guide; you will get lost. See Guides and Outfitters, below, for suggestions.

As mentioned above, **Playa Larga** is an important sea-turtle nesting area, attracting four species of endangered turtles from about April or May through September.

Details: Cayos Zapatillas is nearly an hour by fast boat from Bocas town. Since it's part of the marine park, you have to pay $10 a head to land on the islands or swim offshore. Be sure to ask your tour guide ahead of time if the price he quoted you includes this fee. The German family that owns Pension y Restaurante Bastimentos organizes nature tours of the interior of Bastimentos. The pension is in Old Bank (10 minutes from Bocas town; $2). For details see Guides and Outfitters, below, which also has information on sea-turtle tours.

GUIDES AND OUTFITTERS

Nearly all the guides and outfitters in the archipelago are located in Bocas town, and most of these are found along Calle 3.

There is no shortage of boatmen offering tours of the islands and snorkeling spots. Usually these are organized as day trips with fairly standardized itineraries. A popular tour takes you around Isla Colón to Swan Cay for bird-watching and snorkeling, stops for lunch at Boca del Drago, then lets you snorkel some more down the west side of Isla Colón. Other trips take you to Cayo Coral and Cayos Zapatillas, to the Bastimentos beaches, and so on. A few also offer a tour around the waters off Isla Cristobal, where's there a chance of seeing dolphins.

Tour prices depend on the number of people and the length of the trip, since the main cost is gasoline. Two tour operators, **Transparente Tours**, 507/757-9870 or cell 507/687-3913, and **J&J Boat Tours**, 507/757-9915 or 507/757-9565, jberg1301@cwp.net.pa, have booths next to each other beside Restaurante Le Pirate on Calle 3, making it easy to compare prices and maybe do some haggling. Expect to pay at least $15 per person for a group tour or $75 to $100 if you want the boat to yourself. J&J also offers a sunset rum cruise ($12) if it can rustle up at least nine people. You can also charter a 40-foot boat from them for sportfishing, sightseeing, or scuba diving for $375 per day.

If you're traveling alone or in a small group, you may be better off with one of the many freelance boatmen in the area. One popular character is **Gallardo Livingstone**, 507/757-9388, who charges a flat fee of $60 for a full-day trip. Livingstone is easygoing and professional, knows the islands well, and swears very colorfully in both English and Spanish. If you can't reach him by phone you can try tracking him down through Cocomo-on-the-Sea (see Lodging, below). His brother also does tours.

If you walk down Calle 3 toward the waterfront, you'll likely be approached by boatmen offering their services. Take a look at the boat before you seal the deal. Does it have lifejackets, appear to be in good condition, and have a decent motor? (Some guidelines on horsepower: 75 hp will move you as fast as you're likely to want to go in these little boats, while 15 hp will give you a slow-motion leisure cruise. Time estimates in this chapter are based on a boat equipped with a 75-hp motor.)

No matter who you go with, if you're planning to snorkel make sure decent masks, snorkels, and fins are included if you don't have your own.

Three outfits offer scuba-diving trips and courses. The highly regarded **Bocas Water Sports**, tel/fax 507/757-9541, grpiii@cwp .net.pa, was getting ready to move closer to "downtown" at the time of this writing, but it should still be located on Calle 3. A two-tank, two-site dive costs $50, including everything but lunch. The company also offers four-day dive certification courses for $190. They can arrange package deals with local hotels. You can rent single and double kayaks here for $20 and $25 all day, respectively, or go water-skiing for $40 an hour. **Starfleet Eco Adventures**, 507/757-9630, on Calle 1 next to the Buena Vista Bar & Grill, offers a two-tank, two-site dive for $40. You can take a three-day dive certification course for $195, which includes lunch every day. Starfleet is closed Sunday except by prior arrangement. **Turtle Divers**, 507/757-9594, on Calle 3 in the big wooden building that houses Restaurante Alberto, offers a two-tank, two-site dive including lunch for $45. Turtle Divers also works in conjunction with Mangrove Inn Eco-Resort to offer full packages including room and board. See Lodging, below.

Bocas Water Sports, Starfleet, and Turtle Divers also do all-day snorkeling trips for $15 a person.

Finca Verde

Ancon Expeditions and Finca Verde (see Lodging, below, for contact information) both offer their guests night tours to turtle nesting spots during nesting season, which runs from roughly April or May to September. If you aren't staying at Ancon's lodge or Finca Verde, Bocas Water Sports can make arrangements for an evening visit to Finca Verde.

Tom and Ina, the laid-back German couple that own **Pension y Restaurante Bastimentos** (see Lodging, below), offer nature tours of Isla Bastimentos. Tom is a landscape gardener and tree expert who is quietly passionate about this beautiful place. Another possibility is an unusual nature tour offered by **Bola**, one of the boatmen on Isla Colón. It begins at dawn with a trip upriver on Bastimentos and lasts until early evening. Those who've taken this tour tend to be very pleased with the range of wildlife they've seen. The Claassens at Cocomo-on-the-Sea can put you in touch with Bola (see Lodging, below).

There is some good **surfing** off the northern sides of Islas Bastimentos and Colón. The best sites are accessible only by boat. Since the surf here is quite rough, you should go only with someone who knows what he or she is doing. Unfortunately, no outfitter in Bocas rents surfboards. If you arrive in Bocas with a surfing jones but no board, you may be able to buy a used one from Bocas Water Sports. Ask Chip, one of the owners, to suggest good surf spots. The surfing is best from mid-December to April.

You can rent bikes for $10 for a full 24 hours from Heather at **La Veranda** (see the Lodging section for directions). **Restaurante La Ballena**, right next to Hotel Swan's Cay on the north side of Parque Bolivar, rents bikes for $2 an hour and horses for $5 an hour.

CAMPING

Finca Verde, cell 507/685-0252, Fincaverde@hotmail.com, offers an excellent camping deal. You can camp on the beach there for $3, a price that includes use of toilets, an outside shower, a shelter, and, if you time your visit right, a front-row view of nesting sea turtles. See the Lodging section for information on this nifty spot.

You can also camp in **Parque Nacional Marino Isla Bastimentos** for $5 per tent in addition to the $10-per-person park entrance fee.

You can pay for both at the ANAM office in Bocas town (see Visitor Information, above). If you want to camp on one of the Cayos Zapatillas, you can buy your permits from the ranger there. However, you may still want to check at the ANAM office about current camping conditions and restrictions before venturing out that far.

LODGING

Most of the hotels in the archipelago are in Bocas town, though there are a few on other parts of Isla Colón and on Solarte and Bastimentos. There's quite a variety of accommodations, ranging from simple but clean hostels that charge only a few dollars a night to fairly fancy rooms in modern hotels. The selections below tend to start at mid-range places. All have hot water unless otherwise indicated. There will likely be several more options by the time you read this.

Bocas Town

My favorite place in town is **Cocomo-on-the-Sea**, tel/fax 507/757-9259, a bed-and-breakfast on the water about a five-minute walk northwest of the town center. It offers four large, cheerful rooms in a wooden building designed with simple comfort in mind. The two rooms in front, Calypso and La Palma, have an ocean view, and all share a cozy veranda that juts out into the water. The breakfasts, served on another veranda next door, are delicious and change every day. The place is run by Claus and Dorothy Claassen, a Canadian couple who will make you feel very well taken care of. If you have trouble finding it, tell your taxi driver or passersby you're looking for "Claus." Rates are $40 to $45 per room, with a 10-percent discount after three days.

Ancon Expeditions, 507/757-9226 or 507/757-9850, jonboca @hotmail.com, has a lodge right behind the ANCON field office near the north end of Calle 3. You can also book the rooms through Ancon Expeditions in Panama City, 507/269-9414, 507/269-1915, fax 507/264-3713, info@anconexpeditions.com. The lodge is an attractive two-story wooden structure with a veranda/pier, though by the time you read this a second building set back from the water should be completed, adding 12 more rooms to the four already offered. Of the latter, two have private bathrooms and all are clean, newish, and have air-conditioning. From the model I saw, the addition should be quite pleasant. A package deal including room, three meals and a nature tour costs $66 per person per day, four-person minimum. The price may well go up when the new rooms are completed. If you just want a room the rates are $30 to $55.

Next door to the lodge is **Hotel Las Brisas**, 507/757-9248, a Bocas institution that is feeling the weight of its years. It offers 33 rooms of wildly different quality scattered among three buildings. The main building has a certain weathered charm, but it's a bit gloomy and the rooms have definitely seen better days. The seaside veranda is pleasant, though, with hammocks, wooden rocking chairs, and a breeze that lives up to the hotel's name. Rates are $13 to $25. The new two-story annex down the street has 10 modern, much nicer rooms with shared terraces for $34. Prices at this hotel are flexible.

Hotel Laguna, 507/757-9091, fax 507/757-9092, hlaguna@ chiriqui.com, on Calle 3 about a block south of the park, offers 16 modern, clean, and air-conditioned rooms. There's also a small bistro/cafe. The rooms vary quite a bit; look around before settling on one. Service here can be less than friendly. Rates run $40 for a small room to $70 for a suite with kitchenette. Prices go up $10 from about mid-December to April.

The **Hotel Swan's Cay**, 507/757-9316, 507/757-9090, tel/fax 507/757-9027, swanscayisla@cwp.net.pa, is sort of the Ritz of Bocas town. It's on Calle 3 in the middle of town, just north of Parque Bolívar. The whole place is thoroughly air-conditioned and features an elegant carpeted lobby with wood-paneled walls. Rooms are comfortable and modern, with TV, telephones, and Italian furniture, but the smaller ones are a bit cramped and the whole place is dark. There are 33 rooms in all, none with an ocean view. An annex and swimming pool were in the works at the time of writing. Some may find the hotel staid and the cushy surroundings out of synch with the bohemian ambiance of the rest of Bocas. Rates run $60 to $100.

La Veranda, tel/fax 507/757-9211, heathguidi@hotmail.com, explorepanama.com/veranda.htm, is a charming Caribbean-style wooden house with a wraparound veranda that gives the place its name. It's located at the edge of town on Calle H near the corner of Calle 8, about a block southwest of Cocomo-on-the-Sea. La Veranda is run by Heather, an eager-to-please Canadian who is prodding her place from a comfy and very pleasant backpacker's haven to a B&B. The place is spotless and has fans and mosquito nets. It doesn't have a sea view, but Heather offers tours to "secret" beaches. You can rent bikes here for $10 a day. Attention chocoholics: Heather runs an organic chocolate shop on the premises. Rates are $25 or $35 for a large double room with private bath and continental breakfast, $16 for a room with shared bathroom.

Along with Las Brisas, **Hotel Bahía**, 507/757-9626, is one of the grand old ladies of Bocas, with the accent on the "old." It's right across from the ferry landing at the south end of Calle 3. It was once the headquarters building for the United Fruit Company and certainly has character, but overall it's a dreary place. By the time you read this, however, the place may have been transformed. Three of the 16 rooms had been remodeled in quite good taste, with lovely wood paneling and furniture, and more were supposedly in the works. Bizarrely, though the hotel is only one block from the water, not a single room has an ocean view. Rates are $35 to $40 for a renovated room, $22 for an old one.

For about what you'd spend for a dreary old room at Bahía you can get a more cheerful new room at **Casa Max**, 507/757-9120, about a block west of the ANCON field office. The pension, which has a colorful facade that's hard to miss, is one of the higher-end backpacker places. It has four rooms, with six more on the way. Rates run $20 to $25.

Around Isla Colón

Finca Verde, cell 507/685-0252, Fincaverde@hotmail.com, is a great find for nature lovers who don't mind a remote location. It's located on the northeast side of Isla Colón, with a lovely beach in front and 30 hectares (74 acres) of forest behind. You can watch sea turtles nesting on the beach from March to July. The *finca* offers three large rooms with private bath in a charming wooden building. Electricity here is provided by solar power, and the bathrooms are cold-water only. Two more rooms were being planned at the time of writing.

There's also a bar/dining room on the premises. Several people who stayed here told me they were delighted with the place. However, one normally easygoing pair of visitors said they felt they were treated as less-than-welcome house guests throughout their stay.

The trade-off for having a great location is that the *finca* is a 25-minute drive from town on a dirt road. Unless you catch a ride with the *finca's* staff, round-trip from Bocas is a $12 taxi ride, $2 less if you go with a driver who's struck a deal with the *finca*. If the driver doesn't recognize "Finca Verde," ask him to take you to "Rebecca." This is also a terrific camping spot; see Camping, above. Rates are $40 for up to three people, including breakfast and access to horses, bikes, and snorkeling equipment.

About five minutes by boat from Bocas town, around the southern tip of the island, is the **Mangrove Inn Eco-Resort**, 507/757-9594, manginn@usa.net, bocas.com/mangrove.htm. The inn consists of a series of very basic wooden cabins built on stilts over the water and connected by boardwalks to an open-sided bar/restaurant, also on stilts. Because there are no guardrails, this is not a place for children. The cabins can accommodate from three to six people, have cold-water bathrooms, and feature balconies that look out on the ocean. The view is lovely: the water is like clear glass, and the place is located next to a series of coral reefs. This place is really geared for scuba divers who've arranged packages through Turtle Divers (see Guides and Outfitters, above) who are eager to be near the water and don't care much about their accommodations or being eaten alive by *chitras* (sand flies). Rates are $65 per person, including three meals, transportation from Bocas town, and a daily boat tour. Another $20 gets you the full diving package.

Isla Carenero

The **Buccaneer Resort**, tel/fax 507/757-9042, is on the east shore of Carenero, just a few minutes by boat from Bocas town. This is the archipelago's most upscale hotel. When finished, it will consist of 12 units spread among four cabañas and a pair of two-story buildings set on 10 acres of land. At the time of writing, only one of the larger buildings had been completed, with two units downstairs and two upstairs. The downstairs rooms have screened-in porches. Both upstairs rooms feature a lovely wraparound veranda and wet bars, refrigerators, toasters, and coffeepots. All the rooms are air-conditioned with modern furnishings and bathrooms. There's a tiny beach in front of the resort and a 2,100-meter-deep (6,900-foot) slice of forest behind it. A restaurant and bar were also on the way. The place is run by an American named Thomas Williams, known locally as "Captain Tom." Rates run $65 to $85.

Isla Bastimentos

There are seven pensions in the town of Old Bank. Unless you truly want to live like the locals, the only one you'll probably consider staying at is **Pension y Restaurante Bastimentos**, 507/757-9831, tomina@cwp.net.pa. It's also the only one over the water, near the middle of town. This place oozes rustic, piratical charm, but be advised that accommodations are basic and aimed at the backpacking set. Also, the town is dilapidated, with some trash on the shore and outhouses over the water. Pension Bastimentos has three double rooms with shared bath and a large room, the nicest, with a private bath. The pension and its inexpensive restaurant, which can do vegetarian food, are on a pier that attracts dozens of colorful fish. Shortly before I visited a couple of guests tied fishing lines to their toes at night, tossed the hooks out their window and fished while they slept. Fortunately for them, they didn't snag a barracuda. The place is also the home of the German owners and their teenage daughter. They can take you on nature tours of Bastimentos and boat trips to seven coral reefs within minutes of town. You can rent snorkel gear here for $5. Rates are $10 to $20.

El Limbo (no phone), is about midway between Cayo Coral and Punta Vieja on the east side of Isla Bastimentos. If the Swiss Family Robinson had built a hotel, it would have looked like this. It consists of an extraordinarily picturesque wooden building with four rustic but comfortable rooms, two with stunning ocean views. What makes this place special is that it's smack in the middle of paradise, built along a long, lovely beach with water so tranquil that radiant tropical fish swim right up to the shore. If you really want to get away from it all, this place is for you, but realize you'll be far away from civilization. The only soul as far as the eye could see when I visited

THE TURTLES OF BOCAS DEL TORO

Four species of endangered sea turtles find Bocas as attractive as the tourists do. These are the Pacific green (Chelonia mydas), the loggerhead (Caretta caretta), the hawksbill (Eretmochelys imbricata), and the leatherback (Dermochelys coriacea). They come to lay their eggs on the islands' northern beaches between March and September.

The turtles are officially protected, but they're still sought after for their meat and eggs. Obviously, you shouldn't partake of these yourself or buy anything made of tortoiseshell. But there are more subtle ways you may harm the turtles.

A night trip to the beach is a popular activity during nesting season (see Guides and Outfitters). The most accessible nesting sites are Playa Bluff on the northeast side of Isla Colón and Playa Larga on the north side of Isla Bastimentos. But if you go don't use flashlights, take flash photos, or even wear light-colored clothing. The baby turtles use the full moon to steer themselves into the sea, and artificial light can steer them into the forest, a likely fatal detour.

was Isaac, a self-possessed and friendly 13-year-old acting as manager in the absence of the Argentine owners. He's also your guide for hikes through the dense forest behind the hotel. Presumably, by the time you read this the owners will have figured out better communications between the hotel and Bocas town; when I visited, locals barely knew it existed. Rates are $35 per person. Meals can be arranged for about $10.

A new hotel, featuring well-crafted thatch-roofed cabins set among trees, was under construction farther up the coast at the time of writing.

FOOD

Bocas del Toro offers quite a range of cuisine, considering its size and location.

Las Palmitas, 507/685-1943, is my favorite place to eat in Bocas, but it's often overlooked by visitors since it's tucked away on a side street. Walk all the way south on Calle 3, then turn right at the ferry dock and head up Avenida Sur, a waterfront street, for a couple of blocks. This is a romantic, boho place specializing in Thai dishes (!) and seafood. It's an open-sided wooden place on stilts with a thatched roof and an uneven plank floor that'll make you think you've had even more Italian wine than you have. The most expensive item on the menu is lobster, at $10. Most other dishes are $6 to $8. Try the Thai seafood soup—it's delicious. Between courses you can peer over the railing and watch squid hunt for small fry. The restaurant opens at 4 p.m. every day.

On the north side of the park right next to Hotel Swan's Cay is **La Ballena**, a simple street-side restaurant that serves pretty good pasta. Portions are huge and most dishes are $8 to $10.

The dining room at Swan's Cay is called **Restaurante Alexander**, 507/757-9090, where you can dine in air-conditioned, tableclothed comfort. The cuisine here is Italian, with prices hovering around $10.

Restaurante Alberto, 507/757-9066, is on the second story of the old wooden building just south of park (the Turtle Divers office is on the first floor). It's a pizzeria that serves tasty thin-crust pizzas for about $5. You can sit on the balcony and check out the scene on Calle 3.

The **Buena Vista Bar and Grill**, 507/757-9035, is *the* gringo hangout in Bocas. It serves basic American comfort food, from burgers and hotdogs to brownies and cheesecake. Other offerings include sandwiches (the Jamaican jerked chicken is good), dinner salads and—wonder of wonders—veggie food. Margaritas are a house specialty, but the one I tried wasn't very good. They'll pack a lunch in a cooler for you to take on boat excursions. Please order it the night before you need it. Be warned: The satellite TV is always tuned to a game and, since the couple that runs the place is from San Francisco, emotions run high when the 49ers are playing. The place is closed Tuesdays.

Heike, 507/757-9708, on the west side of Calle 3 near the park, is a cozy little bistro with an equally small but popular menu. Nothing here is over $6. The place is named for the overworked German owner who runs the place with her overworked Panamanian husband. They also rent inexpensive rooms here.

Le Pirate, 507/757-9870, a bar/restaurant on the water next to several boat-tour operators, has enjoyed a good reputation, but I find its offerings so-so. It's in a colorful location, though, and it offers an "executive lunch" for about $4 from 11 a.m. to 4 p.m. Most dinner items are $8.

A popular hangout with locals is **Don Chicho** (officially named El Lorito, but no one calls it that), 507/757-9288. It doesn't have much atmosphere, but it offers cheap local food.

The **Loop** is a fun pool hall/bar two doors down from Hotel Laguna. It doesn't serve food, but it's a laid-back place to have a drink and people-watch.

There are two restaurants right across the channel from Bocas on little Carenero Island. The more colorful one is **El Pargo Rojo**, 507/757-9649 or cell 507/685-2948, which is well worth a visit. They'll send a boat to pick you up if you call ahead of time. The owner, Bernard, is also the cook, and he's a good one. The lobster is excellent, and this is surely the only place within hundreds of miles where you might find homemade pate. Other offerings include sushi, kebabs, and tandoori chicken. Except for the lobster ($10), nothing is more than $7. Bernard is an Iranian who moved to Maryland after the revolution. The bandana he wears gives him the air of a pirate, as do the tales of his many exploits. He also rents rustic cabins for $20 to $30.

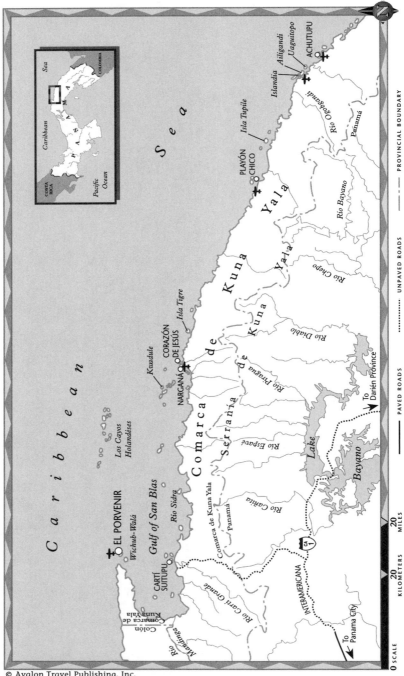

CHAPTER 11

San Blas Islands
(Comarca de Kuna Yala)

Welcome to paradise. Cartoonists who love to picture tropical islands as dots of soft sand with a few coconut palms could have gotten the idea from the San Blas Islands. That image fits countless idyllic spots in this archipelago of nearly 400 islands off the eastern Caribbean coast of Panama. When the sun hits the sea here you'll think of emeralds and sapphires.

The islands are part of the Comarca de Kuna Yala, the semi-autonomous homeland of the Kuna people. Their land also encompasses a mountainous strip of mostly virgin forest on the mainland that runs the length of the archipelago, ending at the Colombian border. It, too, is well worth a visit; see Lay of the Land, below.

But most visitors, like the Kuna themselves, prefer to hang out on the islands. Nearly all the estimated 40,000 Kuna who live in the *comarca* (district) inhabit just 40 of the islands, none of which are very large. As you might imagine, things can get pretty crowded: on many islands, the thatch roofs of the Kunas' bamboo huts almost touch, making walking around a bit of a challenge. You'll probably spend as much of your time as possible on the uninhabited islands, but make time to visit a village. The chance to meet the Kuna, who have one of the most vibrant indigenous cultures in Latin America, is reason enough to visit the San Blas Islands.

MOLAS

Molas *are made from several layers of brightly colored cotton cloth. Kuna women create these works of art using a technique of cutting and sewing sometimes referred to as reverse appliqué. The way the cloth is cut reveals the layers beneath, which all go into creating the overall design. Designs can be abstract or representational.*

What should you look for in a mola? Anthropologist Mari Lyn Salvador conducted a study in which she asked Kuna women themselves that question. A few of her findings:

1. *The design should be balanced and all the spaces filled.*
2. *The lines should be thin and evenly spaced, with smooth edges.*
3. *Stitches should be small, even, and nearly invisible.*
4. *The design should stand out and be easy to see, which is largely a matter of the proper use of contrast and color.*

For more information on Kuna arts and culture, see The Art of Being Kuna: Layers of Meaning Among the Kuna of Panama *(UCLA Fowler Museum of Cultural History), edited by Mari Lyn Salvador.*

A word of warning: If you're looking for Club Med, Kuna Yala is not for you. Even the most "exclusive" accommodations are quite simple, and there's little to do on the islands except swim, snorkel, laze in hammocks, and visit villages. The food is generally bland and basic.

More disturbing, any lingering romantic notions you have about indigenous people's harmonious relationship with nature will get a jolt when you discover how severely the Kuna are overfishing their waters, or see the garbage and sewage they routinely dump into pristine blue waters. (But be sure to take a close look at that garbage, which washes up even on remote islands. Much of it— plastic sunscreen bottles, hair-spray canisters—was not generated by the Kuna, but by folks not unlike you and me.)

On the other hand, there are still plenty of lovely, uninhabited islands in the archipelago, more than you could possibly visit. A big part of the charm of these islands is their very simplicity: you won't find any time-share condos or tacky T-shirt shops here. Nodding off in a hammock slung between coconut palms, watching a Kuna woman sewing a *mola*, and showering by the light of a kerosene lantern can soon seem like a pretty good way to spend a day.

LAY OF THE LAND

The Comarca de Kuna Yala consists of a strip of mountainous coast and a nearby archipelago that stretch 226 kilometers (140 miles) down the eastern Caribbean side of the isthmus to the Colombian border. Nearly all the islands are within five kilometers (3.1 miles) of the mainland. Only a handful of the inhabited ones have much in the way of visitor facilities. Few tourists visit the coast, which is home primarily to Kuna farms and dense tropical forest.

The islands most popular with and accessible to visitors are listed below, organized in four clusters where you'll find visitor accommodations, followed by a description of the most popular of the sparsely inhabited outer cays.

It's possible to visit more than one of these clusters during your visit. However, distances are great enough to make a day trip from one group to another impractical or impossible by motorized *cayuco*, the chief means of transportation for tourists. (*Cayucos*, properly speaking, are dugout canoes, but the term is also used to refer to long, narrow handmade boats.) Unless you have access to a bigger boat, you're probably better off choosing just one area to explore. If your schedule allows, you can also fly to a second area and spend one or more nights there, but that will increase your logistical hassles significantly.

Nusagandi is a 60,000-hectare (230-square-mile)primary-forest reserve owned and run by the Kuna on the mainland. Its headquar-

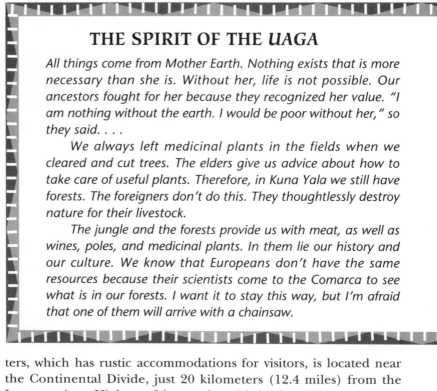

THE SPIRIT OF THE *UAGA*

All things come from Mother Earth. Nothing exists that is more necessary than she is. Without her, life is not possible. Our ancestors fought for her because they recognized her value. "I am nothing without the earth. I would be poor without her," so they said. . . .

We always left medicinal plants in the fields when we cleared and cut trees. The elders give us advice about how to take care of useful plants. Therefore, in Kuna Yala we still have forests. The foreigners don't do this. They thoughtlessly destroy nature for their livestock.

The jungle and the forests provide us with meat, as well as wines, poles, and medicinal plants. In them lie our history and our culture. We know that Europeans don't have the same resources because their scientists come to the Comarca to see what is in our forests. I want it to stay this way, but I'm afraid that one of them will arrive with a chainsaw.

ters, which has rustic accommodations for visitors, is located near the Continental Divide, just 20 kilometers (12.4 miles) from the Interamerican Highway. It's popular with birders. This is the best place in Panama to see the speckled antshrike, black-headed antthrush, and black-crowned antpitta. It's nearly impossible to get to Nusagandi from the islands. Most people drive to the reserve from Panama City, and even that's pretty tough. At the time of this writing, it was unclear if the Kung would continue to welcome visitors to Nusagandi. Contact Ancon Expeditions for current conditions. See Appendix B.

NATURE AND ADVENTURE ACTIVITIES

Snorkeling, swimming, and visiting Kuna villages are just about the only things to do on the islands. Depending on where you stay, your

> The lobster traders are responsible for the deterioration of our main resources—only for the money. Even if we want to control the fishing of lobsters, we won't succeed, because the young people who are involved in this activity are making their living from it.
>
> Our tradition of working together no longer exists. Once, when a decision was made to address a problem, everyone complied unanimously. Now they follow money. We are acquiring the spirit of the uaga (foreigner, outsider).
>
> Once everything is evaluated in terms of money, it changes one's way of being, it makes one selfish. So said our forefathers. Thus we are beginning to deceive our forefathers. That's what I think.
>
> —Cacique General (Head Chief) Carlos López, quoted in *Plants and Animals in the Life of the Kuna,* (University of Texas Press), by Jorge Ventocilla, Heraclio Herrera, and Valerio Núñez.

hotel may be able to arrange a tour of the rain forest near the coast for an extra fee. Transportation within the *comarca* is mainly by motorized *cayuco*. Don't expect to see a life jacket. The seas can get choppy, especially in the dry season. If you're planning to travel long distances by boat consider bringing a life jacket with you.

Diving visibility in these crystalline waters can be better than 30 meters (about 100 feet) on a good day. The best diving and snorkeling are found among the sparsely inhabited outer cays at the western end of the archipelago, where the coral is extensive and indescribably beautiful. The most popular of these are the Cayos Holandéses.

Unfortunately, the Kunas have banned nearly all dive operators from the *comarca*. (See Guides and Outfitters, below, for an exception.) Private individuals who bring their own scuba-diving equipment are still tolerated, especially if they hire local boatmen to take them around. But you should think twice about diving here unless you're traveling with an experienced diver who knows the waters well. The snorkeling, however, can be great. The hotels typically have equipment you can rent or borrow, but it's usually not in good shape. You're better off bringing your own.

THE KUNA PEOPLE

No one knows for sure where the Kuna came from. Some evidence, and Kuna lore, suggests they immigrated to their current home from the Darién several hundred years ago, forced out by other indigenous peoples.

They first settled along the rivers on the mainland, where there are still Kuna living today. Though must Kuna now live on the islands, even they travel by *cayuco* to the mainland to farm and hunt.

The Kuna have done a remarkable job over the centuries of keeping invaders out and holding onto their rich culture. They even fought and won a revolt against the Republic of Panama in 1925, which eventually won them their semi-autonomous status. Today, no foreigner is allowed to own land in the *comarca*.

At the same time, Kunas have gained a greater voice in Panamanian society in recent years. In 1999 a Kuna, Enrique Garrido, became the head of Panama's general assembly.

Visitors are inevitably struck by the beautiful traditional dress of the Kuna women, which is not worn to impress tourists. The Kuna themselves cite the preservation of women's traditional clothing and ornamentation as vital to maintaining their culture.

The most famous part of this dress are the panels of intricately worked cloth that decorate the front and back of the woman's blouse. Known as *molas* ("*mola*" is Kuna for blouse), these panels are prized by collectors around the world (see the *Molas* sidebar). Older women in particular also wear gold rings through the bottom of their nose and tight strings of beads around their forearms and lower legs.

The Kuna are physically striking in other ways as well. For one thing, they are short by European standards, growing to about 150 centimeters (five feet). That doesn't stop basketball from being the most popular sport on the islands. They also have the highest rate of albinism in the world. Known as "moon children," albinos are treated with great respect.

The Kuna have always been wary of outsiders, and that's a major reason they still exist. You can have a relatively inexpensive stay in the San Blas Islands, but don't expect to get anything for free; even taking a photo of a Kuna will usually cost you a dollar.

The Kunas' reticence, and a belief that visitors should pay for the privilege of visiting their homeland, can be off-putting to those who come with stereotyped notions of fun-loving, generous Indians. It's not hard to see the Kunas' point of view, though. Outsiders have been trying to take their home away from them for centuries, and even visitors with more benign intentions often treat them as colorful parts of the scenery. One Kuna official I chatted with on my first visit angrily recounted instances in which he felt Kunas were treated, at best, as so much travel-brochure fodder, concluding: "*No somos animales*" ("We are not animals").

Try to bear that in mind during your stay. At the very least, never take a photo of a Kuna without asking permission first. You'll probably find that if you're willing to accept the Kuna on their own terms, you'll get a glimpse of a fascinating world.

FLORA AND FAUNA

The spectacularly clear water around the islands makes the *comarca*'s underwater flora and fauna the big draw for most visitors. For starters, consider the coral reefs that can make navigating these waters so treacherous: according to the Smithsonian Institution, which until recently had a research facility on the islands, Kuna Yala has more coral species than just about anywhere else in the Caribbean. The coral gardens are magnificent. It's easy to spot colorful staghorn, brain, fan, and leaf coral, among many others. Nearly 60 species of marine sponges grow on the western side of the *comarca.*

Sadly, overfishing has decimated marine life. Five types of lobster are found here, but they are in danger of local extinction because Kuna divers catch them to sell to outside commercial interests. The same thing is happening with other marine creatures, including sea turtles and, beginning in the early 1990s, even small tropical fish, which are ending up in household aquariums in the United States. Marine life in the region, while still impressive, is not what it was even a decade ago.

About 90 percent of the *comarca*'s territory on the mainland is still covered with forest. Though these forests are under pressure, animals still found in them include the collared and white-lipped peccary, Baird's tapir, red brocket (a kind of deer), and iguana.

VISITOR INFORMATION

The archipelago's simple hotels typically offer packages that include all meals and daily boat trips to snorkel or visit a Kuna village. Some hotels allow you to opt out of the full package and fend for yourself for meals and transport: the Hotel San Blas, for instance, charges $35 per person for a full package, but the room alone is just $7 each. However, unless you have your own boat you'll probably find it cheaper, and certainly simpler, to go with a package deal.

Note that the life span of hotels is particularly unpredictable in Kuna Yala. It sometimes seems the more successful the hotel, the better its chances of being shut down. It's one of those things that makes Kuna society such a mystery to outsiders. Both the Hotel Anai on Wichub-Wala and the Hotel Iskardup on Iskardup recently closed, though as this book went to press it looked likely the Anai would reopen. Hotel Iskardup was open so briefly and closed so quickly that ads and articles about it were still running after it shut down. Make sure your hotel of choice still exists before making too many plans.

You'll be extremely tempted to take photos of the Kunas, particularly the colorfully dressed women. But always ask first, and expect to be charged $1 for the privilege. If the Kuna are going to be treated as curiosities, they figure the least you can do is compensate them for it. Be sure to bring small bills with you, which you'll also need to buy souvenirs. (See the sidebar on *Molas*.) You may feel more comfortable taking a photo of a Kuna woman you've just bought something from, and she may not even charge you in that case. You won't be charged for photos of village scenes that don't focus on an individual. Even with the hassle, the San Blas Islands are so photogenic you'll probably burn through a lot of film. Take more than you expect to use.

Bring enough traveler's checks and/or cash to cover any expenses you expect to incur on the islands. There's a branch of the Banco Nacional de Panama on Narganá. It's open from 8 a.m. to 2 p.m. weekdays, 9 a.m. to noon on Saturday. It doesn't have an ATM, but you can cash traveler's checks.

Telephone booths that accept Cable & Wireless calling cards are popping up on the inhabited islands. But you should expect to be more or less cut off from the rest of the world during your stay.

GETTING THERE

Unless you're a glutton for punishment and have access to a great four-wheel-drive vehicle with a winch, you can't get to the San Blas Islands by land. There is a road of sorts that leads from El Llano, on the Interamerican Highway, over the mountains to the west end of the *comarca*. But for most of the way it's little more than a brutally rugged trail, though there's talk of one day improving it. It's sometimes impassable with any vehicle.

The best way to explore the beauty of the islands is by yacht. The second best way is by small, adventure-type cruise ship. See Appendix B for information on the latter.

Several of the huge cruise ships that transit the Panama Canal also stop in the islands. Tourists can outnumber Kunas during these brief visits, which are hardly the ideal way to experience the islands or Kuna culture.

Most visitors who want to stay on the islands come by small plane from Panama City. Flying on these tiny, sometimes aged-looking contraptions can be an adventure in itself, especially while crossing the coastal range. But on a clear day the views are breathtaking, and the flights are mercifully short—usually less than an hour.

Three airlines fly from Panama City to islands and coastal airstrips in the *comarca*. The planes make several stops, so make sure you're in the right place before getting off. If you're staying in one of the archipelago's hotels, transportation by boat between the hotel and the closest airstrip is included with your stay.

Aereo Taxi and ANSA, both subsidiaries of Aeroperlas (507/315-0275, iflyap@aeroperlas.com, www.aeroperlas.com for either), and Aviatur, 507/315-0307, fax 507/315-0316, serve all the airstrips in the *comarca* Monday through Saturday. They run a truncated schedule to the major islands on Sunday.

Airfare is the same on all airlines and is quite reasonable. The most expensive flight, at $88 round-trip, is to Puerto Obaldía, near the Colombian border. You'd go there only if you were on your way to Colombia. (*Note:* At the time of writing, the conflict in Colombia had made Puerto Obaldía a dangerous place, and visitors were being advised to stay well away from it.) Shorter flights cost proportionately less. Roundtrip fare is $55 to El Porvenir or Río Sidra, $56 to Corazón de Jesús/Narganá, and $62 to Achutupu. The one-way fare to all destinations is half the round-trip fare.

NATURE AND ADVENTURE SIGHTS

The four main areas frequented by visitors are listed below, starting with the western islands and heading southeast down the archipelago. The most famous of the lovely outer islands are described at the end of the chapter.

Around El Porvenir—The small island of El Porvenir is the western point of entry for the San Blas Islands. It has little on it besides a landing strip, a couple of government offices, and a somewhat run-down hotel (see Lodging). But because it's isolated from the densely populated islands nearby, its little beach is clean and pleasant. For most people, though, this island is just a transit point.

Clustered just to the south of El Porvenir are **Wichub-Wala, Ukuptupu,** and **Nalunega.** Wichub-Wala and Nalunega both have villages. Ukuptupu is entirely covered with a sprawling wooden complex connected by boardwalks. It was the home of a Smithsonian research facility for 21 years. The Kuna, ever suspicious of foreigners in their *comarca*, finally kicked the Smithsonian out of Kuna Yala in 1998. The research facility is now a rustic hotel. All three islands are just a couple of minutes from each other by motorized *cayuco*. Nalunega is most popular with visitors because it's home to the Hotel San Blas (see Lodging, below). The villages on it and Wichub-

William Friar

Church on Nalunega

Wala make the islands worth a visit if you're staying in this area, but they're too polluted to make swimming inviting.

The idyllic uninhabited and semi-inhabited islands in this part of the archipelago are all east or northeast of this busy hub.

The most popular with visitors is **Achutupu**, also known as Isla de Los Perros (Dog Island). It's a private island with just one small family living on it. (*Note:* Don't confuse this Achutupu with the large, crowded island of the same name much farther east.) Everything about this pristine speck of sand and palm trees is straight out of a postcard. The water is calm and crystalline, with great snorkeling visibility. And the snorkeling here is fun: there's an old shipwreck in shallow water just off the south side of the island. It's overgrown with brilliant coral and has become a playground for a variety of small and medium-sized tropical fish.

Achutupu is surrounded by other lovely islands, and you can often see rustic Kuna sailboats and the occasional sleek foreign yacht gliding around them. If Achutupu isn't perfect enough for you, you can ask your boatman to do some more exploring. You'll have to resist the urge to use up your entire stock of film here.

South of the Porvenir area, just off the coast, is **Cartí Suitupu** (aka Gardi Sugdup), one of a cluster of islands and a bit of coast known collectively as Cartí (aka Gardi). There's a large, vibrant village on the island, which makes this a popular cruise-ship destination. Especially noteworthy is a small museum housed in a thatch-roofed hut. The displays are modest—mostly a few crude posters and a variety of artifacts—but it'll give you a glimpse into the mythology, history, rituals, and daily life of the Kuna. A Kuna man named José Davis, who established the museum along with his father, gives guided tours of the exhibits in English and Spanish. One of the more interesting tidbits you'll pick up is a description of Kuna burials. (The cemeteries are on the mainland, where the Kunas dig underground rooms and string them with hammocks into which the deceased are placed.) You can also visit the other islands in the group.

Details: The flight to El Porvenir is $27 one-way, $55 round-trip. Achutupu and Cartí Suitupu are a short ride by motorized cayuco *from the Porvenir area, so the hotels there include day trips to both as part of their standard packages. There is a $1 per head fee to visit Achutupu, payable to the owner on the island. Admission to the museum on Cartí Suitupu is $1.*

Around Río Sidra—Río Sidra is a densely packed traditional island that doesn't get that many visitors. Its next-door neighbor, Nusatupo, is similar. Most visitors who do come here are on their way to Kuanidup, a gorgeous island a half-hour away by motorized *cayuco*. Actually, there are two Kuanidups. The first is Kuanidup Grande, which is home just to Cabañas Kuanidup (see Lodging), a sandy beach, and hammocks strung between coconut palms. It's "grande" only in comparison to its little sister, Kuanidup Chico, about 300 meters (a bit over 300 yards) away. There's nothing but a single hut, sand, and palm trees on Kuanidup Chico, which is an easy swim away for a moderately fit swimmer. The hotel staff on Kuanidup Grande can also ferry you over if you're staying there.

Details: Río Sidra is about an hour from the Porvenir area by motorized cayuco, *but few people go all that way just for a day trip. Most tourists fly into Río Sidra and stay at Kuanidup, a half-hour away by motorized* cayuco. *The airfare is $27 one-way, $55 round-trip.*

Around Corazón de Jesús and Narganá—Another hub of island life lies about 40 kilometers (25 miles) east of El Porvenir, centered around the inhabited islands of Corazón de Jesús and Narganá. These relatively developed islands—you'll see more concrete buildings than thatch-roofed huts—are linked by a foot bridge. The only things likely to be of interest to visitors are the Banco Nacional de Panama office on Narganá and the airstrip on Corazón de Jesús. Narganá is the more southerly island, closer to the mainland.

Kwadule, a few minutes by motorized *cayuco* from Narganá and Corazón de Jesús, is a tiny private island that is home to the Kwadule Eco-Lodge, the fanciest hotel in the archipelago. "Fancy" is a relative term in Kuna Yala, but this is a place to indulge your deserted-tropical-island fantasies in comfortable surroundings. See Lodging, below, for details. The hotel is the only thing on the island, and you have to be a guest to visit it. **Isla Tigre**, also called Río Tigre, is a few kilometers east of the islands mentioned above. A visit to the traditional Kuna community here is a common tourist destination.

Kwadule Eco-Lodge

Details: It takes about 2.5 hours by motorized cayuco to reach these islands from El Porvenir. Unless you've got a yacht, it's much more practical to come here by plane and spend at least a night or two. The only place you'll probably want to stay is the Kwadule Eco-Lodge (see Lodging, below). Airfare to the Corazón de Jesús airstrip is $28 one-way, $56 round-trip.

Around Achutupu—Don't confuse this Achutupu with the little private island described above. This is a densely populated island quite a bit farther east and south down the archipelago, less than 100 kilometers (about 60 miles) from the Colombian border. It's an interesting place to visit, although as with the other inhabited islands you should be considerate about where you poke your nose and always ask permission before snapping a photo. In the middle of the island is a very large gathering house. These long thatch-roofed buildings are the center of community life in Kuna villages. If you're lucky, a puberty ceremony or community meeting will be taking place on the island during your stay. If you're very lucky, you'll be allowed to observe some of it.

Immediately to the east of Achutupu, about a minute away by boat, is **Uaguitupo**, also known as Dolphin Island. About half the island is taken up by Kuna huts, while the other half is home to Dolphin Island Lodge (see Lodging, below). This part of the island is pretty and offers tranquil views. However, it doesn't offer much in the way of a beach. This is primarily a place to collapse in a hammock for hours on end, and for that it's just about perfect.

About 20 minutes north of these islands are a series of **coral reefs**. If the sea is calm and the visibility good, the snorkeling here is okay. Sadly, though, intensive fishing in the area makes it unlikely you'll see much besides tiny fish. The highlight of my snorkeling trip was watching a school of squid squirt by.

If you stay at the Dolphin Island Lodge—and there's probably nowhere else here you'd want to stay—you'll be offered a trip to the peculiarly named **Islandia.** (That's right: Iceland. Go figure.) This is a microscopic uninhabited island with a thin strip of beach. You'd have more of a sense of getting away from it all if beer cans, plastic bags, and other garbage from the inhabited islands didn't wash up on the shore. Still, it's worth a visit if only for the scenic boat ride,

*Day trips to uninhabited islands are part of standard
hotel packages in the San Blas Islands.*

which gives you good views of the islands, both uninhabited and
packed with huts. There's a good chance of passing a Kuna sailboat
gliding by, with the deep forests of the coastal mountain range as
backdrop. The major inhabited island of **Ailigandi** is a short distance west of Islandia, closer in to the mainland. Your boatman may
take you there if you're curious to check it out.

Potential visitors should note that it's harder in this part of the
archipelago to get completely away from the inevitable garbage and
sewage that plague the islands.

*Details: This section of the archipelago is quite a hike from the other
touristed spots. It's much too far to take a motorized cayuco from any of the
areas described above. Unless you're coming by yacht plan to spend at least
one night here. Airfare to Achutupu is $31 one-way, $62 round-trip.*

Los Cayos Holandéses—These are the best-known of the many gorgeous uninhabited and lightly populated islands toward the western
end of the archipelago. They are 15 kilometers (about nine miles)

277

from the mainland, farther offshore than any others in the archipelago. Yachts like to hang out here, as do snorkelers and (when tolerated) scuba divers. The coral gardens are spectacular, and there are
shipwrecks to explore as well. Unfortunately, the Cayos Holandéses
are not that accessible from the islands with visitor accommodations—there are no cabañas on these remote cays.

You can reach the Cayos Holandéses by motorized *cayuco* from
the Porvenir, Río Sidra, and Corazón de Jesús/Narganá areas (the
Achutupu area is too far away), but it's quite a haul on open sea.
None of the hotels offer a visit as part of their standard package, but
they can arrange a motorized *cayuco* snorkeling trip for you. I
strongly advise you to bring along some kind of life vest if you want
to make the trek. You may be content with exploring islands closer
to where you're staying.

*Details: The cost of a boat trip to the Cayos Holandéses, and the time it
takes, obviously depend on where you're coming from and how many islands
you want to explore. From Kuanidup, for instance, the trip takes at least two
hours each way and will cost $60 just for gas, plus a bit more for the boat-*

Dolphin spotting

278

man's time. It's a safe bet, however, that most boatmen will charge you much less than what Kwadule Eco-Lodge asks for a trip to the Holandéses from the island of Kwadule: a whopping $200 for a large, fast boat.

GUIDES AND OUTFITTERS

There are no formal tour operators on the islands. Visitors usually arrange tours and boat trips through their hotels, which offer a daily excursion as part of their standard packages. You can also hire Kuna boatmen and guides, but almost none of them speak English and some don't even speak much Spanish. Agree on a price and itinerary ahead of time.

You may find it simpler to arrange a trip to the islands through a tour operator in Panama City, who will book the flights and room and make sure a boatman's there to meet the plane. See Appendix B for tour operator suggestions.

As this was written, only one dive operator was offering trips to the San Blas Islands: **Nautilus**, cell 507/613-6557, 507/263-5742, fax 507/263-5892, kbmrossa@sinfo.net. The company is based in Portobelo (see Chapter 9, The Central Caribbean, for details). Two-night, four-dive packages cost $125 to $225 per person. The price depends on whether you want to camp or stay at the Hotel San Blas and whether you fly or come over by boat with Javier's crew. Be advised that the boat trip from Portobelo takes about 2.5 hours on seas that can get quite choppy. If you camp, you'll probably spend the night on Achutupu (the gorgeous island near Porvenir, not the one farther down the archipelago). It's hard to imagine a more idyllic spot. Diving is around the Cayos Holandéses and other sites near Porvenir. Nautilus brings the food over from Portobelo, sparing you from the usual meager fare on the islands.

CAMPING

Camping on the islands is not generally a good idea unless you're with an organized group. There are no developed campgrounds, so your only real option is pitching a tent or slinging a hammock on a deserted island. That may sound appealing, but smugglers, including drug traffickers, have been known to run these waters. You really wouldn't want them accidentally to stumble upon you in the middle of the night. There has also been some concern that Colombian guerrilla activity may be spilling into the *comarca*. Just to be on the safe side, it's probably a good idea to be under a Kuna roof close to a population center during your visit if you're traveling alone or in a small group.

LODGING

Most of the phone numbers listed below are in Panama City, where nearly all the hotels have offices. When you make a reservation, the staff will also arrange for a boat to pick you up from the nearest airstrip. All the hotels offer packages that include room, meals, pickup and drop-off at the airstrip, and a daily boat tour. Some will also make plane reservations for you. Remember that accommodations on the islands range from fairly rustic to very rustic.

Around El Porvenir

The **Hotel San Blas**, 507/262-5410, is the old stalwart among the archipelago's hotels. It consists of 28 bamboo-walled, thatch-roofed rooms on the southern side of Nalunega. There are two kinds of accommodations here. The huts right on the beach have sand floors and offer slightly more privacy, as they are a few inches away from their neighbors. If a breeze is more important than privacy, for the same price you can get a room on the second floor of a larger building behind the huts. Be warned, though, that this is essentially a dormitory with bamboo dividers that don't reach all the way to the very tall thatch roof. If anyone up there snores, you'll soon find out about it. Also, there's not much of a view from the rooms even though you're only a few steps from the beach. The hotel is owned by Luis Burgos, a laid-back Kuna who speaks English and Spanish, but it's essentially run by a tough albino Kuna woman named Griselda, who is actually quite warm once you get past her brusque persona.

Fishing nets drying off densely populated Achutupu Island

The rest of the island is taken up by a village with about 450 inhabitants. One of the charms of this place is living in such close proximity to the Kuna. You're free to wander around the village, but there's enough of an invisible divide between the hotel and the rest of the island to ensure both the Kuna and guests a certain degree of privacy from each other. As with other Kuna villages, this one is none too clean, but the hotel staff rakes the sand around the hotel every day, ensuring that its little patch is tidy. Still, the outhouses over the water on either side of the hotel's small beach should be a tip-off that this isn't a good place to go for a swim (the hotel's own bathrooms are shared and rustic but have plumbing).

You can rent snorkeling equipment here for $6. But you may find yourself more drawn to the hotel's most popular activity: snoozing in shaded hammocks right at the edge of the lapping sea. This is a very relaxing place. You should know, however, that the hotel sometimes has rats. I've never heard of anyone being bitten, but the rustling critters have been known to upset a good night's sleep. Rates are $35 per person, including all meals and a daily boat trip.

Cabañas Ukuptupu, 507/220-4781 or 507/299-9011, is the only thing on the rocky island of Ukuptupu, nestled between Wichub-Wala and Nalunega. The hotel consists of 15 basic but spacious bamboo-and-wood rooms over shallow water, connected to each other by boardwalks. Because it's very easy to walk off the board-walks into the ocean, this is not a place to bring small children. The hotel completely covers this tiny island, so it's more private than the Hotel San Blas. You also miss out on the pros and cons of sharing an island with a Kuna village. As with the Hotel San Blas, bathrooms are shared but have plumbing. The hotel has good views of the ocean and the surrounding inhabited islands. You can rent snorkel-ing equipment for $4 a day. An underwater rock corral houses the lobsters, crab, and other sea creatures you may be offered for din-ner. English is spoken. Rates are $40 per person, including all meals and a daily boat trip.

If both the above are full, the **Hotel Porvenir**, 507/229-9000 or 507/299-9056, on El Porvenir may have to do. Rooms here are drab and run-down, and have zero charm. The staff is friendly, though. As the name suggests, the hotel is located on the island of El Porvenir, which is also home to the area's airstrip and some small government offices. There's nothing else on the island, which means you'll have plenty of peace and quiet—at least until an air-plane lands, since the hotel is almost on the airstrip. The little beach here is pleasant, and the water seems much cleaner than that surrounding the crowded islands nearby. But you'll likely feel quite isolated. Rates are $30 per person, including all meals and a daily boat trip.

Around Narganá/Corazón de Jesús

The **Kwadule Eco-Lodge** on Kwadule Island is pricey, but it com-bines the rustic charm found elsewhere in the archipelago with comfort and cleanliness that's harder to come by. When you fanta-size about a simple tropical island, this is the kind of place you prob-ably picture. Rooms consist of six (you guessed it) thatch-roofed, bamboo-walled huts in a row along the southern side of the island. The difference with these huts is they are built on stilts right over the water—you can see blue sea through the floorboards—and have ceiling fans, electricity, balconies, and private bathrooms. They're spaced just far enough apart from each other to offer a modicum of privacy. Other than sandy beaches, coconut palms, and strategically placed hammocks, the only things on the tiny island are the staff quarters and the bar/dining room. The latter consists of a large open-air building over the water on the north side of the island. That's it. You can walk from one side of the island to the other in a couple of minutes. It's beautiful, and so are the views.

The hotel can arrange visits to the nearby islands for snorkeling, lazing, and village exploring. The catch is that only a visit to the Kuna village on Isla Tigre is included. Prices for other boat trips range from $10 to $15 for nearby islands to $200 for a fast boat to the gorgeous Cayos Holandéses.

Reservations for the hotel are handled through Green World Ecological Tours. Call 507/269-6313 or fax 507/269-6309. Rates run $110 to $120 per person double occupancy, $150 to $168 single. Prices include three meals and a visit to Isla Tigre. There are price breaks for additional nights and a third person in the room.

Around Río Sidra

Cabañas Kuanidup, 507/227-7661, fax 507/227-1396, is probably the best bet for those who want the beauty of a remote island without spending a fortune for the privilege of living simply. The location is gorgeous. The nearest sizable settlement is a half-hour away by motorized *cayuco*, which helps keep the sea here clean and the beaches free of trash. There are eight cabañas with sand floors and the usual thatch roofs and bamboo walls, spaced a few feet away from each other, offering a bit of privacy. Accommodations range from a small cabaña with a double bed to a couple of large ones with four single beds. The cabañas are rustic but comfortable. There are shared toilets and showers in a separate hut and a small open-sided dining room on the opposite end of the island. Lights in the dining room are powered by solar panels, but the cabañas are lit only by kerosene lanterns. The standard package includes daily boat trips to tour the traditional, densely packed island of Río Sidra or snorkel and laze around Achutupu (the one with the shipwreck; see above). *Note:* The hotel doesn't have snorkeling equipment; you'll have to bring your own. The swimming is also fine around the Kuanidup islands themselves. Your only other entertainment will be looking at the blue ocean, the occasional fishing *cayuco,* and the islands off in the distance. You have to be truly in the mood to get away from everything to come here. Rates are $65 per person, which includes all meals and a daily boat tour.

Around Achutupu

The **Dolphin Island Lodge**, 507/225-8435, is in some ways a good blend of the other accommodations in the archipelago. It's small— only seven rooms, with two more that should be completed by the time you read this. It offers seclusion, yet there's an interesting Kuna village just minutes away on Achutupu. The cabañas are large, attractive, and comfortable. They have cement floors instead of the more typical sand ones, plus cold-water showers and sinks. Most have a back porch right on the water, where you can lie in a hammock or write postcards at a little table. A few have toilets in the room, and there are shared bathrooms for the rest. Water pressure here is iffy, which isn't surprising when you consider the water is piped from a remote source on the mainland.

The open-air dining room is on the northern edge of the island, looking out on open sea. The site is pleasant enough to take your mind off the food, which as usual is bland and uninspiring. (Another distraction from the food my last night there was a rat-like rustling up in the dining room's thatch roof.) The dining room and grounds have electricity, but the rooms themselves don't. You're brought a lantern at night, which adds to the romantic charm of the place.

The lodge is owned and run by a Kuna family, the de la Ossas, and service here is personal and friendly. The patriarch is Jerónimo, but you're likely to have more contact with his sons and daughters. One of the sons, Horacio, will be happy to practice his English on you. He learned most of it during a three-month visit to the hippie enclave of Bolinas in Northern California, which he found a fascinating anthropological experience. (He thought it was *"muy interesante"* that there are 60-year-old American women who smoke marijuana.)

While the cabañas are all thatch-roofed, their walls are being converted from bamboo to longer-lasting wood, which is a shame because it's delightful to look through the bamboo slats in the morning and see the sun sparkling on the blue water. There may still be a few bamboo huts left when you visit. Avoid the new cabañas with two units; they offer very little privacy.

Rates are $158 or $173 per person for double or single occupancy, respectively. That price includes round-trip airfare to the island, all meals, and a daily boat trip. Deduct $63 per person if you don't go for the plane ticket. A second night is $80 for double, $100 for single occupancy.

FOOD

Don't expect to find any real restaurants in Kuna Yala. If you're staying on the islands, you'll probably be eating all your meals at your hotel's simple dining hut. As mentioned above, the food generally is not very good. Consider bringing snacks to tide you over. Beer is widely available on the islands, but wine and spirits are not.

Once you've had your third straight meal of tasteless fried fish and rice, you may be tempted to accept your hotel's offer of lobster. Bear in mind that lobster, once a subsistence food for the Kuna, has been so commercially overexploited it's in danger of extinction in these waters. At the very least, do not eat lobster during the mating season, which runs from March to July. Also, even if you have a package deal you'll probably pay extra for lobster, something you may not realize until you're presented with the bill.

It's probably also a good idea to avoid squid. Kuna fishermen typically chase squid out of aquatic caves by dumping bleach into them. Bad for the environment and bad for you.

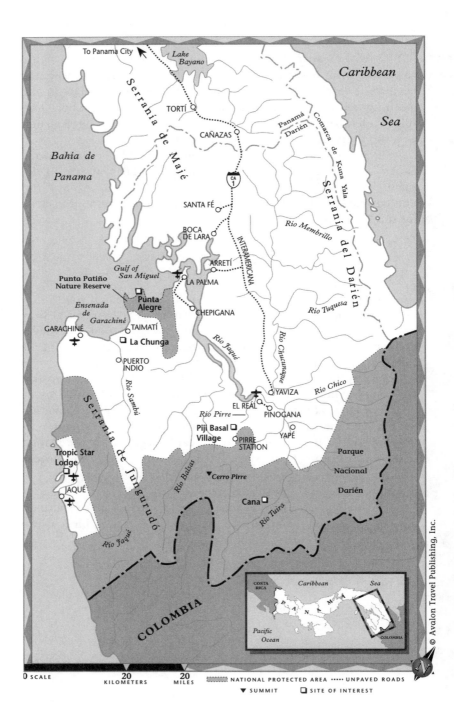

To Panama City
Lake Bayano
Caribbean
Sea
Serranía de Majé
TORTÍ
CAÑAZAS
Panamá Darién
Comarca de Kuna Yala
Bahía de Panama
CA 1
SANTA FÉ
BOCA DE LARA
Río Membrillo
Serranía del Darién
ARRETÍ
Punta Patiño Nature Reserve
Gulf of San Miguel
LA PALMA
INTERAMERICANA
Punta Alegre
Ensenada de Garachiné
CHEPIGANA
Río Tuquesa
GARACHINÉ
TAIMATÍ
La Chunga
Río Jaqué
Río Chucunaque
PUERTO INDIO
Río Sambú
YAVIZA
Río Chico
EL REAL
PINOGANA
Serranía de Jungurudó
Río Pirre
Piji Basal Village
PIRRE STATION
YAPÉ
Río Balsas
Parque Nacional Darién
Tropic Star Lodge
Cerro Pirre
JAQUÉ
Cana
Río Tuira
Río Jaqué
COLOMBIA

COSTA RICA
Caribbean
Sea
PANAMA
Pacific Ocean
COLOMBIA

© Avalon Travel Publishing, Inc.

0 SCALE
20 KILOMETERS
20 MILES
NATIONAL PROTECTED AREA
UNPAVED ROADS
SUMMIT
SITE OF INTEREST

CHAPTER 12

Darién Province

"The Darién." It's still a name filled with magic, even in this decidedly un-magical era.

In many people's minds the magic is of a dark and sinister kind. The Darién has historically been seen as a foreboding, dangerous place, a Conradian wilderness into which explorers venture, never to return.

In modern times, the magic has been perceived in a much more positive light. The Darién is recognized as one of the last bastions of pristine tropical nature. Its biodiversity is so incredible it's been named both a World Biosphere Reserve and a Natural World Heritage Site by UNESCO.

The province of Darién is, at 16,671 square kilometers (6,500 square miles), by far the largest in Panama. Yet only 65,000 people live in the entire region. Parque Nacional Darién alone is enormous, covering 579,000 hectares (1.4 million acres) of wilderness that stretch across the isthmus near the Colombian border. It contains the most extensive lowland tropical forest left along Central America's Pacific coast. It was through this forest that Balboa stepped out onto a cliff in 1513 and became the first European to set eyes on the "South Sea."

No road has ever penetrated all the way through the Darién, and many hope none ever will. The Darién Gap is the only place where the Interamerican Highway, which links North and South America, comes to a complete stop. Wherever there is a road, massive deforestation has followed. Logging, ranching, and farming have decimated enormous tracts of the Darién. If the Interamerican Highway is completed, chances are extremely good that the days of the Darién as a magical place will be numbered.

For now, however, it remains a fantastic nature destination. Try to get there if you possibly can.

LAY OF THE LAND

It's possible to drive into the Darién as far as the town of Yaviza, but there's no reason to do so other than to say you've done it. The road is horrendous, the drive takes a solid day, and all you're going to encounter along the way are vast expanses of deforested land.

The part of the Darién of most interest to visitors lies toward the southeast section of the province, where there are no roads.

River and rainforest

Bachmann/Photo Network

The only way to get around is by plane, boat, and foot. This is where you'll find the part of Parque Nacional Darién most accessible to visitors.

At the heart of the park are Cana, on the east side of 1,615-meter-high (slightly over one mile) Cerro Pirre, and Pirre Station, on its west side. Either place will put you right in the middle of a tropical forest. Cana, the most remote point in Panama, is especially impressive.

The most popular coastal areas are Punta Patiño, on the Gulf of San Miguel, and Piñas Bay, farther down the coast near the Colombian border. Those looking for a trip up a Darién river usually find themselves on the Río Sambú, the Río Mogue, or the Río Jaqué, though many other rivers crisscross this part of the Darién. *Note:* At the time of writing, there was concern about Colombian guerrilla and paramilitary activity on the Río Jaqué. See Visitor Information, below, for suggestions on safe travel in the Darién.

NATURE AND ADVENTURE ACTIVITIES

The great attraction of the Darién is, of course, its magnificent forests and the incredible biodiversity they contain. Hiking, trekking, and bird-watching are what draw most nature tourists. But there are a couple of places along the coast of the Darién where you can find accessible beaches and coral reefs. And, for those into such things, the waters off Piñas Bay offer world-class deep-sea fishing. Kayaking is also possible there.

FLORA AND FAUNA

From rainforests to sandy beaches to cloud forests to mangroves, the Darién has a greater variety of ecosystems than any other place in tropical America. Lush doesn't even begin to describe the vegetation. Flying over the Darién you'll see an endless expanse of forest broken only by the occasional snaking river or a lone flowering tree that's trying to add a splash of bright red, orange, or yellow to the sea of green.

Clea Efthimiadis

Iguanas abound at Punta Patiño

The wildlife is spectacular. Mammals alone include jaguars, ocelots, pumas, margays, jaguarundi, giant anteaters, capybaras, white-lipped and collared peccaries, howler monkeys, white-faced capuchins, spider monkeys, Geoffroy's tamarins, two- and three-toed sloths, and Baird's tapirs. And unlike so many other parts of Panama and the tropics in general, you actually have a fair chance of spotting at least a couple of these.

The Darién is a bird-watcher's dream, one of the best places in the world for spotting birds. Over 400 species have been identified, including plenty to impress even those who think they don't give a hoot about birds. In some places it's actually hard *not* to see flocks of flamboyant blue-and-yellow, red-and-green, great green, and chestnut-fronted macaws. The rare harpy eagle, the world's most powerful bird of prey, lives here, as does the lovely golden-headed quetzal.

Reptiles and amphibians abound as well, including caimans, crocodiles, and beautiful poison-arrow frogs. Then there are the creatures that make some people nervous when they think of visiting the "jungle": snakes. Yes, there are lots of them, including some very venomous ones. The common wisdom is you're very unlikely to see one, and you should count yourself lucky if you do. My personal experience is if you do any amount of serious hiking in the tropics, you will probably eventually come across at least one. Most are not at all aggressive, and if you leave them alone they won't bother you. The most common venomous snake in the Darién is also one of the most lethal: the fer-de-lance, a tan-colored pit viper with a diamond pattern on its skin. They are everywhere in the Darién, though again you probably won't see one. If you do, don't try to play with it.

THE ELUSIVE HARPY EAGLE

*The Darién is one of the last Panamanian homes of the harpy eagle (*Harpia harpyja*), the world's most powerful bird of prey. Deforestation has endangered this magnificent creature, which inhabits lowland tropical forests. So has hunting, especially since harpies don't generally fear humans. It doesn't help that they nest only once every three years, though there have been attempts to breed harpies in captivity. (See the Summit Botanical Gardens entry in Chapter 4.)*

The harpy can grow to be over a meter long from fierce hooked bill to tail, more than half the height of a tall man. Its wingspan can reach 2.1 meters (7 feet). Adults have a distinctive two-pronged crest, making them easy to distinguish from other eagles.

You'd be extremely lucky to spot a harpy even in the Darién, as they rarely soar above the treetops. They hunt within the canopy with remarkable agility given their great size. They favor monkeys, sloths, and other hefty mammals, which they scoop up in their powerful talons at speeds up to 80 kilometers per hour (50 mph).

VISITOR INFORMATION

Unlike other chapters in this book, this one is written with the idea that you will probably travel to the Darién under the auspices of a tour operator with experienced, respected nature guides. I strongly urge you to do so (unless you're going to the Tropic Star Lodge, where you will be in comfortable, modern surroundings).

The Darién is a fantastic place, and you should definitely visit if you get a chance. But it has to be treated with caution and respect. If you venture off on a nature hike by yourself, you have a quite decent chance of getting lost and dying. Seriously. You will also just get much more out of the experience if you're with a guide who can help you spot animals and plants and tell you what you're seeing. And unless you're fluent in Spanish and really know your way around the tropical bush, you will find it hard to communicate with people and get logistics set up for any true Darién adventure.

If you plan on going on a multi-day trek in the Darién, versus staying in a lodge with screens at night, you should take antimalaria medication in advance.

There are human hazards as well. Colombia's civil war has spilled over the border into the forests of the Darién, and there are guerrillas and paramilitaries working in some areas. There are also drug traffickers and run-of-the-mill bandits who hide out in the forest. Knowing which areas are safe and which aren't can be tricky. Again, experienced nature guides can be helpful, since it's obviously in their interest to know if the area they're guiding is potentially dangerous. Border police and park rangers are also a possible source of information. Before setting off on your trip you may also want to check the U.S. State Department's travel warnings, 202/647-4000, www.travel.state.gov/travel_warnings.html. However, you should know that at the time this was written, Cana, which has had no incidents and was considered safe by those on the ground, was on the list of places to avoid. On the other hand, known hot spots such as Jaqué were not even mentioned. Things like that do not inspire much confidence in the State Department's assessment of the situation.

It was considered extremely dangerous at the time of writing to venture on foot beyond Yaviza, where the Interamerican Highway currently ends. (There's no reason to go there in any case.) Other known danger spots included the Colombian border crossing at Puerto Obaldía, which is actually in the Comarca de Kuna Yala; and Paya, near the Colombian border halfway down the Darién. The town of Jaqué and the Río Jaqué were iffy at best, as an influx of Colombian refugees had made the area a potential military target for Colombian paramilitary and guerrilla forces.

There are still three groups of indigenous peoples living in the Darién, many of whom live much as they have for thousands of years. The two main groups are the Emberá and the Wounaan, who are sometimes known collectively as Chocos. They have a very similar culture, though their languages are different. It's possible to visit Emberá and Wounaan in the forest, where the people live in open-sided huts built on stilts. As befits the climate, they traditionally wear very few clothes, but the influx of "civilization" has eroded this practice. There are an estimated 14,000 Emberá and 2,600 Wounaan throughout Panama, though the Darién is their homeland. There is also a small Kuna population in the Darién, and villages inhabited by the descendants of African slaves.

GETTING THERE

Most travel is by small plane. See the individual Nature and Adventure sights below for details.

NATURE AND ADVENTURE SIGHTS

Cana—If you can possibly spare the time and money, you should make a trip to Cana, in the heart of **Parque Nacional Darién.** It's the most remote spot in all of Panama: The nearest human settlement is two to three days away by foot, and there are no roads. Cana is a truly amazing place that offers genuine adventure amid relative comfort, a rare combination.

Cana sits in a forested valley up against the eastern slope of the 1,615-meter-high (slightly over one mile) Cerro Pirre. It was a major gold-mining camp off and on from the days of the conquistadors to the 1960s, but today its only residents are a handful of staffers working at an ANCON field station and a couple of border policemen. Imposing abandoned mines (which you should *not* try to explore) and rusted mining equipment overwhelmed by vegetation give the place a slightly spooky *Heart of Darkness* feel. But for the most part it's an open, airy, and inviting spot that doesn't square with stereotypes the uninitiated may harbor about the forbidding jungle.

The wildlife here is breathtaking. As usual in the forest, if you come expecting a Discovery Channel cavalcade of big critters you're likely to be disappointed. The only thing you're guaranteed to see are some of the most gorgeous birds in the world. But you have a better chance of coming across tropical mammals and other impressive animals here than in most parts of Panama. You have an especially good chance of finding troops of Central American spider monkeys, and you'll often be surrounded by the barks of howler monkeys. It's not uncommon to come across fresh jaguar prints. Jaguars have been known to take a leisurely stroll down Cana's landing strip, but you'd be extremely lucky to spot one during a brief visit.

Herds of literally hundreds of white-lipped peccaries sometimes descend on the station and tear up the turf, rooting for food. When this happens, the staff and visitors have to lock themselves in the lodge. Peccaries, the only creature I've seen Darién guides get a bit nervous about, can be aggressive, and they run faster than you do. Don't make the mistake of thinking they're just cute little pigs.

If you're very lucky, you might also come across a Baird's tapir, the largest land mammal in Central America. At the cloud-forest camp above Cana, a tapir once sat on a guide's tent while the guide was sleeping in it. Both recovered from the surprise.

Cana has been called one of the 10 greatest bird-watching spots on the planet. Even if you have only the slightest interest in feathered creatures, you'll likely be bowled over by what you encounter here. Blue-and-yellow, red-and-green, great green, and chestnut-fronted macaws streak across the valley all day long. Keel-billed toucans, looking like they just flew off a Froot Loops box, peer down at you from the trees.

Just sitting on the porch of the lodge you can see an incredible array of stunning birds, many of them rare elsewhere, searching for food on the ground a few meters away.

Since Cana's elevation is nearly 500 meters (about 1,600 feet), the forest here is premontane, and it's neither as hot nor as buggy as you might expect. The valley offers beautiful views of the surrounding hills, which are covered with lush virgin forest. There's also a cloud-forest camp on the mountain itself, at 1,280 meters (about 4,100 feet), where it can get cool in the evenings.

The lodge at Cana is a barely converted mining camp building that dates from the 1960s. It's a rustic wooden structure containing six basic rooms with little in them besides a bed and a few shelves. Fresh linens are supplied and there are screens on the windows. There are shared bathrooms and showers with running water. A generator provides electricity from 7 to 9 p.m., after which you'll have to rely on candles and flashlights. Accommodations were slated to be much improved—and probably more expensive—by 2002. Initial plans call for six simple but elegantly designed and environmentally friendly cottages with private, composting bathrooms and hydroelectric power.

Five main trails originate from Cana, not counting a short trail near the station that follows railroad tracks to an abandoned locomotive. The **Boca de Cupe Trail** is the longest. Theoretically you could hike it for two or three days to the settlement of Boca de Cupe, but at the time of writing that wasn't a smart thing to do, as there had been Colombian guerrilla activity around that area. But hiking in for a few kilometers is well worthwhile. It's a mostly flat trail offering spectacular birding and the chance of seeing larger wildlife. The **Machinery Garden Trail** is a lovely and exotic two-kilometer (1.2-mile) loop that allows you to check out both nature and the rusting remains of a 19th-century mining operation. The **Seteganti Trail** leads down to the Seteganti River. You can easily explore all these trails during a brief visit.

The **Pirre Mountain Trail** is a somewhat strenuous nine-kilometer (5.6-mile) hike that leads you three-quarters of the way up Cerro Pirre to a cloud-forest camp. The hike takes four to five hours at a reasonable clip. The hike down takes about three hours and can actually be a bit more painful, as the trail is often fairly steep and hard on the legs.

But it's absolutely worth the effort. The trail itself takes you through beautiful primary forest alive with animals. On a single trip

I've encountered large groups of spider monkeys crashing through the trees 40 meters (130 feet) overhead, crossed paths with a deadly fer-de-lance snake (it was a baby, which can actually be more dangerous, but we both minded our own business), and, of course, seen dozens upon dozens of flamboyant birds.

The camp itself is a pretty impressive operation. A full field kitchen is set up in one large thatch-roofed hut, and tents with pads are set up in another. The camp can accommodate about two dozen guests. It's relatively cushy for its location. Generally all you have to take is a day pack; the cook and staff bring the food and water and set up the tents. (Tips are much appreciated; the guides can suggest amounts.) The view of nearby Cerro Setetule and the forested valley from here is breathtaking, and the nights are a riot of forest sounds. Big animals have been known to wander through camp at night.

The truly dedicated can continue a bit farther up the mountain on the **Cloudforest Trail**, but the summit can't be reached from this side of the mountain. There's a slim chance of spotting the rare golden-headed quetzal on this trail.

Guides will take you on all these hikes. Do not attempt to venture out anywhere on your own. The trails are well marked so you probably wouldn't get lost, but there are small but real dangers to avoid in the forest. You have a much better chance of staying out of trouble if you go with a good guide.

It's hard to exaggerate just how special Cana and its surroundings are. It's an enormous expanse of nearly pristine tropical forest, an overwhelming oasis of biodiversity. It's not cheap to get there and the trip is a bit of adventure, but it will likely be the highlight of your trip to Panama.

Details: The only reasonable way to get to Cana is by airplane, and only small chartered planes make the trip. Visits are generally arranged through tour operators, who offer package deals that include everything from airfare to guides and food. See Guides and Outfitters, below. The trip over takes about an hour and 15 minutes. The view is incredible. Planes land on a grass landing strip that ends in the mountain, which can make takeoffs and landings adventures in themselves.

Pirre Station (Rancho Frío)—The area around Pirre Station, an ANAM ranger station in Darién National Park, offers an experience of the Darién similar to what you'd find at Cana. While Pirre is in the lowlands and Cana is in the foothills, they are on opposite sides of Cerro Pirre and share many of the same birds and other wildlife. Both have good trails, including ones that lead up onto Cerro Pirre.

Cana has a bit more to offer, however, and the conditions at Pirre Station are far more rustic. On the other hand, a trip to the Pirre area can be arranged far more cheaply. If you have to choose between the two and you're willing to spend the money, you're probably better off visiting Cana. (They're only about 20 kilometers, around 12 miles, apart, but no trails connect them.)

Getting to Pirre Station can be an adventure. You must first get to El Real, a small town in the middle of the Darién in which you won't care to spend much time. It's possible to reach El Real by boat, but most visitors coming from Panama City fly in.

To get to Pirre Station from El Real, you can take a one-hour boat ride up the Río Pirre to the Emberá village of Piji Basal. From there it's a two-hour hike to Pirre Station. Expect to encounter serious mud if you come during the rainy season. You can also hike the entire way in, but the trail from El Real is rough and overgrown, and you shouldn't attempt it without a guide. Sometimes the road is impassable.

Pirre Station is just within the boundaries of Parque Nacional Darién. The birding is excellent here. Specialties include such beauties as lemon-spectacled and scarlet-browed tanagers, white-fronted nunbirds, and crimson-bellied woodpeckers. Mammals you have a chance of spotting include sloths, spider and howler monkeys, white-faced capuchins, and Geoffroy's tamarins.

Three **trails** originate from the station, which is surrounded by primary forest and little else. One follows a river by the station down to a six-meter (20-foot) waterfall about 15 minutes away. The second leads to a clearing where you can do some bird-watching. The most severe takes you on a three-hour hike up to a ridge on Cerro Pirre. Along the way you may encounter red-and-green macaws, a group of spider monkeys, or other creatures that will make the trip worth the effort. You can camp up here, but you need to bring your own gear. Do not hike anywhere in the area without a guide. If you get lost or hurt, you have a very real chance of not making it back out.

The station building itself is very rustic. It consists of two rooms. You'll be sleeping on bunk beds in one room that are nothing more than a foam mattress on a wooden frame. You have to bring your own sheets and towels, and you'll be sharing the accommodations with the park rangers. At the time of writing the only toilet was an outhouse and you had to bathe in the river, but flush toilets and showers were being installed. (*Note:* Please bring biodegradable shampoo.) The only light was supplied by kerosene lanterns and battery-powered fluorescent tubes. There is no electricity.

Unlike many places in the Darién, it's possible to visit Pirre Station on your own without tremendous hassle or expense. However, I recommend going with a good tour operator, as you're likely to have a safer, more enlightening trip and won't have to deal with making all the considerable arrangements.

If you decide to try the place on your own, the usual routine is to fly into El Real and contact Chicho Bristan, who is in charge of the ANAM office in the town. (You should contact ANAM headquarters in Panama City ahead of time to get permission and check on local conditions; see Appendix B for information on ANAM.) Chicho will help you find a boat and captain to take you upriver to Piji Basal. Expect to pay $70 to $80 one way, including gas. In El Real you will also have to buy whatever supplies you weren't able to bring on the plane. You can find basic supplies such as beans, pasta, and bottled water. Note that you will have to bring in all the water you'll need during your stay unless you bring a water purifier or purification tablets. In Piji Basal you can hire Emberá porters for about $5 each to tote your supplies in for the one-hour hike to the station.

The rangers will prepare food for you for a small tip. Expect to pay $15 a night ($10 for the bed, $5 for the cooking). It'd be a nice gesture to bring food for the rangers, too. They're your hosts during your stay, and you'll have a more enjoyable time if you've won their good will. If you've come without a guide, you can hire a ranger to take you on the trails. Again, do not venture far on a trail without a knowledgeable guide.

Details: *Aeroperlas, 507/315-7500, 507/315-7580, iflyap@aeroperlas.com, flies from Panama City to El Real on Monday, Wednesday, Friday, and Saturday mornings. Aviatur, 507/315-0307, fax 507/315-0316,* *makes the trip on Tuesday, Thursday, and Saturday mornings. The flight takes about an hour, slightly more if the plane makes stops along the way. The fare is $34 one-way, $69 round-trip, on either airline. If you go for a package deal with a tour operator, transportation, food, and guides are included and the tour operator will make all the arrangements.*

Punta Patiño Nature Reserve—Punta Patiño is, at 30,000 hectares (74,000 acres), the largest private reserve in the country. Owned by ANCON, it's a great place to come if you want to get a taste of "coastal Darién," which has a much different feel from the interior. Punta Patiño offers quite a range of vegetation and wildlife, and it has the best tourist infrastructure in the Darién outside of Tropic Star Lodge.

The reserve is on the Gulf of San Miguel, a little over an hour by boat from La Palma, the tiny, rustic provincial capital of Darién Province. Guests stay in ANCON's 10 surprisingly comfortable cabins, two of which are air-conditioned (the rest have fans). Each cabin has a terrace and a cold-water bathroom with shower. A generator supplies electricity from the evening until 6 a.m. Food is served in a new, rather stately lodge.

You're almost guaranteed to see capybara, the world's largest rodent, and gray foxes at night toward the end of the rainy season (late December through January). Sightings drop off thereafter. Other big mammals you might see include the tayra (a lanky weasel with a long, bushy tail), Geoffroy's tamarin, and collared peccaries. There are also lots of iguanas. Bird specialties at Patiño include trogons, boat-billed herons, and night herons.

At Patiño you'll find primary and secondary forest (both lowland and premontane), mangroves, black-sand beaches, and even large coconut plantations. Notable trees include the massive cuipo, whose blossoms burst into bright red or orange at the end of the dry season, and the spiny cedar, which has sharp spikes covering its trunk.

Large swaths of Patiño, about a third of the reserve, were badly deforested before it became a protected area. But nature is making a surprisingly strong recovery in the disturbed areas. A large reforestation project is underway, and ANCON is also working to preserve red and black mangrove here.

There is one main trail, the **Sendero Piedra de Candela** (Flintstone Trail), a loop that takes about an hour to walk. It takes you through dry forest where birders can hunt for mannakins, common black hawks, woodpeckers, and tanagers. It's also a good place to spot Geoffroy's tamarin and, at night, red-eyed tree frogs.

There is a great deal of primary tropical lowland forest behind the ANCON station. Visitors are taken back part of the way by "tractor taxi," a tractor with a wagon hitched to it. It's easy to spot caimans near the swampy road into the forest.

Visitors to Patiño often make boat trips to the human settlements in the area. There is an **Emberá village** up the nearby Río Mogue. You can arrange to spend the night in someone's home if you want a really rustic experience. You'll be sleeping in an open hut on stilts, and you will be absolutely devoured by insects. I don't recommend it, but if that's your thing at least coat yourself with insecticide at night. You should also be taking antimalaria medication. This village is a bit more rustic and less touristy than La Chunga (see the following sight), which is on the Río Sambú a lengthy ocean ride south. The descendants of African slaves live in another fishing village, **Punta Alegre**, on a point a short boat ride north of Punta Patiño.

Details: There is a private airstrip at Punta Patiño itself, but only chartered aircraft land there. The nearest commercial airstrip is at the provincial capital of La Palma. Aeroperlas, 507/315-7500, 507/315-7580, iflyap@aeroperlas.com, makes the trip from Panama City every morning except Sunday. Aviatur, 507/315-0307, fax 507/315-0316, flies over on Tuesday, Thursday, and Saturday mornings. The fare on either airline is $34 one-way, $69 round-trip. The flight takes about 45 minutes. From La Palma you have to take a boat ride down to Patiño, which will be arranged if you go with a tour operator. Ancon Expeditions offers a three-day, two night package to Patiño for $550 per person for two people, $480 per person for four people, $425 per person for six people, and $350 per person for eight or more people. The price includes lodging, airfare, guided hikes in the forest, tours of an Emberá village on the Río Mogue, a visit to Punta Alegre, and meals.

The Río Sambú and La Chunga—The Sambú River makes for a memorable boat ride. Its wide, muddy mouth opens into the Ensenada de Garachiné, a cove that in turns opens into the Pacific Ocean. The mouth is about midway between Punta Garachiné to the south and Punta Patiño to the north. The river is bordered by

Local boatmen guiding visitors to the Emberá village of La Chunga

an intricate tangle of mangroves, behind which rise lush green towering trees. It's a beautiful sight. Even though there are settlements along the banks and many small fishing boats plying the waters, there's no doubt you're in Mother Nature's living room here.

It's easy to spot birds sailing overhead or hanging by the water as you motor upriver, particularly such water-loving fowl as herons, egrets, frigate birds, pelicans, and cormorants. You'll probably see at least a couple of hawks perched high atop the tallest trees. Toucans and parrots are a bit harder to spot, but they're around. And the occasional splash and burble in the river will set your mind wondering exactly what is lurking in there.

The heavily touristed Emberá village of **La Chunga** is about an hour upriver. It's located along the banks of the Río La Chunga, a sluggish but no less scenic little river that empties into the Sambú. (A *chunga* is a kind of black palm. Ask a villager to point one out to you.) The village is about a 20-minute walk down a wide, flat path from where the boat drops you off.

You may have mixed feelings about visiting La Chunga. The village, which has a population of about 300 people, has obviously been shaped with tourists in mind. Most of the tourists come from small cruise ships that offer a taste of the Darién as part of a trans-canal itinerary. If you slip into the village ahead of a tour group, you'll see women taking off their blouses and bras and men kicking off their jeans to look appropriately Indian for their visitors. Decked out in little more than short skirts or loin coverings, they dance around as tourists snap their photos. The whole thing looks as uncomfortable for the villagers as it will probably feel to you.

On the other hand, the residents of La Chunga have managed to turn their village into one of the most comfortable places to stay in the Darién. "Comfort" is a relative term where the Darién is concerned, but amazingly enough this place has real flush toilets and running water. Four solid thatch-roofed, bamboo-sided cabins on stilts are rented out to visitors. The rooms, officially known as the **Hotel Emberá**, are a short walk from the village proper, set in a little clearing where medicinal plants are being grown for the edification of visitors. The cabins have two rooms, each equipped just with two wooden beds topped by a foam mattress and mosquito nets. One of the cabins has double beds; the rest are singles. Showers are in a neighboring hut and consist of a cold-water spigot.

Your host is Ricardo Cabrera, *cacique* (chief) of La Chunga and 11 other villages. Ricardo is a warm, sweet guy who speaks great English. (He's the only one in the village who speaks more than a word or two.) It's startling to hear American slang from him until you learn he spent six months in Southern California helping a missionary document the Emberá language. He can arrange guided hikes on which you might see all kinds of critters, including crocodiles in a nearby lake, golden-headed quetzals, peccaries, "and, of course, snakes."

A group of up to five people can hire a fishing boat for $180 and pursue corvina, a delicious saltwater fish that's a Panama staple. The largest you're likely to catch will weigh in at a little over two kilos (about 4.5 pounds). If you do decide to fish, one hopes you'll avoid the practice that at least one villager told me was great sport: hooking a manta ray and watching its frantic efforts to escape.

When a tour group is expected, Emberá and Wounaan come from nearby settlements to join the villagers in selling handicrafts at tables set up around the village. If you're in the market for a souvenir, you can find some well-made items at good prices, and you know the money is going right to the needy source. Popular items include rosewood figurines, tightly woven baskets and bowls, and tagua nuts (also known as ivory nuts) carved in the shape of forest animals.

Details: *Unless you're coming by boat from Punta Patiño or somewhere else, you'll probably be flying to Sambú, where you can hire a boat to take you to La Chunga. Aeroperlas, 507/315-7500, 507/315-7580, iflyap@aeroperlas.com, makes the trip on Monday, Wednesday, and Friday mornings. Aviatur, 507/315-0307, fax 507/315-0316, flies there on Tuesday, Wednesday, Thursday, and Saturday. The price is $36 one-way, $72 round-trip, for either airline. The flight takes about 45 minutes. Aviatur offers an overnight package that includes all transportation, meals, a guided jungle tour and Emberá dances. You arrive mid-morning and leave before noon the next day. High season rates, which apply from December through March, are $196 per person for up to three people or $150 per person for groups of four or more. Rainy season rates are $153 per person for up to three people and $138 per person for a group of four or more. Additional nights are $45 per person, regardless of season or party size. Note: Be sure to ask for Lily when you call Aviatur about this package. If you've made your own transportation arrangements, you can also try booking your stay directly through Ricardo Cabrera, the cacique. The price is the same, minus the airfare. Ricardo can be reached through the one telephone in the village. The number is 507/299-6083. However, be advised that the phone is often out of order. If Ricardo knows you're coming, he'll arrange for a boat to pick you up and take you to La Chunga, but don't be surprised if you have to wait around for a while.*

Tropic Star Lodge and Jaqué—Tropic Star Lodge is an exclusive, world-famous deep-sea fishing resort perched above lovely **Piñas Bay,** 56 kilometers (35 miles) from the Colombian border on the Pacific coast. It's the kind of place movie stars frequent—it was one of John Wayne's favorite haunts back when. Over 170 world deep-sea fishing records have been set here, more than anywhere else on the planet. Tropic Star held over 40 records at the time of writing, mostly for black, blue, or striped marlin and Pacific sailfish. The place has been owned by the Kittredge family since 1976. Your hosts are Terri Kittredge Andrews and her husband, Mike Andrews.

There is a reason for nature tourists to care about this luxurious place, even if they don't care for fishing (though they may be interested to note that the billfish caught here are tagged and then released). Tropic Star has begun to experiment with keeping the lodge open during the rainy season, from about August to the end of November, for "green season" tourists interested in enjoying the beautiful surroundings without necessarily going fishing. You should expect rain, though August and September aren't as wet as later months.

While still quite expensive, rates during the green season are far below those during the regular season. Also, fishing packages are normally for an entire week, while green-season visitors have the option of staying for two to five nights.

Guests have free use of kayaks to explore the bay or travel up the Río Piñas, and snorkeling equipment to explore a nearby coral reef. A trail has been cut through the forest down to a white-sand beach about a half-hour walk away. In all there are about three kilometers (nearly two miles) of trails on Tropic Star's vast property, a peninsula covered mainly in primary forest. Don't expect to see too much wildlife. Hunters from nearby villages have wiped out much of what was once here. However, the owners have found jaguar prints on the beach over the years.

The staff can also arrange a trip up the **Río Jaqué**, which winds up toward the Colombian border through wilderness broken only by the occasional Emberá village. Trips start at the river's mouth near the town of Jaqué, 10 kilometers (6.2 miles) southeast of Tropic Star Lodge.

Warning: At the time this was written, visiting Jaqué and heading up the river was not a good idea. The Colombian civil war had pushed hundreds of refugees over the border into Jaqué and its surroundings. Stories were appearing in the Panamanian press saying that some of these refugees had been placed on Colombian death lists, and there was concern the war might spill over the border into this area.

Months after this crisis started no such incursion had happened. By the time you visit, the problem may have long since disappeared. But you should check out the situation before setting out on trips in the area. Even in the best of circumstances you should

not head too close to the Colombia border, nor wander away from the river into the forest. The staff at Tropic Star and the border police at Jaqué are probably your best sources of current local information. You can also check the U.S. State Department's travel warnings, 202/647-4000, www.travel.state.gov/travel.warnings.html, but you should note that at the time of writing this area was not even mentioned, while other spots that had not seen any trouble were on the list of places to avoid.

None of these problems had affected Tropic Star Lodge as this was written, though the lodge was taking some extra security measures just to be on the safe side.

Green-season tourists have the option of going deep-sea fishing on Piñas Bay on one of the lodge's yachts. Rates are $275 for a half day, $475 for a full day. Prices include crew and tackle but not tips. Each boat can carry up to six passengers.

The lodge itself is, as you might expect, quite comfortable. Rooms and cabins are air-conditioned, with twin beds and private baths. All have a view of the bay. A hillside three-bedroom house with a sunken living room can also be rented. The food is gourmet, with five-course candlelit dinners served at night. The grounds are well groomed and lovely, and there's a swimming pool and bar. There are no telephones, fax machines, or televisions at the lodge so that guests can have a true sense of getting away from it all. Expect pampering: The place can accommodate only 36 guests at one time, but it has a staff of 80.

Those who come for the fishing will be pleased to note that trips are made on 9.5-meter (31-foot) Bertrams. The prime black-marlin season runs from mid-December through April. Pacific sailfish are caught year-round, with April through July especially good months.

Details: *The basic fishing package includes seven nights of lodging, six days of fishing, and three meals a day, including wine with dinner. The rate depends on the number of people in the boat. From December to the end of May the weekly per-person rates are $2,300 (four people in a boat), $2,700 (three people in a boat), $3,350 (two people in a boat) and $5,550 (one person in a boat). Those not fishing pay $1,300 for the week. Rates are slightly less in June and July, when there is also the possibility of shorter trips. Note that spaces usually book up a year ahead of time.*

Add another $300 per person for the charter flight and ground transportation in Panama City. Boat pickup and drop-off from the airstrip to the lodge, about 15 minutes away, is included.

Nightly green-season rates, from about August to the end of November, are $140 per person double occupancy or $220 per person single occupancy. Children's discounts are available. The minimum stay is two nights. Rates include pickup and drop-off at Piñas airstrip, but you are responsible for your own ground transportation in Panama City. The air charter service does not run during the green season: you must take a commercial small plane to Piñas. Tropic Star can make the arrangements for you. The fare is $41 one-way, $83 round-trip. Aeroperlas, 507/315-7500, 507/315-7580, iflyap@aeroperlas.com, makes the trip on Tuesday and Saturday mornings. Aviatur, 507/315-0307, fax 507/315-0316, flies over on Monday, Wednesday, and Friday mornings. The flights takes about an hour. (Make sure you get off at the right airstrip; the plane sometimes lands in Jaqué first.) For reservations and more information, contact 800/682-3424, www.tropiscstar.com, tslorl@aol.com.

GUIDES AND OUTFITTERS

The most prominent Darién guide outfit is **Ancon Expeditions**, 507/269-9414, 507/269-9415, fax 507/264-3713, ecopanama@sinfo .net, www.anconexpeditions.com. The company also runs the ANCON lodges at Cana and Punta Patiño. They are known to have most of the best Darién guides in the country. At the top of the heap is **Hernan Araúz**, a second-generation Darién explorer with a passion for this place. His many credits include nine trans-Darién expeditions. He's also considered one of the premier birding guides in the entire country. **Rich Cahill** is another experienced Ancon guide, with seven trans-Darién expeditions. I've traveled with Rich in the Darién and found him to be a conscientious, safe, friendly guide with an infectious love of the forest. He's a lot of fun to hike with.

Ancon Expeditions offers a number of packages in the Darién. In addition to those described in the individual nature/adventure sights above, these include a three-day, four-night all-inclusive package to Cana for $1,330 per person for two people, $960 per person for four people, $900 per person for six people, or $775 per person for eight or more people. Other trips include a four-day, three-night trip to Pirre Station for $375 per person for two people, $325 per person for four people, $275 per person for six people, or $225 per person for eight or more people. The price includes all in-country transportation and meals.

They also offer major treks, including a 14-day Darién Explorer Trek. This trek takes you by foot and dug-out canoe to the best-known nature hot spots in the Darién. It costs $2,400 per person, with a minimum of four people and maximum of 12.

At the time this was written, Ancon Expeditions was offering a Trans-Darién Trek once a year. This takes you by foot and dug-out canoe from the Caribbean to the Pacific, following a route similar to that taken by Balboa when he discovered the "South Sea." It costs $2,495 per person, with a minimum of four people and a maximum of 12.

These major treks are true adventures, but you'll be traveling in a certain amount of style. Porters carry all your gear (it's for your safety, as you wouldn't want to trip and break a leg in the middle of the Darién—it has happened), and the guides bring along a para-medic and satellite phone. Still, you should be in good shape and willing to rough it a bit.

Guerrilla and paramilitary activity along the Colombian border can affect these treks, particularly the Trans-Darién one. Contact Ancon Expeditions for current conditions and schedules.

Another top Darién guide, and perhaps the finest birding guide in Panama, is **Willie Martinez.** His company, Nattur Panama, 507/225-7325, fax 507/225-7314, panabird@sinfo.net, offers extensive trips that take you to the Darién and other parts of Panama. The shortest trip being offered at the time of writing was a four-day, three-night camping trip in the area around El Real that cost $477 per person, minimum of four people. Prices include all meals and transportation.

LODGING AND FOOD

See the individual Nature and Adventure sights, above.

APPENDIX A
TRAVEL BASICS

WHAT TO BRING

Most parts of Panama are hot and humid year-round. You'll want to bring lots of thin cotton clothing. Be sure your travel wardrobe is not all shorts and skimpy tops, though; dress in Panama is conservative (see the Culture section of Chapter 1, Panama: An Overview). Also, lightweight long-sleeved shirts and long pants provide protection from the sun and insects. Make sure you have subdued-colored clothes for hikes and bird-watching trips—light, bright clothing scares off wildlife. Bring at least one semiformal outfit if you want to go to restaurants or clubs in the cities.

If you're planning to go on treks or long hikes, be sure to bring sturdy hiking boots. U.S. Army surplus boots are the footwear of choice for Darién trekkers. If you go trekking with a tour company, check ahead of time to see what equipment they'll provide and what you're expected to bring. Generally you won't have to bring your own tent. They'll usually take care of providing clean water, too, but you may want to bring along water-purification tablets just in case. Consider bringing along a bedroll or light sleeping bag even if you're not planning on doing serious camping. It can make a good blanket or pillow if you have to spend a night in a place without decent linens.

If you're planning to spend any length of time in the outdoors, you should bring one or two water bottles, a hat, and sunscreen. It's surprisingly hard to find strong insect repellent in Panama. Be sure to bring some. The best stuff contains a high concentration of DEET and is easy to find at camping or Army surplus stores. (*Note:* DEET is not safe for small children.)

You'll be surprised how much the air can cool off in some regions of Panama. Even parts of the Darién can get fairly chilly at night, and temperatures in the western highlands sometimes

309

approach freezing. Bring some warm clothes. A light sweater or fleece along with a waterproof windbreaker or parka is a useful combination. If you think you'll spend much time island-hopping, consider bringing a life jacket. These are not often standard equipment.

Panama can get quite a bit of rain even in the dry season. If you're planning to do much hiking, bring along a rain poncho, preferably of breathable fabric. You may also want to bring along a small umbrella for when you're out and about in town, or you can just do what the locals do: Wait for the rain to stop.

If you forget anything, you'll have little trouble buying most of what you need in Panama, especially in Panama City.

ENTRY AND EXIT REQUIREMENTS

Passports, Tourist Cards, and Visas

Foreign nationals entering Panama must have a valid passport and proof of an onward ticket. U.S. citizens do not need a visa to enter Panama, but they do need a tourist card. These cost $10. If you're flying to Panama from the U.S., you can buy one at the airport through your airline. If you come to Panama by bus from Costa Rica, the bus company should have tourist cards. If not, get one from a Panamanian consulate or embassy before your trip. Do not show up at the border without a tourist card.

Visa and tourist-card requirements for other countries change constantly. Check with the nearest Panamanian consulate or embassy for current requirements.

A tourist card entitles the bearer to stay in Panama for 30 days. You can extend your stay for another 60 days, but to do so is a bit of a bureaucratic hassle. (As this was written, legislation to eliminate the laborious extension process described below was inching its way through the Panamanian government.)

A few days before the tourist card expires, go to an immigration office to apply for a *prórroga de turista* (tourist extension). The main office in Panama City is at Avenida Cuba and Calle 29 Este, 507/225-1077. Hours are 8 a.m. to 3 p.m., but you should try to come first thing in the morning as the whole process can take a couple of hours. You won't want to come back a second day. The official name of the place is the Ministerio de Gobierno y Justicia, Dirección de Migración y Naturalización.

Bring your passport, tourist card, a photocopy of the passport page that shows your photo and personal details, a photocopy of your passport page showing the entry stamp for Panama, two passport-size photos, and proof of an onward airplane or bus ticket. You will have to fill out a simple Spanish form (if you don't speak Spanish, bring a phrase book if you've got one). You will be charged $11 to process the form and create your file. At the end of this ordeal you'll be presented with a laminated ID card good for 60 days.

That's not the end of it. Four days before you leave the country, you then have to get a *permiso de salida* (exit permit) and a *paz y salvo* (a certificate indicating you don't owe Panama taxes). Be sure to take your passport, Panama ID card, and other travel documents. Note that only those who've extended their stay have to go through this process; if you are in Panama for 30 days or less, you don't need a *permiso de salida* or *paz y salvo.*

The first step is to get the *paz y salvo* from a tax office. In Panama City, it's an ugly high-rise building on Avenida Cuba between Calle 35 Este and Calle 36 Este. The name of the building is Edificio Hatillo. You're looking for the Ministerio de Economía y Finanzas, Dirección General de Ingresos. It's not well marked, but it's on the ground floor to your left as you face the building. Hours are 8:30 a.m. to 4 p.m., but again, come early so you can finish the whole procedure in a single day.

Pick up the *paz y salvo* form from the table on your right as you enter the office. Take a number and fill out the middle section of the form, where it says "*extranjeros*" (foreigners). When your number is called, a clerk will take the form, run your name through a computer to make sure you're not a tax cheat, then print out an official-looking certificate. You pay $1 at another desk, where the form will be stapled into your passport.

Then you have to go back to the same immigration office that issued your tourist extension. (*Note:* If you go to a different office, you will have to go through the entire extension process described above all over again.) The main immigration office is down the street from the tax office. You'll be asked for your passport and the *paz y salvo*, and a *"permiso de salida"* stamp will be entered in your passport. Done at last. The departure tax is $20.

In David

If you're in western Panama when it's time to extend your tourist card or leave the country, you may want to handle the immigration formalities in David, the provincial capital of Chiriquí, rather than return to Panama City. Note, however, that if you did not get your *prórroga de turista* in David, you'll have to go through the entire registration process described above all over again before you can get your *permiso de salida* and *paz y salvo*. Also, the bureaucrats in the little immigration office in David seem particularly unhelpful. You're probably better off taking care of all this in Panama City if possible.

That said, the immigration office in David, 507/775-4515, is tucked away in a small, squat building near the corner of Calle C Sur and Avenido Domino Diaz A. (better known as Avenida Central, not to be confused with Calle Central). A few blocks away from the Hotel Nacional, it's open 8 a.m. to 3 p.m. weekdays.

If you need to get a *paz y salvo*, before going to the immigration office stop by the Oficina de Ingresos of the Ministerio de Hacienda y Tesoro, 507/774-2868, around the corner from the post office near Parque Cervantes in downtown David. You can get a *paz y salvo* here. Hours are 8:30 a.m. to 4:30 p.m. weekdays.

The Costa Rican Consulate, 507/774-1923, is in a little nondescript house a short walk east of the immigration office, directly across from Restaurante El Fogón. There's a Costa Rican flag flying outside. Hours are 8 a.m. to 2 p.m. weekdays.

HEALTH AND SAFETY

Immunization Requirements and Health Precautions

It's extremely unlikely you'll contract a serious disease in Panama. Health conditions are generally good, especially for a developing nation. Panama City and the area around the former Canal Zone are particularly safe.

However, if you're planning to spend a considerable amount of time in rural areas, especially if you're going to be camping, there are several things you can do to make sure you stay healthy.

The most important of these is to avoid insect bites as much as possible. Always use insect repellent in the countryside, particularly in the evenings and early mornings. Sleep in screened-in rooms or use mosquito netting. Wearing long-sleeved shirts and long pants will also reduce insect bites. Some hikers tuck their pants into their socks, tape up the gap with masking tape, then spray insect repellent on their clothes. This lowers the risk of bites from ticks and chiggers. Consider bringing a little masking tape with you, or buy some in Panama. Powdered sulfur sprinkled into boots and on pants is considered the best precaution against chiggers.

Outside of Panama City and the area around the former Canal Zone there is a slight risk of malaria. In the Darién, the Comarca de Kuna Yala (San Blas Islands), the Lake Bayano area, and parts of Gatun Lake there is a chloroquine-resistant strain, and mefloquine is recommended if you're going to be spending a significant amount of time in these regions. The highest-risk areas west of the Panama Canal are the rural parts of Bocas del Toro and Veraguas provinces. Chloroquine is considered effective against the strains found there.

If you're only planning to spend a few days in these areas and know you'll be sleeping under mosquito nets or in screened-in rooms, you may not want to fool with malaria prophylaxis. If you do decide to take the medication, though, remember that you have to start taking it at least a week before you leave on your trip.

Dengue fever is on the rise in Panama, though the incidence of infection is still low. The only prevention is to avoid insect bites, as the disease is carried by mosquitoes.

There are still some cases of yellow fever in Panama, though the chances of contracting the disease are remote. The U.S. Centers for Disease Control recommend a yellow-fever vaccination for visitors to Panama. It's not required, however, and is not suitable for everyone (those allergic to eggs, for instance). Again, the disease is carried by mosquitoes.

There was an outbreak of hantavirus in the eastern Azuero Peninsula in early 2000. Serious measures were being taken to address the problem at the time this was written, and presumably it will be under control by the time you visit.

Any time you travel in the developing world it's a good idea to make sure your regular vaccinations are up to date. You may also want to consider vaccinating yourself against hepatitis A and B.

For current information on health conditions in Panama, contact the Centers for Disease Control in Atlanta, Georgia, at 877/FYI-TRIP or www.cdc.gov.

Food and Drinking Water

It's safe to drink water out of the tap almost everywhere in the country. The destination chapters alert you to the few places where that still wasn't a good idea at the time of writing, such as Bocas del Toro. Never drink untreated water from a stream or lake, no matter how pristine it looks.

Hygiene standards in restaurants tend to be fairly high, particularly in Panama City. You're unlikely to get so much as a stomachache. But if a place looks dirty or unpopular, you're probably better off going elsewhere. Obviously, you take your chances if you eat food from street vendors. If you can't resist, make sure whatever you munch has just been fried at high temperature. It's not a good idea to eat ice cream and other milk- or water-based sweets from street vendors.

Sun

Panama is near the equator, and you can burn amazingly quickly even on a cloudy day. Limit your exposure to the sun, especially around midday. Pale visitors have been known to turn bright red after less than half an hour in the noonday sun. Wear lots of sunscreen and a hat anytime you go outdoors. You're particularly susceptible to sunburn on the water; don't let a cool breeze make you forget that.

Crime

Panama is by and large a peaceful, mellow place despite its absurdly undeserved reputation as some sort of danger zone. You'll likely be safer in Panama City than you would in any comparably sized city back home. However, extreme unemployment and poverty make Colón, Panama's second-largest city, unsafe for tourists. You have a very good chance of getting mugged if you wander around here. You should probably avoid that city altogether for the foreseeable future.

Even in Panama City, you should avoid the poorer neighborhoods, such as Chorrillo, and be alert in transitional ones, such as the historic Casco Viejo area.

Rural areas are generally quite safe, though if you rent a car you should not leave valuables unattended in it when you go for a hike in remote areas.

Hitchhiking

Hitchhiking is not common in most parts of Panama, and it's just as dangerous there as it is in your own country.

Illegal Drugs

Panama is legendary for its marijuana and notorious as a transshipment point for cocaine and other drugs. Don't let that fool you into thinking the consumption of illegal drugs is treated casually in Panama. If you're caught you could very well find yourself spending years in a squalid, overcrowded prison. Dealers have also been known to set up gullible tourists for a bust, sometimes in the hope of sharing a bribe with a corrupt cop. Resist all temptations to sample the local products. It's an extremely foolish risk to take.

Hiking Safety

Rule number one: Never, ever hike alone. It's surprisingly easy to get lost, and in some parts of Panama—such as the Darién—getting lost can be fatal. Also, rain-forest trails can be very slippery, and you don't want to be stuck alone in the forest with even a twisted ankle. I'm embarrassed to admit how many times I've wiped out on what looked like an easy trail or gentle stream crossing.

Almost every hiker new to the tropics worries about snakes. As has been mentioned several times throughout the book, it's rare to come across a snake while hiking and extremely rare to be bothered by one. But there are several things you can do to make it even less likely you'll be bothered by a slithering critter.

First, be careful stepping over tree falls, which attract snakes (not to mention stinging insects). Also be careful around piles of dried leaves. If you want to gather some to start a fire, shuffle your boot-clad feet through them before picking them up.

This should go without saying, but don't play with snakes in the tropics. Some people seem irresistibly drawn to disturbing the creatures, which usually just want to be left alone. A European tourist I was hiking with in the Darién once tried to use his walking stick to prod a baby fer-de-lance we came across. The fer-de-lance is a deadly pit viper, and even the babies can be lethal. The guide and I managed to save the guy from his foolish, possibly suicidal, curiosity.

In the extremely unlikely event you are bitten, try not to panic. Poisonous snakes don't always inject venom when they strike. Obviously, you should get to the nearest hospital as soon as possible. Do not try slashing at the wound and sucking out the poison, as usually this is ineffective and can actually make things worse. If possible, keep the site of the wound elevated above your heart and head.

In general, be careful where you put your hands and feet when you hike. Many plants have sharp spines and the like and may harbor aggressive ants, poisonous caterpillars, and other nasties.

You have a reasonable chance of coming across a scorpion even in semirural hostelries. Usually the sting isn't dangerous, but it's quite painful. To be on the safe side, shake out your shoes and clothes before putting them on. When I'm traveling in the countryside, I stuff my socks into my shoes before going to bed at night. In the canal construction days, workers slept with their boots under their pillows.

Be prepared for cold, wet weather even in the dry season. Carry a rain poncho and bring lots of plastic bags to keep your gear dry. You need to be particularly careful in the highlands. Hikers have died of exposure when they were stuck overnight in the highlands on a day that started out hot but approached freezing after the sun went down. Bring warm clothes with you.

Panama has Africanized bees—the so-called "killer bees"—which can be aggressive and dangerous. Keep well away from any bees you come across. If you disturb them and they start chasing you, try to run through dense brush. They will have a hard time following you. Do *not* jump into a body of water to escape them; they will wait for you to surface. (I know someone who died precisely this way in Panama—when he came up for air, the bees got down his throat.)

Take precautions against bug bites. See Immunization Requirements and Health Precautions and What to Bring, above, for tips.

Always camp in a tent, even on the beach. Vampire bats bite mammals, and they carry rabies. They're sneaky buggers, and you probably won't know you're bitten until the morning, when you find blood on your head or toes.

Treat even small scratches with antibiotics; wounds quickly become infected in the tropics.

TRANSPORTATION

To and From the Country
By Air

Most visitors to Panama arrive by air. Miami is the major U.S. gateway city to Panama, though Houston, Los Angeles, and New York are also important gateways. The flight from Miami to Panama City takes a little under three hours.

Panama's national airline is COPA, 800/892-2672 (in the United States), 507/227-5000 (in Panama), reservas@copaair.com, www.copaair.com. It has flights to the United States and many destinations in Latin America. Other carriers serving Panama at the time of writing included American Airlines, Continental Airlines, Delta Air Lines, and Eva Air.

The airport in David, Aeropuerto Enrique Malek, also has flights to and from San José, Costa Rica. (David is in western Panama, near the Costa Rican border.)

Note: You would be surprised how many tourists think they're booking a flight to Panama City, Republic of Panama, and end up in Panama City, Florida. No joke. Double-check that your reservation is for the right country.

By Bus

Two bus lines make the run between Panama City and San José, Costa Rica. The buses are large, comfortable, and air-conditioned.

The Panaline Bus, 507/227-8648, leaves from the Gran Hotel Soloy, at the corner of Avenida Perú and Calle 30 Este in Panama City. The bus leaves at 12:30 p.m. every day, arriving at 4 a.m. in San José. The fare is $25. The office is in the lobby of the hotel and is open from 8:30 a.m. to 5 p.m. weekdays, 9 a.m. to 2 p.m. Saturday, and 10 a.m. to 2 p.m. Sunday. You should make reservations as far ahead of time as possible. The bus continues all the way up to Nicaragua.

The Tica Bus, 507/262-2084, arrives and leaves from an area next to Hotel Ideal on Calle 17 Oeste near congested Avenida Central in Panama City. The bus line's shabby office is adjacent to the hotel. There's one bus that leaves for Costa Rica every day at 11 a.m., arriving at 3 or 4 a.m. the next day in San José. The ticket costs $25 one way. You need to make a reservation two or three days ahead of time, in person, and you must present your passport. The bus continues all the way up to Mexico.

A third bus line, Tracopa, 507/775-0585 (David), has one daily bus from David to San José, Costa Rica. It leaves at 8:30 a.m. and arrives about 4:30 p.m. Tickets are around $13 one way. The Tracopa office is at the David bus terminal and is open 7 a.m. to noon and 1 to 4 p.m. daily.

Within the Country
By Bus

Long-distance buses offer a cheap, convenient, and often surprisingly comfortable way to get around the country. At the time of writing there were four main bus terminals in Panama City serving different destinations.

Large, air-conditioned buses to David, near the Costa Rican border, leave from the Terminales David-Panama, across from the Mercado del Mariscos (fish market) near the western end of Avenida Balboa. Buses to David leave every hour to 1.5 hours from 6:15 a.m. to 8 p.m., followed by expresses at 10:45 p.m. and midnight. The return schedule from David is slightly different. The trip takes seven hours by regular bus ($11), about six hours by express ($15). The ticket information number in Panama City is 507/262-9436. In David call 507/775-2974 or 507/775-7074.

The terminal for buses from Panama City to Colón is at Calle 28 and Avenida 3 Sur (Avenida Justo Arosemena). As noted elsewhere, I do not recommend visiting Colón. However, those who want to go to Portobelo or Isla Grande by public transportation would take a Colón-bound bus and transfer at Sabanitas, on the Boyd-Roosevelt Highway (Transístmica). See Chapter 9, The Central Caribbean, for information.

Buses from Panama City to the interior of the country—including the Pacific beaches, Azuero Peninsula, and points farther west—departed from the Terminal de Buses al Interior in the Curundu district at the time this was written. However, by the time you read this all these bus lines should be leaving from the new Gran Terminal Nacional de Transportes in Albrook, not far from the domestic airport.

Orange-and-white buses from Panama City to various points in the canal area leave from the SACA Bus Terminal, 507/212-3420, on Calle 9 de Enero near Avenida Central, close to the Legislative Palace. There is frequent daily service to Summit Gardens (55 cents), Gamboa (65 cents), the Amador Causeway (30 cents), Miraflores Locks (35 cents), and many other locations.

Note: It's possible the new Gran Terminal Nacional de Transportes may affect the schedule and departure locations of some of the other buses mentioned above.

By Air

Most points in Panama are well-served by small commercial planes. The main domestic airport, Aeropuerto Marcos A. Gelabert, is in the Albrook district (formerly a U.S. Air Force base) of Panama City. Most cab drivers won't know it by name: ask to go to the "*aeropuerto*" in Albrook. Be sure to stress you want to go to Albrook, or you may be taken to Tocumen International Airport. (*Note:* Don't be confused if you come across an old map showing the domestic airport in the Punta Paitilla district: the airport was moved to the new location in 1999.)

There are five major domestic carriers. The combined weight

limit for carry-on and check-in luggage on these flights is 25 kilograms (55 pounds). The limit is strictly enforced for your own safety. You'll even be asked how much you weigh—don't fib.

Aeroperlas, 507/315-7500, 507/315-7580, iflyap@aeroperlas.com, www.aeroperlas.com, is the largest and has the most destinations. Its subsidiaries, Aereo Taxi and ANSA, serve all the airstrips in the Comarca de Kuna Yala (San Blas Islands). Both can be reached at 507/315-0275, 507/315-0276, iflyap@aeroperlas.com, www.aeroperlas.com.

Aviatur, 507/315-0307 through -0314, fax 507/315-0316, flies primarily to the San Blas Islands, Contadora, and the Darién.

Mapiex Aero, 507/315-0888, is Panama's youngest airline. It flies to David, Bocas del Toro, and Changuinola.

Note: As this book went to press, the U.S. State Department had just issued a travel warning that "called into serious question the safety standards of small air carriers flying domestic routes." It recommends that traveler's consider other means of domestic transportation.

By Taxi and Auto

Taxis are cheap and plentiful in many parts of the country, particularly the cities. You shouldn't fool with buses or rental cars within Panama City; you can take a taxi almost anywhere you want to go for under $2; be sure to agree on the fare ahead of time.

Rental cars are a reasonable option for longer trips. Note that for the western highlands and other remote, rugged areas, you will often need a four-wheel-drive vehicle, which are available in Panama City and other major urban areas but can be hard to come by due to their popularity.

COMMUNICATIONS

Language

The official language of Panama is Spanish. English is not as widely spoken as one might think given the long United States presence in the country and its role as an international trade center. In fact, even in Panama City it's harder to find someone fluent in English than it was 20 years ago. That said, you'll usually have little trouble getting around even if you don't speak Spanish. You can often find someone who speaks at least some English, especially in the fancier hotels and restaurants. Outside of the cities, you'll find the most English speakers in Bocas del Toro and the fewest in the Comara de Kuna Yala (San Blas Islands).

Telephone Service

The country code for Panama is 507. Do not dial 507 when making calls witin the country.

Pay phones pop up in the most unlikely places, including dirt-poor villages and islands in the middle of nowhere. Instructions on using the phones are in English and several other languages, but finding one that actually works can sometimes be a problem. Also, many of these phones accept only prepaid calling cards. These cards, Tarjetas Telechip, are widely available in stores and come in various denominations. Look for a Telechip logo with the words De Venta Aquí ("For Sale Here") on shop doors or windows.

The international access code to call the United States from Panama is 001. Check a local phone book or call the international operator (106) for other access codes and for help making a call.

Calls within the country cost 15 cents for the first three minutes.

Mail Service

Mail service between Panama and other countries is not too speedy. A postcard sent from Panama takes at least five to 10 days to reach the United States, longer to more distant destinations. Postcards to the United States cost 25 cents. Airmail letters weighing up to 20 grams (0.7 ounces) cost 35 cents. Add 5 cents to the above for Canada addresses and 10 cents for European ones. Some of the more expensive hotels sell stamps. Note that bulky packages sent to or from Panama sometimes get "lost" in the mail. Post office hours are generally 7 a.m. to 6 p.m. weekdays, 7 a.m. to 5 p.m. Saturday. Post offices are closed on Sunday.

Internet Access

Internet cafés are increasingly common in Panama. You will have little trouble finding one in the cities, and they're beginning to pop up in fairly remote areas as well. Charges are rarely more than a couple of dollars an hour. Most of these cafés use Windows-based machines, but Macintoshes are sometimes available as well.

ELECTRICITY

Panama's voltage is almost universally the same as it is in the United States: 110 volts. Sockets are two-pronged, and you don't need an adapter for U.S. appliances. There are still a few places that use 220 volts, however, so if you have any doubt ask before you plug in. Note that short blackouts and power surges are common in Panama. If you're traveling with sensitive equipment, such as a laptop computer, you should bring a surge suppresser.

MONEY MATTERS

Currency

Panama's currency is the balboa, and chances are you already have some in your wallet. The balboa's rate of exchange is tied to the dollar. In fact, Panama does not print paper money, so the U.S. dollar is legal tender in Panama. Panamanian coins (one-, five-, 10-, 25-, and 50-cent pieces) are the same size, weight, and color as American ones and are used interchangeably with them. You may see prices quoted with either a "B/" or "$" before them. Both mean the same thing.

Despite Panama's status as a world banking capital, you will find it virtually impossible to exchange foreign currency into dollars/balboas in Panama. Spare yourself a major hassle and bring only dollars to Panama.

Banks

Banks are generally open from 8 a.m. to 2 or 3 p.m. weekdays, 9 a.m. to noon on Saturday. ATMs are located throughout Panama; look for red signs that read Sistema Clave. Banks will cash traveler's checks. The easiest to cash are American Express traveler's checks.

Credit Cards

Credit cards are widely accepted in the cities, especially in the more upscale places. Simpler hotels and restaurants are often cash only. The farther away you are from an urban center, the less likely it is you can use credit cards. Bring lots of small bills with you in more remote parts of Panama, such as the Comarca de Kuna Yala (San Blas Islands), where credit cards are not accepted and larger denominations are hard to break.

Taxes and Tipping

A 10-percent tax is added to all hotel room bills. Room prices quoted in this book do not include tax unless specified. Panama sales tax is 5 percent.

It's customary to tip 10 percent in restaurants. Bellhops, porters, and others who perform services for you should be tipped. Taxi drivers do not generally expect a tip.

TIME ZONE

Panama is on Eastern Standard Time. (There is no daylight savings time in Panama.) Put another way, Panama time is five hours behind Greenwich mean time. Panama is always one hour ahead of Costa Rica, something to remember when you're crossing the border.

MAJOR HOLIDAYS

- January 1st: New Year's Day
- January 9th: Martyr's Day
- Carnaval: The four days leading up to Ash Wednesday
- Good Friday: Friday before Easter Sunday
- May 1st: Worker's Day

- November 3rd: Independence from Colombia
- November 10th: First Call for Independence from Spain
- November 28th: Independence from Spain
- December 8th: Mothers' Day

If you are in Panama around Christmas, New Year's, Carnaval, Semana Santa (the week leading up to Easter), or the November independence holidays, be prepared for celebrations and business closures even on days that are not officially listed as holidays. Also note that when holidays fall on a weekday they are often celebrated on a Monday to create a long weekend.

BORDER CROSSINGS

There are three border crossings between Panama and Costa Rica, at Paso Canoa, Río Sereno, and Guabito. The border at Guabito, on the Caribbean coast, connects with the Costa Rican town of Sixaola and is mainly of interest to visitors traveling from Costa Rica to Bocas del Toro.

At the time this was written, the civil war in Colombia had made the one Panamanian border crossing with Colombia, at Puerto Obaldía at the very eastern tip of the Caribbean coast, far too dangerous to attempt. If you want to go to Colombia from Panama, you should fly.

Paso Canoa

The border crossing at Paso Canoa is on the Interamerican Highway and is the route taken by most visitors coming from or going to Costa Rica. It's about an hour by bus from the terminal in David, the provincial capital of Chiriquí Province. See Chapter 7, Western Highlands: West of Volcán Barú, for information on David. A taxi between Paso Canoa and David will cost around $18 to $20, maybe less if business is slow.

Paso Canoa is a grim little border town with nothing to offer visitors and no places to stay. There's an IPAT office at the border that's open from 6 a.m. to midnight. You will likely find the "help" here useless, unfriendly, and indifferent, especially if it's manned by a grumpy old grandpa who'd rather watch TV than answer your questions, as it was the last time I visited. It's not the best introduction to Panama for those coming from Costa Rica.

A branch of the Banco Nacional de Panama is near the immigration office. It's open 8 a.m. to 3 p.m. weekdays, 9 a.m. to noon Saturday. It's near immigration. There's an ATM, but they don't change Costa Rican colones. If you need to change colones, you'll be told to look for the man wandering around carrying a money pouch. If changing money on the streets of a grungy border town doesn't sound like a smart thing to do—and it probably shouldn't—change your colones into dollars before entering Panama.

Río Sereno

This little-used border crossing is an alternative to Paso Canoa for those coming from or going to the western highlands of Panama. You're likely to be the only gringo in town. There's nothing much of interest to tourists there. The nearest major junction in Panama is at Volcán, 42 kilometers (26 miles) away. The drive, on a beautiful but dangerous road, takes nearly two hours. The pickup-taxi ride costs about $20, and you'll be sharing the ride. Buses run from 5 a.m. to 5 p.m. every 45 minutes to Volcán (around $3) and David (around $4).

If you want to drive to Río Sereno from David, take the turnoff to Concepción from the Interamerican Highway and head up toward Volcán. Stay straight past Volcán; the right fork heads up toward Cerro Punta.

The immigration office in Río Sereno is on a hill not far from the town plaza. It's near the radio tower and shares a building with the police station; hours are 7 a.m. to 5 p.m. every day. You need an onward ticket, proof of carrying $500, and a tourist card or visa to enter the country at this crossing.

If you end up stuck at the border, Posada Los Andes, which from the outside looks more like a factory than a hotel, can supply you with a basic room for $9 to $15. It's on the town plaza.

Lovely as the drive is, the border crossing is inconvenient and the road isn't safe. You're better off taking the far less attractive but more convenient route through Paso Canoa.

APPENDIX B
ADDITIONAL RESOURCES

TOURIST INFORMATION

Instituto Panameño de Turismo
P.O. Box 4421
Panama 5, Panama
507/226-3015, 507/226-7000, fax 507/226-3483
www.panamatours.com and pantours@sinfo.net, and
www.ipat.gob.pa

SOME TOUR OPERATORS AND GUIDES

There are many tour operators and guides in Panama, of wildly different quality.
The ones listed below are among the most prominent and well-established.

Ancon Expeditions
Calle Elvira Mendez
Edificio El Dorado
Panama City, Panama
507/269-9414, 507/269-9415, fax 264-3713
info@anconexpeditions.com
www.anconexpeditions.com
This is the top nature-tour company in Panama. It's known for
employing some of Panama's best guides, particularly in the
Darién. You can also try contacting a couple of the guides directly:
Hernán Araúz, 507/618-6979 (cell), 507/268-0438 (home), bird-
er@sinfo.net; and Rich Cahill, Cahill2000@hotmail.com, 507/264-
8086, 507/630-4297.

Aventuras 2000
Edificio Mabeal y Vicosa, No. 4
Apartado Postal 5375
Panama 5, Panama
507/227-2000, 507/263-5208, fax 507/263-5195
Juan@colon2000.com
www.colon2000.com
This new company, which absorbed the now-defunct Eco Tours, is the official tour operator of Colón 2000, an ambitious tourism complex in the Caribbean city of Colón that will include a cruise-ship port, shopping mall, a Radisson hotel and casino, etc. Because of this connection, Aventuras 2000 will cater primarily to cruise-ship tour groups. But it may be of interest to the independent traveler since it's likely to be one of the biggest tour operators in the Panama Canal area, particularly on the Caribbean side of the isthmus. No price information was available at the time this was written, and it was too early to evaluate the quality of its tours. However, most of the tour descriptions posted at the time this was written were for half-day excursions intended to give tourists a brief introduction to attractions, not an in-depth exploration.

Chiriquí River Rafting
Entrega General
Boquete
Chiriquí, Panama
507/720-1505, fax 507/720-1506
rafting@panama-rafting.com
www.panama-rafting.com
Chiriquí River Rafting enjoys a terrific reputation as a safe, highly professional operation, and at the time of writing it was the only company in Panama offering true white-water rafting.

Iguana Tours
Avenida Belisario Porras, near Calle 72 Este
Panama City, Panama
507/226-8738, 507/226-4516, fax 507/226-4736
iguana@sinfo.net
Iguana Tours enjoys a good reputation for its nature and adventure tours. Its specialties include trips to Isla Iguana off the Azuero Peninsula, but it offers tours all over the country.

Carmen Martino

Apartado 1606
Balboa-Ancon, Panama
507/276-6487, cell 507/617-6342
cmartino@sinfo.net
Carmen is a freelance birding guide with a solid reputation.

Nattur Panama

Apartado 5068
Balboa-Ancon, Panama
507/225-7325, fax 507/225-7314
panabird@sinfo.net
This group is headed by Willie Martinez, who is recognized as one
of the very best birding guides in Panama. The company offers a
wide range of nature tours throughout the country. Its unique
offerings include stays at Martinez's own ecological retreat in the
species-rich Fortuna area. (See Chapter 8, Western Highlands: East
of Volcán Barú, for information.)

Panama Jones

Calle Ricardo Arias (near Hotel Continental)
Panama City, Panama
507/265-4551
In the United States: Panama Discovery Tours, P.O. Box 130,
Clarita, OK 74535, 800/PANAMA-1 (United States and Canada)
pdt@iamaerica.net
www.panamacanal.com
Panama Jones prides itself on personal and attentive service. Its
nature trips range from very soft adventure to ambitious treks.

Pesantez Tours

Apartado 55-0716
Paitilla, Panama
507/263-8771, 507/223-5374, 507/263-7577, fax 507/263-7860
pesantez@sinfo.net
Pesantez is a long-established company that enjoys a good reputation. It specializes in tours of Panama City and cultural tours rather
than nature expeditions.

José Saenz

Based in Panama City, Panama
507/614-7811, fax 507/251-0698
saenzjose@hotmail.com

José is a taxi driver, but if you spend any amount of time in Panama you'll realize he's an important part of the tourist infrastructure. I highly recommend him, as do many others. He's punctual, responsible, polite, dependable—and a safe driver. These are qualities to prize among Panama taxi drivers. He'll pick you up or drop you off at Tocumen International Airport for $20, and if you give him enough notice he'll even make hotel reservations for you. He charges $7 an hour for Panama City tours. He also does tours all over Panama, including Chiriquí, the Azuero Peninsula (his specialty; that's where he's from), and Bocas del Toro. Rates for this vary. Besides his air-conditioned cab, he has access to a 14-passenger minibus and a pick-up truck with a double cabin for surfboards and such.

Scubapanama

Apartado 6666
Balboa, Panama
507/261-3841, 507/261-4064, fax 507/261-9586

Panama's biggest diving outfitter.

Sergesa

Based in Panama City, Panama
tel/fax 507/230-0108
sergesa@sinfo.net

This company primarily offers birding trips in the Panama Canal area, but it also offers trips to Portobelo, San Lorenzo, and Cerro Campana as well as tours of Barro Colorado Island. The vice president of the group is Anayansi ("Ana") Castillo, who is also a Panama Canal Authority guide. She is an accomplished naturalist and an excellent, well-respected guide.

CONSERVATION GROUPS

ANAM (Autoridad Nacional del Ambiente/National Authority of the Environment)
Apartado 2016
Paraíso
Ancón, Panama
507/232-7228, 507/232-7223.

ANCON (Asociación Nacional para la Conservación de la Naturaleza /National Association for the Conservation of Nature)
Apartado 1387
Panama 1, Panama
507/314-0060, fax 507/314-0061
ancon@ancon.org
www.ancon.org.

Smithsonian Tropical Research Institute (STRI)
Street Address: Earl S. Tupper Research and Conference Center, Roosevelt Avenue, Ancon
Mailing Address: Apartado 2072, Balboa-Ancon, Panama
507/212-8000

Sociedad Audubon de Panamá (Audubon Society)
Apartado 2026
Balboa-Panama, Panama
507/224-9371, fax 507/224-4740
audupan@pananet.com
www.orbi.net/audubon

SMALL SHIPS

For those who can afford it, a trip on a small, adventure-type cruise ship can be a terrific way to explore Panama, particularly its more inaccessible parts. These ships are quite different from mammoth "Love Boat"-style cruise ships. For one thing, they're small, usually accommodating fewer than 100 passengers. Because of this they can give visitors a much more intimate and eco-friendly experience of the natural surroundings than larger ships can. They also tend to be more oriented towards adventure travel and the natural and human history of the places they visit. Some offer scuba-diving, snorkeling, sea kayaking, water-skiing, and other active sports. Cruises generally run only in the dry season.

The following are some of the more popular cruise operations:

American Canadian Caribbean Line offers an 11-night cruise aboard the 100-passenger *Grande Caribe*. The itinerary includes the Perlas Islands, San Blas Islands, coastal Darien, Portobelo, Isla Taboga, and a Panama Canal transit. Prices: $2,500–3,100. Offered March–April. Contact info: ACCL, P.O. Box 368, Warren, RI 02885, 800/556-7450, info@accl-smallships.com, www.accl-smallships.com.

Classical Cruises offers a seven-night cruise aboard the 44-passenger *Panorama*. The itinerary includes Parque Nacional Isla de Coiba, the Azuero Peninsula, coastal Darién, a Panama Canal transit, and Costa Rican destinations. Prices: $5,000–5,500. Offered January–March. Contact info: 800/252-7745 or 212/794-3200, classical-cruises@travdyn.com, www.classicalcruises.com.

Linblad Expeditions offers two different Panama cruises aboard the 60-passenger *Temptress Voyager*. Both place an emphasis on natural history. The first is a seven-night cruise that includes Parque Nacional Isla de Coiba, the Perlas Islands, a Panama Canal transit, and Costa Rican destinations. Prices: $3,100–5,000. Offered January–April. The other lasts 10 nights and adds coastal Darién and the San Blas Islands. Prices: $5,000–7,500. Offered December–February. Contact info: Linblad Expeditions, 720 Fifth Ave., New York, NY 10019, 800/397-7740 or 212/765-7740, explore@expeditions.com, www.expeditions.com.

You can also book a seven-night Christmas or New Year's cruise on a Temptress ship directly through **Temptress Adventure Cruises.** These run $2,000–3000. Contact info: Temptress Adventure Cruises, 6100 Hollywood Blvd., Suite 202, Hollywood, FL 33024, 800/336-8423, infor@temptresscruises.com, www.temptresscruises.com.

Tauck World Discovery offers a six-night cruise aboard *Le Ponant,* a 60-passenger sailing/power yacht. The itinerary includes the Perlas Islands, the San Blas Islands, Parque Nacional Isla de Coiba, a Panama Canal transit, and Costa Rican destinations. Prices: $3,200–7,200. Offered January–March. Contact info: Tauck World Discovery, 276 Post Rd. W., Westport, CT 06880, 800/788-7885, info@tauck.com, www.tauck.com.

EMBASSIES

For a complete list of the many embassies in Panama, see a Panama City telephone directory under "Embajadas." All of the embassies listed below are in Panama City.

Canada
Avenida Samuel Lewis and Calle Gerardo Ortega
507/264-9731

France
Plaza de Francia, Casco Viejo
507/228-7824, 228-7835

Germany
Calle 50 and Calle 53 Este
507/263-7733

United Kingdom
Calle 53 Este
507/269-0866

United States
Street Address: Calle 37 and Avenida Balboa, Panama City
Mailing Address: Apartado 6959, Panama 5, Panama
507/207-7000

RECOMMENDED READING

A Day on Barro Colorado Island, by Marina Wong and Jorge Ventocilla (Smithsonian). A slim volume that contains a trail guide to and an overview of Barro Colorado Island. It's on sale at the Smithsonian Tropical Research Institute's headquarters in Panama City.

A Field Guide to the Mammals of Central America and Southeast Mexico, by Fiona A. Reid (Oxford). A useful guide to the habits, distribution, and description of thousands of mammals.

The Golden Isthmus, by David Howarth (Collins). Also published as *Panama: Four Hundred Years of Dreams and Cruelty.* Contains fascinating tidbits on the exploits of Spanish conquistadors, Elizabethan adventurers, and bloody buccaneers. Becomes inaccurate and unreliable as it enters the modern era.

A Guide to the Birds of Panama, by Robert S. Ridgely and John A. Gwynne, Jr. (Princeton). The Bible of Panama bird-watching. It costs around $40, but it's a must for anyone half serious about birding. Also contains information on birds found in Costa Rica, Nicaragua, and Honduras.

A Neotropical Companion: An Introduction to the Animals, Plants, & Ecosystems of the New World Tropics, by John Kircher (Princeton). A long, detailed explanation of just about anything you'd like to know about the New World tropics. It's written in clear language that gets into nuts and bolts but is not intimidatingly technical. Reading it will deepen your experience of the tropical forest.

The Path Between the Seas: The Creation of the Panama Canal, 1870–1914, by David McCullough (Simon and Schuster). The definitive history of the Panama Canal. An astonishing book that reads like a thriller.

A People Who Would Not Kneel: Panama, the United States, and the San Blas Kuna, by James Howe (Smithsonian). Gives interesting insights into the history and culture of the Kuna.

Plants & Animals in the Life of the Kuna, by Jorge Ventocilla, Heraclio Herrera, and Valerio Núñez, translated by Elisabeth King (University of Texas). This book is notable in that it not only describes nature in Kuna Yala but does so as much as possible from the point of view of the Kuna themselves, in their own words.

SOME SPANISH TERMS
FOR NATURE TRAVELERS

ardilla, squirrel
buho, owl
cacique, chief
cascada, waterfall (also *chorro*)
cayuco, dugout canoe
chitra, sand fly
comarca, district, reservation
conejo pintado, agouti paca (literally "painted rabbit")
cusumbí, kinkajou
extranjero, foreigner, outsider
finca, refers both to a farm and to a country house
gato solo, coatimundi/white-nosed coati (literally "lone cat")
gavilán, hawk
guacamayo, macaw
hormiga, ant
lagarto, caiman
loro, parrot
macho de monte, Baird's tapir (literally "man of the mountain")
manigordo, ocelot
mariposa, butterfly
mono, monkey
mono araña, spider monkey
mono aullador, howler monkey
mono cariblanco, white-faced capuchin
mono tití, Geoffroy's tamarin (aka red-naped tamarin)
ñequi, agouti
oso perezoso, sloth (literally "lazy bear")
rana, frog
rancho, a thatch-roofed hut, sometimes also called a "*bohio*"
saíno, peccary; also, *puerco de monte* (literally "mountain pig")
sapo, toad
sendero, trail
tigre, jaguar
tortuga, turtle
trucha, trout

INDEX

ABOUT THE AUTHOR

John McNally

William Friar grew up in Panama and is the author of *Portrait of the Panama Canal* (Graphic Arts Center Publishing). He has also lived in India and Denmark and has traveled to more than 40 other countries on five continents.

William began his journalism career as a stringer for the Metro desk of the *New York Times*. These days he works as a reporter and columnist for Knight Ridder Newspapers in the San Francisco Bay Area. His work has appeared in the *Los Angeles Times, Miami Herald, Arizona Republic, San Jose Mercury News, Orange County Register, Oakland Tribune, Houston Chronicle,* and other publications.

A graduate of Stanford University and the Columbia University Graduate School of Journalism, William lives in San Francisco. He can be reached at wsfriar@hotmail.com.

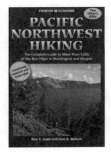

FOR TRAVELERS WITH
SPECIAL INTERESTS

GUIDES

The 100 Best Small Art Towns in America • Asia in New York City
The Big Book of Adventure Travel • Cities to Go
Cross-Country Ski Vacations • Gene Kilgore's Ranch Vacations
Great American Motorcycle Tours • Healing Centers and Retreats
Indian America • Into the Heart of Jerusalem
The People's Guide to Mexico • The Practical Nomad
Saddle Up! • Staying Healthy in Asia, Africa, and Latin America
Steppin' Out • Travel Unlimited • Understanding Europeans
Watch It Made in the U.S.A. • The Way of the Traveler
Work Worldwide • The World Awaits
The Top Retirement Havens • Yoga Vacations

SERIES

Adventures in Nature
The Dog Lover's Companion
Kidding Around
Live Well

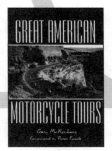

MOON HANDBOOKS

provide comprehensive coverage of a region's arts, history, land, people, and social issues in addition to detailed practical listings for accommodations, food, outdoor recreation, and entertainment. Moon Handbooks allow complete immersion in a region's culture—ideal for travelers who want to combine sightseeing with insight for an extraordinary travel experience.

USA

Alaska-Yukon • Arizona • Big Island of Hawaii • Boston
Coastal California • Colorado • Connecticut • Georgia
Grand Canyon • Hawaii • Honolulu-Waikiki • Idaho • Kauai
Los Angeles • Maine • Massachusetts • Maui • Michigan
Montana • Nevada • New Hampshire • New Mexico
New York City • New York State • North Carolina
Northern California • Ohio • Oregon • Pennsylvania
San Francisco • Santa Fe-Taos • Silicon Valley
South Carolina • Southern California • Tahoe • Tennessee
Texas • Utah • Virginia • Washington • Wisconsin
Wyoming • Yellowstone-Grand Teton

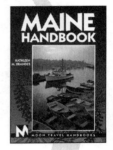

INTERNATIONAL

Alberta and the Northwest Territories • Archaeological Mexico
Atlantic Canada • Australia • Baja • Bangkok • Bali • Belize
British Columbia • Cabo • Canadian Rockies • Cancún
Caribbean Vacations • Colonial Mexico • Costa Rica • Cuba
Dominican Republic • Ecuador • Fiji • Havana • Honduras
Hong Kong • Indonesia • Jamaica • Mexico City • Mexico
Micronesia • The Moon • Nepal • New Zealand • Northern Mexico
Oaxaca • Pacific Mexico • Pakistan • Philippines • Puerto Vallarta
Singapore • South Korea • South Pacific • Southeast Asia • Tahiti
Thailand • Tonga-Samoa • Vancouver • Vietnam, Cambodia and Laos
Virgin Islands • Yucatán Peninsula

www.moon.com

Rick Steves shows you where to travel and how to travel—all while getting the most value for your dollar. His Back Door travel philosophy is about making friends, having fun, and avoiding tourist rip-offs.

Rick's been traveling to Europe for more than 25 years and is the author of 22 guidebooks, which have sold more than a million copies. He also hosts the award-winning public television series *Travels in Europe with Rick Steves*.

RICK STEVES' COUNTRY & CITY GUIDES
Best of Europe
France, Belgium & the Netherlands
Germany, Austria & Switzerland
Great Britain & Ireland
Italy • London • Paris • Rome • Scandinavia • Spain & Portugal

RICK STEVES' PHRASE BOOKS
French • German • Italian • French, Italian & German
Spanish & Portuguese

MORE EUROPE FROM RICK STEVES
Europe 101
Europe Through the Back Door
Mona Winks
Postcards from Europe

WWW.RICKSTEVES.COM

ROAD TRIP
USA

Getting there is half the fun, and Road Trip USA guides are your ticket to driving adventure. Taking you off the interstates and onto less-traveled, two-lane highways, each guide is filled with fascinating trivia, historical information, photographs, facts about regional writers, and details on where to sleep and eat—all contributing to your exploration of the American road.

"Books so full of the pleasures of the American road,
you can smell the upholstery."
~ BBC radio

The Original Classic Guide
Road Trip USA

Road Trip USA Regional Guide
Road Trip USA: California and the Southwest

Road Trip USA Getaways
Road Trip USA Getaways: Chicago
Road Trip USA Getaways: New Orleans
Road Trip USA Getaways: San Francisco
Road Trip USA Getaways: Seattle

www.roadtripusa.com

TRAVEL ✦ SMART®

guidebooks are accessible, route-based driving guides. Special interest tours provide the most practical routes for family fun, outdoor activities, or regional history for a trip of anywhere from two to 22 days. Travel Smarts take the guesswork out of planning a trip by recommending only the most interesting places to eat, stay, and visit.

"One of the few travel series that rates sightseeing attractions. That's a handy feature. It helps to have some guidance so that every minute counts."

~ San Diego Union-Tribune

TRAVEL SMART REGIONS

Alaska
American Southwest
Arizona
Carolinas
Colorado
Deep South
Eastern Canada
Florida Gulf Coast
Florida
Georgia
Hawaii
Illinois/Indiana
Iowa/Nebraska
Kentucky/Tennessee
Maryland/Delaware
Michigan
Minnesota/Wisconsin
Montana/Wyoming/Idaho
Nevada
New England
New Mexico
New York State

Northern California
Ohio
Oregon
Pacific Northwest
Pennsylvania/New Jersey
South Florida and the Keys
Southern California
Texas
Utah
Virginias
Western Canada

Foghorn Outdoors

guides are for campers, hikers, boaters, anglers, bikers, and golfers of all levels of daring and skill. Each guide contains site descriptions and ratings, driving directions, facilities and fees information, and easy-to-read maps that leave only the task of deciding where to go.

"Foghorn Outdoors has established an ecological conservation standard unmatched by any other publisher."
~ Sierra Club

CAMPING Arizona and New Mexico Camping
Baja Camping • California Camping
Camper's Companion • Colorado Camping
Easy Camping in Northern California
Easy Camping in Southern California
Florida Camping • New England Camping
Pacific Northwest Camping
Utah and Nevada Camping

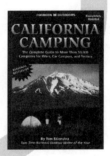

HIKING 101 Great Hikes of the San Francisco Bay Area
California Hiking • Day-Hiking California's National Parks
Easy Hiking in Northern California
Easy Hiking in Southern California
New England Hiking
Pacific Northwest Hiking • Utah Hiking

FISHING Alaska Fishing • California Fishing
Washington Fishing

BOATING California Recreational Lakes and Rivers
Washington Boating and Water Sports

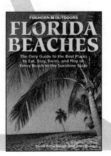

OTHER OUTDOOR RECREATION California Beaches
California Golf • California Waterfalls • California Wildlife
Easy Biking in Northern California • Florida Beaches
The Outdoor Getaway Guide For Southern California
Tom Stienstra's Outdoor Getaway Guide: Northern California

WWW.FOGHORN.COM

CiTY·SMaRT™

The best way to enjoy a city is to get advice from someone who lives there—and that's exactly what City Smart guidebooks offer. City Smarts are written by local authors with hometown perspectives who have personally selected the best places to eat, shop, sightsee, and simply hang out. The honest, lively, and opinionated advice is perfect for business travelers looking to relax with the locals or for longtime residents looking for something new to do Saturday night.

A portion of sales from each title
benefits a non-profit literacy organization in that city.

CITY SMART CITIES

Albuquerque	Anchorage
Austin	Baltimore
Berkeley/Oakland	Boston
Calgary	Charlotte
Chicago	Cincinnati
Cleveland	Dallas/Ft. Worth
Denver	Indianapolis
Kansas City	Memphis
Milwaukee	Minneapolis/St. Paul
Nashville	Pittsburgh
Portland	Richmond
San Francisco	Sacramento
St. Louis	Salt Lake City
San Antonio	San Diego
Tampa/St. Petersburg	Toronto
Tucson	Vancouver

www.ricksteves.com

The Rick Steves web site is bursting with information to boost your travel I.Q. and liven up your European adventure. Including:
- The latest from Rick on what's hot in Europe
- Excerpts from Rick's books
- Rick's comprehensive Guide to European Railpasses

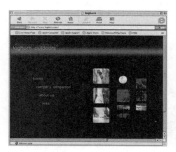

www.foghorn.com

Foghorn Outdoors guides are the premier source for United States outdoor recreation information. Visit the Foghorn Outdoors web site for more information on these activity-based travel guides, including the complete text of the handy *Foghorn Outdoors: Camper's Companion*.

www.moon.com

Moon Handbooks' goal is to give travelers all the background and practical information they'll need for an extraordinary travel experience. Visit the Moon Handbooks web site for interesting information and practical advice, including Q&A with the author of *The Practical Nomad*, Edward Hasbrouck.